DISTORTION

BOOKS BY TERRI BLACKSTOCK

THE MOONLIGHTERS SERIES

1 *Truth Stained Lies*
2 *Distortion*

THE RESTORATION SERIES

1 *Last Light*
2 *Night Light*
3 *True Light*
4 *Dawn's Light*

THE INTERVENTION SERIES

1 *Intervention*
2 *Vicious Cycle*
3 *Downfall*

THE CAPE REFUGE SERIES

1 *Cape Refuge*
2 *Southern Storm*
3 *River's Edge*
4 *Breaker's Reef*

NEWPOINTE 911

1 *Private Justice*
2 *Shadow of Doubt*
3 *Word of Honor*
4 *Trial by Fire*
5 *Line of Duty*

THE SUN COAST CHRONICLES

1 *Evidence of Mercy*
2 *Justifiable Means*
3 *Ulterior Motives*
4 *Presumption of Guilt*

SECOND CHANCES

1 *Never Again Good-bye*
2 *When Dreams Cross*
3 *Blind Trust*
4 *Broken Wings*

WITH BEVERLY LAHAYE

1 *Seasons Under Heaven*
2 *Showers in Season*
3 *Times and Seasons*
4 *Season of Blessing*

NOVELLA

Seaside

OTHER BOOKS

Shadow in Serenity
Predator
Double Minds
Soul Restoration
Emerald Windows
Miracles (The Listener/The Gifted)
The Heart Reader of Franklin High
The Gifted Sophomores
Covenant Child
Sweet Delights

DISTORTION

(MOONLIGHTERS SERIES, BOOK TWO

New York Times Bestselling Author
TERRI BLACKSTOCK

 ZONDERVAN®

ZONDERVAN

Distortion
Copyright © 2014 by Terri Blackstock

This title is also available as a Zondervan ebook. Visit www.zondervan.com/ebooks.

This title is also available in a Zondervan audio edition. Visit www.zondervan.fm.

Requests for information should be addressed to:

Zondervan, Grand Rapids, Michigan 49530

Library of Congress Cataloging-in-Publication Data

Blackstock, Terri, 1957-
  Distortion / Terri Blackstock.
    pages cm. -- (Moonlighters series ; Book 2)
  ISBN 978-0-310-28314-0 (trade paper)
  1. Moonlighting--Fiction. 2. Women private investigators--Fiction. 3. Murder--Investigation--Fiction. I. Title.
  PS3552.L34285D57 2014
  813'.54--dc23

                                            2013037375

Scripture quotations taken from the Holy Bible, *New International Version*®, *NIV*®. Copyright © 1973, 1978, 1984, 2011 by Biblica, Inc.™ Used by permission. All rights reserved worldwide.

NEW AMERICAN STANDARD BIBLE®, © The Lockman Foundation 1960, 1962, 1963, 1968, 1971, 1972, 1973, 1975, 1977, 1995. Used by permission.

Any Internet addresses (websites, blogs, etc.) and telephone numbers in this book are offered as a resource. They are not intended in any way to be or imply an endorsement by Zondervan, nor does Zondervan vouch for the content of these sites and numbers for the life of this book.

Cover design: James Hall
Cover image: Getty Images
Interior design: Mallory Perkins

Printed in the United States of America

14 15 16 17 18 19 20 /RRD/ 20 19 18 17 16 15 14 13 12 11 10 9 8 7 6 5 4 3 2 1

This book is lovingly dedicated to the Nazarene.

CHAPTER 1

J uliet Cole watched her husband through the windshield, wishing he'd stop brooding. His jaw popped as he stood at the gas pump, scowling at the dollar amount of the fuel going into the U-Haul truck. She couldn't say she blamed him for his foul mood tonight. This was the fourth time in the last year he'd taken the day off from his practice to help her sister Holly move, and it had been a long day.

A white Camaro pulled up between her silver Caravan and the U-Haul truck Bob was about to return, illuminated by the gas station's lights. The man inside looked toward Bob, then turned to peer at Juliet. Did she know him? Just in case, she lifted her fingers in a wave. The man looked away and pulled on through.

Bob put the gas pump back into its cradle. He grabbed the receipt, then climbed back into the box truck. He pulled out without a word, expecting her to follow. Maybe when the truck was returned and he was back in the van, she could coax him into a better mood.

She followed him down the highway where sleazy clubs with neon signs lined the streets, Friday night partiers' cars crammed into the parking lots. Juliet would have preferred a safer location after dark, but this was the only U-Haul store that had the size truck they needed, and they'd been instructed to return it to the same place they'd rented it. Her husband's left-turn signal came on, and she pulled in behind him. There were no lights in the parking lot. Uneasy, she clicked on her locks.

Though the parking lot was empty, she pulled between the white lines of a parking space, facing the depository box forty feet away. Bob drove the truck to the empty space among the other rental trucks, off to her left at the back of the lot. He jumped down from his seat and slammed the door. Then he trudged across the asphalt to put the key in the night depository.

Another car pulled into the lot, drove just past the building, and did a U-turn, putting the driver on the side of the depository box. He stopped in front of the box, obstructing Juliet's view of Bob. The car's interior light didn't come on; the man didn't get out of the car. Juliet stiffened, her hand on the door. Was he talking to Bob?

A blast as quick as a balloon pop jolted her. She strained to see. Her car sat at an angle to the box, her headlights aimed to the left, barely illuminating the driver. He had turned sideways, his back to her, and was leaning out the window closest to Bob. Another blast, then another, shook her breathless. As he turned back to the steering wheel, she saw the quick outline of a gun.

Dread choked her. Tires squealed and the car screeched off, leaving thick darkness in its wake. Then she saw him . . . a hump on the ground.

"Bob!" She fumbled for the door handle, then the lock.

Throwing the door open, she stumbled out of the van. "Bob!" she screamed. "Oh, God, please don't . . ." She went toward him, walking at first, then running.

As she fell to her knees beside him, Juliet gasped at the blood pooling around his head. He wasn't moving. Screams shredded her throat. Her phone—where was her phone?

Trembling, she lifted his head, warm liquid coating her fingers. Blood? *No . . . please, God . . .* The exit wound—she tried to apply pressure, but the wound was too big. She groped for a pulse, couldn't find one.

"Help! Somebody, please . . . !"

No one came. Her phone. Was it in her purse in the van? She carefully laid Bob's head back down, then forced herself to abandon him and stumbled back to the van. She grabbed her purse with bloody hands and groped for her phone. She pulled it out, tried to punch in the digits as she ran back to him. It took three tries to get the number right, but she finally hit CALL.

"Bay County 911, what is your emergency?"

"Help!" she said, breathless. "My husband's been shot!"

The maddeningly calm dispatcher demanded to know an address. Juliet had no idea. "The U-Haul place. He's bleeding!" she cried. "Hurry, please!"

"Ma'am, I need an address. Which U-Haul store?"

"The U-Haul store . . . on Highway 57." She looked around for a sign or some kind of landmark. "Across from RK's Plumbing Supplies, near the KFC. Please hurry!"

She screamed again for help from someone, anyone on the street, but her cries were ignored. Cars drove by, their drivers oblivious. Silhouettes passed in the streetlight, indifferent pedestrians ignoring her screams as her husband's life slowly bled away.

CHAPTER 2

The parking lot had filled with police cars, their blue lights strobing. Juliet felt as if she were outside her body as police and EMTs surrounded her husband. She shivered, freezing. Why wouldn't they load him into an ambulance?

They had told her he was dead, but she knew he wasn't. He would be okay if they just got him to the hospital. They could replace the blood he'd lost, use a defibrillator, revive him somehow. Bob did it for patients all the time. Why wouldn't they listen?

She sat in the back of a police car, the door open, staring at him across the parking lot, desperate to cover him.

He must be cold. She wanted to shoo away the crime scene photographers who stood over him as if he were just some object. A policeman knelt on the pavement next to where she sat, trying to pry information from her, but she didn't know how many times she had to tell him. "Please," she wept, her voice raspy and hoarse, "get him to the hospital and maybe—"

"Ma'am, I'm sorry, but we have to leave him there. It's a homicide scene. We'll take him soon. Right now I need to ask a few more questions."

Hadn't he asked her enough already? *"What?"*

"You were carrying a gun in your car."

She met his eyes, wondering if he thought *she* had shot Bob. She had given them permission to search the van because she had no reason not to. "Yes . . . it's registered. I have a concealed weapons permit. I work part-time as a private investigator. It wasn't my gun that shot him. You can take it. Test it." She looked at the eaves on the building. "There's a camera on that building. If you get the security video, maybe you can see who did this."

"We're working on that."

"I didn't shoot my husband."

"I wasn't suggesting that you did. What kind of investigative work do you do?"

She tried to organize her thoughts. "Mostly desk-type stuff. Background searches, workers' comp fraud, adoption searches, divorce cases . . . that kind of thing. Do we really have to go over this right now?" She waved a hand toward her husband's body. "He's just lying there. How can you leave him lying on the ground? His head . . ."

The officer's gaze softened as he got to his feet and blocked her view. She leaned to see around him. "Ma'am, I think it would be best if I took you to the police station."

"No, please! I want to stay with him!"

"Ma'am, it's not doing you any good to stay here. It can take a long time for them to examine the crime scene. We're looking for evidence that can lead us to his killer."

"A white car," she said again. "I told you, it was a white

car. The man, he was white—really pale . . . and he . . . he had greasy hair that strung into his eyes. He was wearing . . . a T-shirt, I think. Please . . . just go find him!"

"Ma'am, we've called it in and we have people looking for him. The white car, have you ever seen it before?"

"No, I don't think so." She stared toward her husband. Why had she agreed to rent the U-Haul from this place? They should have just hired movers for Holly. She thought of Bob sulking at the gas station, not even looking at her. The tightness on his face as he pumped gas.

The white Camaro . . . the man staring at Bob, then glancing at her.

"Wait," she blurted. "It was a Camaro. A white Camaro."

"A Camaro? You're sure?" he said.

"Yes. We stopped at the gas station." She pointed up the road. "The one a block up. We put some gas in the truck. You have to return it full. There was a guy there in a white Camaro. He looked at us. I thought he might know Bob, but he didn't wave or talk to him."

"Was it the same man who shot your husband?"

She touched her throat. "Yes, I think so. He must have followed us here."

The cop quickly spoke into the radio, turning his back to her.

What did it mean? If someone in a Camaro had followed them from the gas station . . . Had the man figured her husband was an easy mark, going to a dark, unlit place?

She begged God to make this a silly nightmare from which she would wake. To get Bob up off the ground . . .

But it wasn't a dream.

CHAPTER 3

Holly stood in the middle of her new living room, surveying the boxes that had been unloaded and left for her to unpack. Cathy and Michael were unloading dishes in the kitchen, something that embarrassed her. She never liked for her successful sister to see her Solo cup aesthetic, and it horrified her that Michael, her boss and mentor, was getting a close-up look at the true state of her life. She'd rather they didn't know that she ate mostly off paper plates and drank from plastic cups she'd picked up at convenience stores. Cathy had a fully stocked kitchen the first time she moved into an apartment of her own. Her plates all matched her cups and bowls, and she displayed them in doorless cabinets like art. Holly was grateful that her cabinets had doors.

At twenty-eight, Holly knew she should be living like an adult rather than a high school dropout. She had graduated from high school—barely—and she'd lived a minimum-wage lifestyle since she opted out of college. Though her sister Juliet had been so helpful every time she moved, her brother-in-law was getting fed up with her. But what else could she do? Six months pregnant, she couldn't lift heavy boxes. And she had barely scraped up enough to cover the down payment on this house, much less the money to hire real movers.

Overwhelmed, she walked through the house, dodging boxes, and found her brother, Jay, kneeling in the master bedroom, patching the hole in the drywall. "Is that going to work?" she asked, standing at the door.

Jay looked up at her. "Oh yeah, it'll be fine. Just let it dry a day or so and then you can slap some paint over it." He stopped spackling and nodded toward the photography equipment she had unpacked on her bare mattress. "What's all that?"

"Tools of the trade," she said.

"Taxi driving?"

She laughed. "No, my other trade. I use them for surveillance."

"That's some expensive equipment. Does Michael pay for it?"

"Yeah, thank goodness. Those zoom lenses make my job a lot easier when I'm watching subjects."

He scraped the extra joint compound back into the bucket, then looked up at her. "So this is getting to be a real thing? Not just a hobby?"

"Seriously?" she said. "You're just now getting that?"

"I mean, I knew you were all helping Michael. But I didn't know he'd made actual investments in you."

"Yeah, imagine that. Somebody investing in me."

He got up and wiped his hands. "You know what I mean."

Holly went to the bed and loaded the equipment back into her camera case. "He's even paying us now. Not much. Just ten bucks an hour, whenever we can put time in. But we're

TERRI BLACKSTOCK9

kind of liking this gig. Even Juliet, though she'd probably
never admit it."

"So . . . how do you do surveillance from a big yellow taxi?
You must stand out like a sore thumb."

She shrugged and snapped her case. "A taxi fits right in at
the hotels, where cheating spouses like to go. And when I get
a taxi call, I can leave and make a run. For everything else,
Michael has an agency car he lets me drive."

"What'll you do when you have the baby?"

"Take him-slash-her with me."

"Great."

"Nothing to worry about, bro. It's utter boredom most of the
time. I vow not to take him-slash-her on any high-speed chases."

"Okay, that doesn't make me feel better."

"Trust me, Jay. I'll be even more protective of my baby
than I am of Jackson."

Jay nodded, clearly remembering that she'd risked her life
for his five-year-old son.

"Besides, I like being called a PI a whole lot better than
Taxi Driver. It sounds better at parties."

"And it's important to sound good at parties," he said in a
dull voice. "So . . . did the previous owners leave any paint cans?"

She shook her head. "I don't think so. I haven't seen any."

"Then you may have to paint this whole room."

She looked around at the dingy brown paint. "Can you
believe somebody actually chose this color?"

"Forty years ago it was popular."

"I'll just paint the whole room."

"Or move a piece of furniture in front of this patch-up
job," Jay said. "The main thing is just to get you settled before
the baby comes."

Before the baby comes. That phrase lodged in her heart, quickening her pulse. Would she be ready in time? She went into the room across the hall, the one she had chosen as the nursery. It was empty. She had nothing to offer her child. No diapers, no shoes, no little outfits. And it wasn't like her friends were the type who gave showers. Some of them didn't even *take* showers. She would need a rocking chair, a crib, a changing table . . . but all those things cost money.

She jumped when she realized that Cathy stood behind her. Her beautiful sister. Cathy's long black shampoo-commercial hair, her dark beach tan, and her glamorous eyes were no worse for having spent the day sweating.

"Holly, what's wrong?" Cathy asked.

Holly blinked back the mist in her eyes. "Just thinking about getting this place ready before the big day."

"You still have three months. It'll be fine. This place is a lot nicer than where you moved from."

"Yeah, but let's face it. I couldn't have gotten it if it wasn't a foreclosure. And it's the worst house on the street. It needs so much work."

"Well, the work's going to get done. You'll be in a safer area. And you'll own it."

She sighed. "I couldn't have done it without Juliet and Bob. But he was really irritated with me today."

"He just seemed distracted."

"By the absurdity of my being a mother?"

"No, probably by a patient or something. You know him. He's a great surgeon because he completely focuses on his work. He was just focusing on getting the job done. We all wanted you in this place."

Holly went into the little bathroom next to the bedrooms.

Looking in the mirror was such a surreal experience these days. She hardly recognized herself. "How will I ever get ready to have a baby?"

"You'll be fine."

Holly breathed a laugh. "Juliet wants me to go to church with her Sunday. It was kind of a condition of her helping me get the house."

Cathy looked at the floor. "Yeah, I kind of figured she'd pull something like that."

Holly shrugged. "You know, it's not *going* that bothers me so much. I mean, I can get up Sunday morning and meet her at the building. I can walk in and sit for a sermon. It's not that."

Cathy lifted her eyebrows. "Then what is it?"

"It's that I'm pregnant and I'm not married, and I'm walking into a place where people don't take well to that kind of thing. At least my friends don't judge me. I just have this vision of walking in there trying to act all pious, like I belong, and having everybody in the congregation turn around and scream, 'Fraud!'"

Cathy chuckled. "It won't be like that. They'll probably just ignore you."

"Yeah, there's that too." Holly looked back in the mirror, rethinking the neon pink ends on her blonde hair, the tattoo of a huge butterfly on her left bicep, and the smaller butterflies on the inside of her arm down to her wrist . . . all things she'd done to make the statement that she was different than the preacher's kid she used to be who'd sat like a robot in church. But if she had to go Sunday, she'd rather blend in.

Cathy sighed and put her arms around her, smiling at Holly's reflection in the mirror. "Maybe it's changed since we were kids."

"Juliet says it has. That her church is full of oh-so-wonderful people."

"And if anyone's mean to you, they'll have her to contend with. It won't be bad."

"Then why don't *you* come?"

"Juliet isn't holding anything over my head." Cathy laughed, let go of her. "Maybe I'll go anyway."

Holly turned, hope rounding her eyes. "Would you? It would make me feel so much better if you were there, just to have someone on each side of me. Maybe they wouldn't notice that I have this bump."

Cathy touched Holly's stomach. "That 'bump' is a precious child."

"Tell me about it. I'm the one who feels him kicking."

"Could be a girl."

"So what do you say? Will you come?"

Cathy just sighed and looked at her for a long moment.

"Michael can come too," Holly added. "We could pack a pew."

Cathy laughed at the reference to those revivals their father used to do, where each church member was tasked with filling up a pew each night. Holly remembered inviting everybody who came into the Laundromat next to the church, just so she could have her own pew. She promised them there would be cheesecake and door prizes, but none of them ever came.

Michael stepped into the doorway, and Cathy's face lit up. "Michael, what do you say? Holly wants us to go to Juliet's church with her Sunday. Wanna come?"

"Sure. Count me in." He slid his arms around Cathy's waist, kissed the top of her head.

Holly glanced away. She was happy for their relationship,

but it sometimes reminded her that she'd done everything backwards. She should have found someone like Michael *before* she got pregnant. Now the chances of finding a soul mate had gone down drastically.

But wasn't that how everything in her life worked?

"So you'll come?" Holly asked.

Taylor Swift's chorus of "Romeo and Juliet" rang out suddenly from the kitchen—Holly's ringtone for Juliet. "My phone!" Holly pushed past Cathy and headed for the kitchen. "They're probably on their way back," she said as she grabbed the phone and swiped the screen to answer. "Hey, Sis, what's up?"

She heard screaming, sobbing, and Juliet blurted out something that Holly couldn't understand. Pressing the phone to her ear, she shouted, "Juliet, what is it?"

More hysterics. Holly motioned for Cathy to turn off the radio, and she put the phone on speaker. "Juliet, I can't understand you. Speak slower."

"He shot him!"

"Shot? Who?"

Suddenly everyone was around Holly. Cathy and Michael and Jay, staring at her, waiting to hear what was going on. Michael spoke up. "Juliet, who shot who?"

"Bob. At the U-Haul place. This man . . . he just drove up and just . . . shot him."

"Did you call the police?"

"Yes, they're here . . . I mean, there."

Cathy grabbed Holly's hand to pull the phone closer. "Juliet, where are you?"

"They're taking me to the police station. But Bob's still there, on the ground in the parking lot, and they won't take him to the hospital. I begged them to. They could save him . . .

give him blood . . . they're saying he's dead but they haven't even tried . . ."

Holly gaped at the others, speechless. Mouths fell open, hands went to their faces.

"Honey, we're coming," Cathy said. "Do you know what precinct?"

They heard Juliet asking the cop transporting her, then she came back to the phone. "The main one. My car. I don't know what they're going to do with it."

"Don't worry about it. We'll meet you there," Cathy said. "Honey, it's going to be all right."

"No, it's not!" Juliet cried. "They won't even put him in an ambulance. They're just leaving him there . . ."

Holly covered her mouth, unable to stand it. Cathy looked white. Jay had his splayed hand in his hair. Michael said, "Juliet, we're on our way over. Just hold on."

Holly grabbed her purse from the kitchen counter. "Let's go!" she cried. "Who's driving?"

"I am," Cathy said.

Jay stopped her. "What about the kids?"

"What about them? Zach is babysitting. They're fine."

"But . . . what if they hear about this on TV? Another murder in the family. Jackson's over there with them. It'll terrify him. And Zach and Abe . . . he's their father!" His face twisted. "How could this happen to our family again?"

Holly rolled her hands into fists. The thought of her nephews suffering penetrated her panic. "Why don't you go over to Juliet's and keep them occupied?"

Jay hesitated. "But I want to go be with Juliet too."

Cathy grabbed up her bag and took out her keys. "Jackson's your son—don't you want to be with him right now? Besides,

I'm an attorney. Juliet needs me. And Michael will be helpful at the police department, so he needs to come."

"I'd get the kids," Holly said, "but I'll be a basket case. I won't be able to hide anything from them."

"She's right," Cathy told her brother. "She's too emotional."

"Okay, I'll go," Jay said. "But keep me informed of every little thing. I mean everything. Do you hear me?"

"Yes, we will," Cathy said. "Just hurry."

The moment Holly and Michael were in the car with Cathy, she punched her accelerator and flew to the police precinct.

CHAPTER 4

Time moved like still frames in a blurry slideshow: the white Camaro, Bob on the ground, police lights flashing, fluorescent lights in the precinct, painted cinder-block walls. Juliet was freezing. It must be twenty degrees in the interview room . . . but that was impossible. This was Florida, and it never got down to twenty. Especially not in August.

She had called her family from the police car, but she couldn't remember what she'd told them.

The door flew open, and Cathy and Holly burst in. Only two years younger than Juliet, Cathy always looked so polished and stoic and *ready*, as if she got up every morning prepared to fight an epic fight. Holly, on the other hand, looked as if she'd just staggered in from a rave, her blonde and pink hair stringing into her face and her pregnant belly straining against her T-shirt.

They both burst into tears as they threw their arms around her. "Are you all right?" Cathy asked. "Did he hurt you?"

"No," Juliet muttered. "He didn't come near me. I don't think he even got out of his car. Just shot Bob and drove away."

"Did he try to rob him?" Cathy asked.

Juliet shook her head. "I don't think he touched him. I heard the shots. Saw the handgun."

"Did he say anything?" Holly asked.

"I didn't hear it if he did. It all happened so fast. I knew that place was dangerous. I never should have rented the truck there."

"You're freezing," Cathy said, shedding her sweater and putting it around Juliet's shoulders. "You're in shock." She slid her chair next to her sister and put her arms around her to warm her up.

"The boys," Juliet said. "They were expecting me home."

"Jay went over to your house," Cathy said. "He's keeping the boys away from TV until you get home."

Juliet nodded. "Okay, good. He . . . he didn't tell them . . . about the shooting, did he?"

"No, of course not," Holly said. "Jay knows better than that. We'll let you do it when you're ready."

Juliet's vision blurred, and for a moment the world seemed to tilt to the left.

"You have blood on you." Cathy's voice seemed far away. "Oh, honey, I should have brought you a change of clothes."

Juliet looked down at herself, shaking her head to clear her vision. There was blood on her jeans, her shirtsleeves, her hands. Her husband's blood.

Images flashed through her mind of Jackie Kennedy with blood on her elegant suit as her husband's life drained out of him. The convertible . . . the grassy knoll . . . the book depository . . .

"I have to change clothes. Can't let the boys see me. I have to go to your house first, Cathy. Have to borrow something."

"Of course."

"I've told them everything I know. I want to go back there. To the parking lot."

Cathy took Juliet's face in her hands and made her look into her eyes. "Honey, we can't go there. That's not where you need to be."

"But I have to . . . he might need . . ."

"Sweetie, I know this is hard for you. But they told us when we came in. Bob is dead."

"But they didn't *do* anything to help him!"

"Honey, he didn't have a pulse when they got there. He was gone. You know that, don't you?"

Juliet's head ached. She twisted her face, suppressing the horror of that truth. She did know that. She had held his head herself, had tried to wake him . . .

Oh, God, why does it have to be true?

She looked down at the blood on her hands and let out a long, low, broken wail. "Oh, God . . . no!"

Cathy pulled her into her arms and held her.

"You're going to be okay," Cathy said in a hard whisper. "We'll get through this."

Juliet didn't want to get through it. She wanted to go backward, through those blurry slides in that random slideshow to the last time Bob had met her eyes and smiled . . .

When *was* that? She couldn't remember.

"I'll see if they need you anymore," Cathy said. "Maybe we can take you home."

Juliet racked her brain for that moment when her husband hadn't been distracted or impatient. Cathy let go, and

Holly took her place. Cathy left the room, but Juliet couldn't remember why. "He was just walking . . . to put the key in the box . . ."

"I should have done it," Holly whispered. "I should have been the one to take the U-Haul back."

Juliet wasn't sure why that made her angry. "And what good would that have done?"

"I don't know. Maybe . . ." Holly's voice trailed off.

Juliet got up. Her legs felt weak, shaky. "Why haven't they found the guy? I told them everything. If they'd looked for the car when I first told them . . . if they'd come sooner . . ."

"I'm sure they're trying to find him," Holly said weakly.

"Michael. Where is he? I need to tell him everything. Maybe he could find the guy."

"He's here. He went to talk to his brother upstairs. He's on this."

CHAPTER 5

Michael Hogan found his brother Max on the second floor of the police department, in the Major Crimes Unit. As he stepped into the doorway, his gaze gravitated to the desk that had once been his. Ironic that it was now his brother's desk.

Max was on the phone, jotting down notes, his expression somber. Max's partner, Al Forbes, a middle-aged man who was overweight and wore a perpetual wince as though in pain, was just getting off the phone. Michael crossed the room. "Hey, Al. Are you two assigned to the Cole murder?"

"Yeah, it's ours," Al gruffed. "We're trying to track down white Camaros registered in town. Sounds like just another drug murder, though. Probably a crackhead looking for cash."

Michael had figured as much. The area where Bob was shot had half a dozen murders every year. "Was he robbed?"

"Doesn't look like it. Still had his wallet on him. Had cash

20

in it, all his credit cards. Wife was pretty sure the guy didn't even get out of the car."

Michael heard Max hang up, and he crossed to his brother's desk and sat on the edge. "Hey, man. What can you tell me about Bob Cole's murder?"

Max finished writing and looked up at him. "I figured you'd be here. It's a shame. Wrong place at the wrong time."

"But if there was no robbery, what was the motive?"

"Who knows? Juliet says she saw the shooter at the gas station earlier. Maybe Bob insulted him or something."

Michael hadn't heard that part. "Did she see them talking?"

"No, she says they didn't get close to each other then, either."

Michael looked at the back wall, where a line of dry-erase boards held notes for each open case. Bob didn't even have a column yet. "If she saw him at the gas station, he must have been following them. It wasn't random."

"Might be that he planned on robbing him after he shot him. But when she started screaming, maybe he thought he should just get out of there."

Michael considered that.

Max got up. "Is her family here?"

"Yeah, they're downstairs with her now."

"She's pretty shaken up. That family's been through a lot. Cathy all right?"

Before Michael could answer, Cathy burst in like she owned the place. "Max, she's freezing. She's in shock. Do you have a blanket?"

"Sure, I'll get it." Max got one out of the closet and came back with it. "She can take it home. She's got blood all over her."

"How is she?" Michael asked Cathy.

"She's a wreck." She turned back to Max. "Have you finished questioning her? Can I take her home? She needs to tell the kids before word gets out."

Max slid his hands into his pockets. "Yeah, go ahead. I was just following up on some of what she told us. Trying to get the security video at the gas station, talking to the owner of the U-Haul property. Soon I need to develop a more detailed timeline with her leading up to the shooting, and get more info about Bob."

"You know where to find her."

"Yeah, she can leave now."

Michael put his arm around Cathy's shoulder and realized she was freezing too. The sweater she'd been wearing earlier was gone. She'd probably given it to Juliet. He wished he had a jacket so he could warm her up.

Michael tried to refocus. "I was with Bob most of the day, helping Holly move. He was all business—spent a lot of time on his phone—but he's a doctor. That's his life, right?"

"Did you hear any of those calls?"

"No. He took them outside, sometimes sitting in his car. I figured he was talking to patients. You can confirm that with phone records."

"Yeah, I'm waiting for those now." Max looked down at Cathy. "I'm really sorry you're having to go through this again."

Cathy's eyes filled with tears, but she blinked them back defiantly. "Me too."

"You taking Juliet straight home?" Michael asked her.

"Not right away. We'll detour by my house and let her clean up before the kids see her. Michael, will you stop by sometime? Maybe you can help jog her memory for clues."

Michael nodded and glanced at his brother, watching for his usual bristling. "Sure, I'll do whatever I can. Max, I'll let you know if she remembers anything else."

Max had the grace not to do the whole "stay out of our way and let us do our job" routine that he often did. Maybe Max was giving Michael grace because he was so close to this family.

"And hey, I could do some of the footwork you don't have the manpower for," Michael said.

"I think we can handle it. But let's stay in touch."

It was the best Michael could hope for.

CHAPTER 6

Juliet hadn't realized she was freezing until Cathy brought the blanket. Her sister opened it and draped it around Juliet's shoulders, cloaking her in warmth. "They said I could take you home," Cathy said. "Come on, we'll keep this around you so people won't see the blood. Let's go."

Juliet stood and looked around, feeling as if she'd forgotten something. Her purse, where was it?

"They've got your stuff," Cathy said. "We can get it on the way out."

Juliet didn't remember them taking her purse. She wondered how long she'd been here . . . how long since her husband died. The reality that Bob was dead bounced around in her brain, but she still couldn't grasp it.

"Juliet, you okay?"

She shook out of her thoughts and looked up at Michael. "Michael, we can't let him get away with this. This person . . . this monster . . ."

"We won't," Michael assured her. But how could he promise her anything? No one knew better than Michael that bad guys didn't always get caught.

They led her out of the interview room. But she'd taken only a few steps when Max Hogan emerged from the stairwell. He'd been the one to corral her into the interview room when she'd arrived, and he'd recorded her statement, taking copious notes and asking questions.

"Juliet, I'm going to let you go," he said, "but I'll need to get back with you tomorrow. Call us if you think of anything else. We'll keep you informed about the case."

The case. Her husband—the love of her life—was now a case.

They escorted her out to Cathy's car, and Juliet climbed into the passenger seat, hoping she didn't get blood on Cathy's leather seats. Michael left in his own car, hopefully to track down leads.

Juliet sat with the blanket wrapped tightly as the car jostled her. She looked out the window at the night sights flying by. If this hadn't happened, where would they be now? They'd be back home with the boys, who would be begging for ice cream before bed. She'd be asking Abe and Zach if they had really brushed their teeth. Asking Bob if he wanted to sleep in tomorrow morning.

She would have herded the boys into the shower, folded a load of laundry, planned tomorrow's lunch, gotten the kids to bed. Then she would have collapsed in bed next to her husband, his warmth making blankets unnecessary. Tomorrow they would have risen to another day in their perfect little oblivious lives.

"Juliet? Honey?"

Juliet drew her gaze from the glass to Cathy. "Hmmm?"

"Are you hungry?"

"No." She couldn't eat a thing. Her stomach felt like stormy ocean waves. "Where do you think they'll take him?"

Cathy was quiet. "Let's not think about that right now. He's been moved. You don't have to worry about him."

The morgue, then. Juliet supposed she'd have to talk to the funeral home tomorrow to get him moved again. The thought exhausted her. So much to do.

She thought of Bob's mother, living in an assisted-living apartment near his sister, two states away. She would have to call her and tell her what happened. Break her mother-in-law's heart.

Her gaze drifted out the window again. Lights blurred by, red, green, black, blue . . . cars . . . vans . . . trucks. There! A white one. Not a Camaro. A Mustang.

Where was this murderer who'd gutted her family?

Cathy took her home and let her shower, which she did on autopilot. When she got out, wet, she wasn't sure if she'd washed, but the blood wasn't on her anymore. She dressed in Cathy's clothes—a white blouse and black sweater, and jeans that mercifully fit.

There was no time to waste. She had to go to her sons. News traveled so fast in this digital age. She imagined Zach getting thoughtless texts from his friends. She hoped Jay had taken their phones.

What in the world would she say to them?

Dad's dead . . .

No, she had to tread more softly.

God took Daddy home.

But that wasn't less cruel.

An evil man had a gun . . .

She brought her cold hand to her mouth. She couldn't do it. Maybe she could get Jay to do it. He'd had to break horrible news to his own five-year-old son. She'd watched through the window, just a few months ago, as he told Jackson that his mother was dead.

No, she couldn't put it off on her brother. It was her job. She had to just say it and let them hurt. There were no Band-Aids for this. Nothing to clean and doctor their wounds. Nothing to make it hurt less.

They pulled into the driveway beside Jay's car. She drew in a deep breath and prayed that God would minimize their torture and provide divine anesthesia.

And please help my legs hold me up.

The children wept when she told them their dad wouldn't be coming home. When it was done, she had no memory of what she'd said. Her head felt like an echo chamber with unrehearsed snatches of conversation bouncing through it. Twelve-year-old Zach retreated to his room to deal with his agony alone. Abe, only nine, became her shadow, unable to leave her side. The whole family—Cathy, Holly, Jay, and his little boy, Jackson—quietly moved in for the night, unwilling to leave her alone with this tragedy.

It was after midnight before Abe fell asleep on her bed. She slowly extracted her arms from around him and slid off the mattress.

The house was quiet. Everyone seemed to be sleeping. Still dressed in the clothes she'd gotten at Cathy's, she stepped into the hall. There was no light shining under Zach's bedroom door, but she opened it and looked inside. Her son slept on top of his covers, still fully dressed down to his shoes. He lay stomach down, his pillow wadded under his face as though he'd cried himself to sleep.

She got a blanket from a chair by the window and covered him.

She slipped out of the room and walked quietly down the stairs. Someone had left a lamp on in the living room. She went to turn it off, then realized Cathy was sleeping on the couch. Her sister could have shared the guest room with Holly, but she'd probably waited up in case Juliet couldn't sleep. She had already covered herself with the throw Juliet kept over the couch.

Juliet turned off the lamp. She went up the hall, into her husband's study, and quietly closed the door behind her. She flipped on the light. The room looked recently used, as though Bob had just stepped out for a moment and would be right back. It was where he spent most of his time when he was home. He had a twenty-seven-inch monitor on the desk, connected to his laptop. Someone's MRI image was up on the screen. Was that person scheduled for surgery next week? She would need to make sure someone notified them.

The thought made her sick.

She sat at Bob's desk in his comfortable executive chair, the one she'd ordered for him. "I'm so sorry, honey," she whispered. "I wish you hadn't been mad at me on your last day."

She longed to touch the bristle of whiskers on his jaw, to hear his breath beside her as he slept, to hear his voice. A box sat on his desk, the personal effects they had given her when she'd left the police station. Cathy must have set it here when they'd come home.

She pulled it toward her and looked inside. His car keys,

his cell phone, his wallet with his cash and credit cards. Why hadn't the shooter taken it? What had he wanted?

She pulled out Bob's phone and turned it on. There had been four calls from the same number, all before he was shot. She clicked on his voice mail and saw the list of old messages. The most recent was from the same number that had called four times this afternoon. She clicked on it and put the phone to her ear.

"Bob, we're getting impatient with you." The male voice was unfamiliar, deep, raspy. "You're putting yourself in danger. But we won't stop with you. We can make an example of your children too."

Juliet caught her breath and stiffened.

"You're making a lot of people very nervous," the voice went on. "Nervous people can be cruel to children."

Juliet dropped the phone as if it had stung her. She got up, unsteady, and stared down at it.

The door swung open. "Mom?"

Abe stood there, his hair mussed, shadows deepening the circles under his eyes. She crossed the room and grabbed him, pulled him closer. Her face felt suddenly hot, and the world seemed to tip again.

"Mom, what is it? You're shaking."

"Juliet?" Cathy's voice came from the living room.

"Cathy!" Juliet tried to think. She had to let Cathy hear the message, but she didn't want to scare Abe. Pulling Abe with her, she went back to the desk and clutched the phone again.

"What is it?" Cathy asked at the doorway.

"It's him—you've got to listen." Her hands shook as if she were moving through water. She punched the message again and handed it to her sister.

Cathy took the phone and listened, her face draining of

color as the message played. She lowered the phone from her ear, glanced down at Abe, then back at Juliet. "I'm calling the police. This wasn't just some random act. It was premeditated."

"But . . . what do they want?"

Cathy opened a desk drawer and pulled out a pen. She wrote down the number that showed on the caller ID.

"Mom, what is it?"

Juliet didn't know what to tell him. "Just . . . somebody calling your dad."

"But what did he say?"

"It doesn't matter. The police need to know."

"Why doesn't it matter?" Abe demanded. "I want to hear."

"No, I need you to go back to bed. It's two in the morning. You need to sleep."

Abe started to cry. "But I want to be with you."

Juliet had no idea what to do. She looked at her sister, feeling helpless.

Cathy took charge. "Okay, I'm calling the police, but after they come, we're going to leave here. You can come to either my house or Jay's, but I don't think it's a good idea for you to stay."

Juliet nodded. Yes, that seemed right. With a threat against her children, she couldn't stay. "*We can make an example of your children too.*"

What was this about?

Tears stung her raw eyes, but for Abe's sake she tried to blink them back. "Honey, I need you to go up and pack a bag."

"In the middle of the night?"

"Yes. Aunt Cathy's right. I don't feel safe here."

"But . . . do you think the killer is gonna come here?"

Terror rounded her son's eyes, and she hated herself for it.

"No, I'm sure he won't. But we don't know what's going on, and we just want to be safe."

"Safe from what?"

Why was she saying all the wrong things? She should have figured out some explanation that wouldn't have frightened him. Her face twisted, and the vein in her forehead throbbed. She couldn't stop the tears. "Come on," she said. "Let's just go upstairs and find you a bag."

As she led her son upstairs, she heard Cathy already on the phone with Max. She went into Abe's room and turned on the light, found a suitcase in his closet, and pulled it down. She zipped it open and laid it on the bed. "I think . . . you have some clean jeans in your drawer. I just hung some shirts up this morning. Grab them, and get some underwear and socks—"

"What are you doing?"

She turned. Zach stood in the darkness of the hallway, where she could barely see him. "I'm sorry we woke you."

"We have to pack," Abe said, wiping tears. "We have to leave so we'll be safe."

"What?"

"The police are coming," Abe added.

Now Zach came into the room, and Cathy heard another door open. She supposed everyone was waking now. She knew Zach wouldn't accept evasions any more than Abe would. She would have to be straight with them. "I have to talk to the police about a message someone left on Dad's phone today," she said. "I just found it. And because it makes me think that his shooting wasn't . . . just some random act . . . I don't feel safe staying here. I just think we need to go somewhere else for a little while."

Zach was silent for a moment, taking it in. "I want to hear the message."

Of course he did. "I'm sorry, honey, but we need to leave the phone alone until the police get here. Right now, I need you to stay with Abe and help him pack, and then go pack your own bag."

"Where are we going?"

Her head throbbed so hard she could barely speak. "Uncle Jay's house. But don't tell anybody. No texting friends, no phone calls. We need to keep this quiet, okay?"

The kids both nodded.

She heard Cathy calling. "The police will be here soon. I have to go down. Help each other, okay?" She came out of the bedroom and saw Holly and Jay standing in the hallway. They'd clearly heard.

"I'll help them get packed," Holly said.

Jay hugged her. "You guys are welcome at my house as long as you want to stay. Jackson and I will love it. And bring Brody."

Juliet hadn't even considered the dog. "Okay, thanks."

Jay and Holly both looked at her with questioning eyes, but they seemed to understand that she couldn't explain anything right now. Cathy called from downstairs, and Juliet hurried down.

"I called Max and told him," Cathy said. "I played it for him over the phone. He's going to come by and question you some more, see if he can jog loose some memory. I also called Michael. He's working on trying to find out who owns the phone that left the message. I already did a reverse lookup, but it's not showing up. It's probably a disposable cell phone."

"Then how will he trace it?"

"Someone used a credit card to activate it. If we get lucky and they used their real name, he can get it. He can also get the billing address for the card."

Juliet nodded. "So he'll call as soon as he knows?"

"Of course."

Juliet tried to think. "What . . . what do you think they wanted from Bob?"

"No idea. But we're going to find out."

"Why didn't I think to get the Camaro's tag number?"

"You were in shock. Besides, it was dark."

Juliet's soul felt crushed beneath the feet of an unseen enemy. An enemy who had murdered her husband and was threatening her children. But anger loomed greater than grief at the moment. She hoped it would get her through the night.

CHAPTER 7

Michael rarely slept when his friends were suffering. He'd gone days without sleep when Jay's wife was murdered—until he and Jay's sisters solved the crime—and now that Juliet was grieving her husband, he found that sleep eluded him again.

He especially hated seeing Cathy in pain. She had suffered enough when Joe was murdered. They had all suffered.

How strange that three of four of these siblings had lost their loved ones to murder. It was too much of a coincidence, but he couldn't make the crimes fit together. His own brother Joe, who'd been engaged to Cathy, had been murdered by a drug dealer he'd been investigating. Leonard Miller had been acquitted by his jury, even though there were eyewitnesses.

Jay's wife's murder had been completely unrelated to Joe's. And Bob's seemed unrelated to both of them. A guy driving up in a parking lot and gunning him down. A threat by telephone.

Michael's training as a police detective had honed his instincts, but they weren't guiding him now. He had to focus on facts. He just didn't have enough of them.

He checked the clock: 2:30 a.m. Too late to call his friends, but he didn't care. He had to narrow down this search. He looked through the contacts on his computer, found the name of his contact who worked for T-Mobile. When Michael was still on the force, he had solved the case of her uncle's murder, and she'd told him if he ever needed a favor, she'd be glad to help. He hoped she'd meant it.

He called her cell phone and waited as it rang. If she let it go to voice mail, he'd have to wait until morning. But that would be too late. They needed this information now.

After three rings, someone picked up. "Hello?" It was a whispered greeting. He'd clearly wakened her.

"Hey, Bette, is that you? This is Detective Michael Hogan."

He heard rustled linens, then her voice came louder. "Hey . . . what is it? It's the middle of the night."

"I'm very sorry to wake you. I just need some information fast."

"What kind of information?"

He hated this. "Remember when you told me if I ever needed a favor I could call you?"

"Of course."

"Well, I need one now. I need for you to tell me who activated a T-Mobile prepaid phone. And I need a billing address."

Her voice dropped again. "I'm not supposed to give that information out. Is this a police case?"

"Yes," he said.

"But I thought you weren't on the police force anymore."

"I'm not, but my brother is working a homicide case.

Happened tonight. I'm a PI, helping with the legwork. We need this information fast, because others have been threatened. The sooner we get him off the street, the better."

"But I don't have access to any of that at home. I don't work until morning. Can you wait until then?"

"No, I can't. Is there anyone working tonight you could contact to get that information?"

She waited for a long moment. Finally, she said, "Yeah, there is somebody. Let me make a call and I'll get back to you. Give me the phone number."

He gave it to her. "I really appreciate it, Bette. Thanks a lot."

While he waited, he opened his database of car tag registrations and typed in "white Camaro" for Bay County. Two hundred came up, of all model years. How would he ever narrow it down?

He rubbed his eyes and tried to think. It was possible that the U-Haul store had security cameras in its parking lot, but he doubted it, since the lot was so poorly lit. Max had probably already gotten the video from the gas station. If he could see the white Camaro, they might be able to narrow down the model year and any markings on the vehicle, and possibly the tag.

The phone rang, and he snapped it up. "Hogan."

"Detective, it's Bette." She sounded perkier. "I got the info you wanted."

He almost jumped out of his chair. "Great. Let me have it."

"The person who activated the phone was a George Hadley. Activated it with a Visa card under that name, but I couldn't get the number. The billing address is 2133 Tidewater Road, Panama City. Does that help?"

"Tremendously. Thank you so much, Bette. I really appreciate it."

"Don't tell where you got the info, okay? I don't want to lose my job. My husband just got laid off, so we need it. But to solve a homicide . . . well, you know how I feel."

"I do. There's a grieving family who thanks you."

When he hung up, he called his brother. Max was already at Juliet's. When he gave him the name and address, Max sounded impressed. "How in the world did you get that?"

"Called in a favor."

"You and your favors. Well, I would have gotten to it, but you saved me some time."

"Yeah, let's just hope the guy used his real name. I'm about to cross-check it with property records, see who owns that house."

"Could be renting."

"Yep. We'll see," Michael said. "I'll let you know what else I come up with. How's Juliet?"

"Shaken. They're about to leave the house. Probably a good idea."

"I agree. This is getting more and more interesting."

"Yeah, too bad. I like boring on weekends."

When Michael hung up, he pulled up his database of property records and found the owner of the address on Tidewater. It was owned by an Erica Harper. Further checking revealed that she was fifty-two, divorced, and lived in the home. No one by the name of George Hadley had ever lived there that he could tell. Erica had raised three boys there—Steven, Caleb, and David, all of whom had been Marines and served in Iraq and Afghanistan. All three of them had rap sheets since getting out of the service—all drug offenses—and two had been dishonorably discharged.

It wasn't clear if any of them still lived there. He checked the auto registration under each name. No white Camaro.

There was no George Hadley with a Bay County tag. Either the name was an alias, or someone who didn't live there had used that address.

It was a start.

His e-mail program chimed. Who would be writing him at 3:00 a.m.? He checked and saw it was a notice from Cathy's blog, *Cat's Curious*. He might have known she was still up.

He clicked the link and read her new post.

> Unbelievably, I come to you today buried deep in another personal tragedy. Like we were two years ago when Joe was murdered, my family is mired in shock.
>
> As much as I'd like to dissect the events here, I can't yet. All I know is that evil is rampant in this world. No one is immune. Psychopaths, sociopaths, and scores of people who assign no value to life are stalking their prey, with chilling agendas. Survival in these times requires much vigilance. Be careful out there.
>
> And if you pray, pray for my family. We're in desperate need. I'll write more about it later.

Michael rubbed his eyes and drew a long breath. Tomorrow this post would go viral, but no one had weighed in on it yet. He put his cursor in the comment box and typed, "Go to bed, Curious Cat. Lots to do tomorrow."

In seconds, he saw her answer. "I will if you will."

He smiled for the first time since before the murder. Knowing these exchanges in the comment section of her blog were public, he chose not to answer again. But Cathy knew better than to think he'd go to bed. He had to dig for answers, and if he found them, maybe the pain in her family wouldn't keep her up nights. If any of what he found could bring her and her siblings peace, then it was worth the sleep he sacrificed.

It was an honor to do that for her.

CHAPTER 8

Morning came too soon for Holly. After moving with her family to Jay's big house at three thirty in the morning, she'd finally settled into a fitful sleep. The baby kicked as if he knew something was drastically wrong in his family. Now she felt weak and exhausted.

Since Jay was taking the day off to stay with Juliet, Holly left at around eight to check in with Michael and see if there was anything she could do to help. He sent her across town to begin surveillance of David Harper, one of the three brothers whose mother lived at the address on Tidewater Road. Although the person who'd activated the phone didn't seem to exist, Michael had done a detailed data search about the three brothers. Today he would follow Steven, and Cathy would tail Caleb. He gave Holly David's address—a run-down house on Mongrave Street—and she sat on his street for an hour. No movement.

Each of the three brothers, Michael had explained, had

rap sheets that included distribution of drugs and petty theft. David also had an arrest for auto theft, but he'd somehow squirmed out of that conviction. Even though his black Ford truck was a recent model, it looked as if it had seen better days. Its front fender was dented, and the back bumper was crunched. Scratches and scrapes marred the paint.

When the driver finally came out and climbed into the truck, he didn't fit Juliet's vague description of the shooter. He was huge, probably six-five, and he wasn't pale. She had mentioned greasy hair, but this guy had a buzz cut. But Holly hoped that one of the brothers would lead them to the shooter with the white Camaro.

"Turning right on Walton Boulevard. Left on Marina at 9:23 a.m." Michael had taught her to dictate the route she followed into a voice recorder when doing surveillance, just in case she had to retrace her steps. To him, writing a detailed report for their clients was almost as important as doing the investigative work itself. Without it, he said, none of what they uncovered would stand up in court. He'd stressed this morning that the same thing applied here too, even though they didn't have a client to please.

She stayed back—two cars between them—as he headed into an area where she'd been many times before. It was a high-crime area, but she often had fares here—people who didn't own cars or who'd had their licenses suspended. A lot of the cabdrivers in town avoided this area, but she knew these people had to get places too. She had once been one of them.

She dictated every turn, distances driven, landmarks. So far, she didn't think David had spotted her, even though her cab stood out like a helicopter in a parking lot. As he took a long stretch without turning, she went over what she knew

about him. Twenty-eight years old, unemployed. The truck
had probably cost a lot new. How would an unemployed guy
have bought such a vehicle, unless maybe he'd bought it used,
already beaten up?

He turned down a street she knew to be a short residential
street, so she hung back at the stop sign, watching to see where
he would go. He slowed at a house, parked on the street. He
got out, pulling a baseball cap low over his forehead as he
crossed the lawn to the front door.

Someone drove up behind her and tapped their horn impa-
tiently, so she drove straight, bypassing that street and going
around the block to come up the back way. The house he'd
entered looked abandoned, but there were cars parked in the
yard. Windows were boarded shut, glass broken. The front
porch steps had long ago rotted out, but there were two other
cars in the driveway. No Camaro. Did someone live here?

As she passed the house, a girl bounced out the front door.
Holly looked away, hoping she wouldn't realize that Holly had
been casing the house. The girl yelled, "Hey!" and ran toward
the street, waving her arms.

Holly groaned. As she slowed, she tried to think up a good
story.

The girl ran out in front of Holly's cab, putting her hands
on the hood. "Hey, I need a ride. I have money."

Holly closed her hand over the gun in her door pocket.
"Where you want to go?"

"Gulf Highway," the girl said. "I thought I was gonna
have to walk or hitchhike. You're a godsend."

Holly wanted to laugh. She'd never been called that before.
"Okay," she said. "Get in." As the girl got in the backseat,
Holly glanced at her in the rearview mirror.

"This is too good to be true," the girl said. "Literally, I'm walking out thinking I'd give my right arm for a ride, and there you are."

"I saw cars at that place. Nobody there could give you a ride?"

"I'd be scared to ride with any of them. Besides, the dudes in there are only interested in scoring."

So it was a drug house. "So can you be more specific with the address?"

"The Admiral Motel, 54 Smith Road, right off the highway. Near Walmart."

Holly jotted down the address and headed that direction. "How'd you get over there if you don't have a car?"

"I had a ride there, but my boyfriend took off without me."

Holly framed her in the rearview mirror. The girl was clearly high on something. She jittered like she'd just had fourteen cups of black coffee. Or one hit of crack. A thin sheen of perspiration covered her skin.

"Cramer," the girl read from the license on Holly's visor. "That your name?"

"Yeah," she said. "What's yours?"

"Bree. How does that thing work?" She was pointing at the meter attached to the dashboard. Holly told her a little about it. Bree moved across the backseat, rolled the window down, let it blow her hair, then rolled it back up. She slid to the center and put her arms up on Holly's seat. She was like a child, distracted by shiny objects.

"So how come you were there? Did somebody call you?" the girl asked, rapid-fire.

Holly shrugged. "Couldn't find the address of the guy who called. Just as well."

"My mother prays for me all the time and says that when things like this happen it's because God is looking out for me." Bree laughed bitterly.

"She's right."

In the mirror, Holly saw Bree's narrow gaze. "You don't look religious."

Holly chuckled. "Pink hair, tattoos, pregnant. I know, right? But I do believe that stuff."

The girl still jittered, but she kept her eyes on Holly.

"So . . . back at that house where you were," Holly ventured. "I saw a truck I know. My friend David's. Big guy. You know him?"

The passenger wiped the sweat off her forehead. "Yeah, I know Dave. How do you know him? You go to school with him?"

"No," Holly said, "but we're the same age."

"He's all right when he's not too jacked up. He's worse than me."

Holly glanced at her again. "Crack?"

"Yeah, mainly. Hey, do you have any smokes on you?"

"No, I quit smoking when I found out I was pregnant. Hardest thing I ever did."

"Figures," Bree said. "I left mine in my boyfriend's car."

"So he just dumped you there?"

"Sorta. Took me over there and stayed in the car, and when I stayed too long, he took off. Jerk."

Holly pulled a business card out of her purse and handed it to her. "You can call me anytime. You shouldn't walk home from that area."

"I don't always have money, especially when I come out of that place. I have it today because I just got my disability check."

Disability? The girl didn't look disabled.

"So that guy Dave," Holly tried again. "I haven't seen him in a long time. What's he been doing?"

"Got me."

"He lose his job?"

The girl laughed. "Which one?"

"The last one. Didn't he used to work over at . . ." She hesitated, as if she couldn't think of the name of the place.

"Big Ten Tires?" the girl asked.

Holly nodded. "Yeah, that was it."

"No, he got fired. Stole money from them. Said they weren't paying him enough. He smokes everything he makes."

Holly frowned and stared through the windshield as she drove. So this guy was a dope addict who couldn't hold a job? He'd spent every penny he had and then stolen to get the drugs he needed? Did this guy and the guy who shot Bob just need money?

"Hey, you know anybody who has a white Camaro?"

The girl shook her head. "I don't think so."

"Nobody?"

"None of my friends do, I know that. Why?"

"I just remember Dave being friends with somebody who had one. I can't remember his name."

"Got me." The girl seemed distracted, anxious. She hadn't hooked her seat belt, and she was moving across the seat, getting up on her feet, turning to look out the back window, leaning up on the front seat, like an undisciplined child.

"You should really hook your belt," Holly said with a smile.

"Yeah, okay." The girl fiddled with the belt, as if she couldn't remember how to hook it.

Wishing she'd gotten more information out of her, Holly dropped her off at the Admiral, a hole-in-the-wall motel, then watched her go up the stairs and into a room. It looked a little like a place Holly had lived last year.

She checked her watch and decided to head back to the drug house to see if David was still there. If she watched him long enough, maybe he'd connect with the guy in the white Camaro. Otherwise it might be days . . . weeks . . . before they figured out who killed Bob. Juliet needed answers before then, especially with these mysterious threats hanging over her head.

Holly felt that she'd done pretty well as a private investigator. Michael had taught her a lot since she first started working for him months ago. She'd helped him solve a number of cases—even though they were boring, mundane ones. She felt like a spy, driving her cab and working as a PI behind the scenes, but she liked it that way. It fit her.

The extra money Michael paid her came in handy, especially at a time like this, with a new house and the baby on the way.

She found the street again, but David's truck was gone. Great. She should have come up with a reason to not give the girl a ride. Now she'd lost him.

She headed back to his house, hoping he had gone home and she could start over with her surveillance, but his truck wasn't there either. It was just as well. There was only so much she could do in a bright yellow cab.

CHAPTER 9

The voice mail left on Bob's cell phone had given Michael and the police a few leads, but as hard as he tried, Michael couldn't find any patterns or connections that clicked things into place.

He'd left home early this morning to follow Steven Harper, the middle brother who still used the address on Tidewater. During the night, Michael had texted Juliet the driver's license pictures of all three Harper brothers, but she didn't recognize any of them. That didn't mean one of them wasn't the killer.

The blue sedan Michael was following pulled into the parking lot of an out-of-business fast food restaurant. Michael made a quick left into the parking lot of a liquor store across the street and two doors down. He idled there a moment, picking up his camera and zooming in. But Steven just sat in his car, smoking a cigarette with his window down. Was this a dead end? Was the guy jerking him around? Had he spotted him?

Just in case Steven was watching, Michael went into the store and peered out the tinted window.

"Help you?" the cashier asked.

"Just a minute." Michael put his phone to his ear as if listening to a call. The clerk went back to whatever he was doing and ignored him.

A car pulled into the parking lot where Steven sat and crept up beside him. It was a navy blue minivan. Michael quickly turned his phone on video camera and zoomed in as he watched them exchange something through the windows.

Man! If only he had his real camera with the zoom lens that would capture their faces, but he'd left it in the car. This was clearly a drug deal. Was Steven buying or selling? It was hard to tell.

The minivan drove off, but Steven stayed put, toking on another cigarette.

"You gonna buy something or what?" the clerk asked Michael, irritated.

Michael turned back to him, glanced around the store. "I don't think you have what I came in here for," he muttered. "Thanks anyway."

"Yeah, no problem."

Michael pushed through the door and, without looking across the street, got back into his car. He adjusted his rearview mirror, grabbed his camera, and caught Steven in his viewfinder.

And then he saw it. A white Camaro, turning in. Michael's heart pounded. He zoomed in and started snapping, desperate to see who was behind that wheel as Steven and the driver talked and exchanged something. He pulled the Bluetooth out of his pocket, stuck it in his ear. He tapped it, turning it on, then pressed Max on speed dial.

His brother didn't answer, so Michael waited for voice mail. "Max, it's Michael. Call me. I found the white Camaro." The Camaro was facing him, so he couldn't get the tag number. He waited until they'd finished making the exchange, then pulled out to the street. When the Camaro pulled out, Michael followed as soon as there was a break in the traffic. He set down his camera, got his flip cam, and began videotaping as he drove.

There were two cars between them, but he passed one. "Come on, man," he said to the car in front of him. "Move!" The white Camaro turned, and Michael followed. Now it was just the two of them on the street. He kept taping. The tag was XFM 320. He set the camera down, grabbed a pen, and wrote it on his hand without looking. Then he called Max again.

This time his brother answered. "Whatcha got, Michael?"

"I got a tag number," he said.

"For what?"

Clearly, Max hadn't heard his message yet. "The Camaro. XFM 320. I just watched him making a drug exchange with Steven Harper—one of the brothers who uses Tidewater as his address."

Max laughed. "Nice work! Could be our man."

"Run the tag, see who owns the car. I can't do it because I'm driving."

"Will do," Max said. "I'll call you back."

Michael followed at a distance, letting three cars get between them. When the Camaro pulled into a vacant parking lot, Michael parked some distance away, watching. So if this was the guy who'd pulled the trigger on Bob, then it could've been about drugs—the guy was either a buyer or a seller. So what did that mean? Had he killed Bob for drugs? Was he hoping to get Bob's prescription pad? Cash? But if so, why didn't he get out of the car and rob him?

No, Bob had been in jeans and a T-shirt. He hadn't been carrying anything but his wallet, his phone, and some change. The shooter must have seen Juliet following Bob at the gas station, so it wasn't like she had unexpectedly interrupted the robbery.

After he saw them at the gas station, why would he follow them unless he thought Bob would be a safe mark, that Juliet couldn't possibly defend him or herself—and that her screaming wouldn't be enough to bring unwelcome attention before he got what he wanted? And if he assumed all those things, why hadn't he immediately jumped out of the car and shaken Bob down?

His phone beeped, and he tapped his Bluetooth. It was Max. "Did you find him?" Michael asked.

"Yeah, it's registered to a Jerome Henderson, twenty-two years old. Been in jail like four times since he was twelve. Once for three years."

"You got a picture? Driver's license?"

"Yep."

"How about texting it to me?" Michael said.

"All right. You have a make on the guy?"

"Yeah, he's sitting in a parking lot right now, probably using the dope he just bought. If you come make an arrest now, you might be able to catch him with the drugs. Then you could get him in a lineup."

He half expected Max to balk at the step-by-step suggestions, but maybe his brother was growing up. "All right, stay with him until we can get there."

Michael hung up, glad his brother was finally treating him

with respect instead of trying to compete with him on every case Michael had any part in. It was something. Since Joe's death, Max and Michael had had a hard time relating to each other.

It was Michael's fault that Joe's killer had walked away scot-free. If he hadn't screwed up the case, Leonard Miller would be sitting on death row right now. Michael's family had never forgiven him, though they pretended to. Communication had been strained between them ever since.

Cathy had forgiven and defended him, even though she'd been devastated by the murder. She'd become Michael's closest friend, and now . . . well, now it was more. He couldn't shake the guilt that she'd been his brother's girl first, but he just hoped that from his place in heaven—and Michael had no doubt Joe was there—Joe loved them both enough to be okay with it.

Michael had been working on finding Leonard Miller, without any luck. He'd hoped to watch him until he committed another crime, and help put him away once and for all. Now he felt the same sense of injustice. He wouldn't let another killer walk away. Juliet was like family to him. He couldn't stand to see her hurting like this.

If they were able to arrest the guy in the Camaro, that would be huge. When Max interrogated Henderson, he might be able to get to the reason behind the shooting. It wouldn't bring Bob back, but at least filling in the blanks and knowing his killer faced justice would give her some closure.

He knew too well that grief without closure left open wounds that never quite healed. He didn't want that for Juliet.

CHAPTER 10

Juliet hated planning funerals, and she'd never intended to plan Bob's. She'd always hoped she would go first, after living a nice long life with him. But she had no choice now. She'd spent the afternoon meeting with the pastor and funeral director, then at home she'd riffled through pictures of Bob, choosing some that could be used at the service. She'd tried to include Zach and Abe in the planning, but Zach had wanted nothing to do with it. She didn't blame him.

She'd talked at length with Bob's devastated mother and sister, and her cell phone had rung off the hook with condolences from Bob's friends and colleagues and their church family. She'd finally turned the phone to silent and stopped taking the calls. She hoped her friends understood.

Sapped of energy, she lay on the bed with her arms around Abe when the doorbell rang.

What now? Had some of her friends tracked her down?

She heard the door opening downstairs, voices, then little footsteps on the stairs. Jackson appeared in the doorway. "Aunt Juliet, Daddy wanted me to tell you that Mr. Michael is here. He needs to talk to you."

Juliet sat up. "Okay, I'm coming." She looked down at Abe, whose eyes were red and puffy. "You okay, honey?"

He just nodded.

Jackson came to lean on the bed. "Want to play Angry Birds with me, Abe? You can teach me level six. Daddy doesn't know how to do it."

Abe pulled himself up. "Okay."

Satisfied that Abe wouldn't be alone, Juliet went downstairs. Michael was in the kitchen with Jay, talking in a low voice. He had dark circles under his bloodshot eyes, and she knew him well enough to know he hadn't slept since Bob's murder. "Juliet, we found a guy in a white Camaro," he said. "They were able to make an arrest."

She sucked in a breath. "Really?"

"Yes. Max needs you to come see if you can identify him in a lineup. There's no guarantee it's him, but he is connected to the people who made the call."

Juliet looked around for her purse. "Has he said anything? Did he confess?"

"No. They only got him on drug charges. He'd just bought a large quantity of cocaine, and he had a big envelope of cash. They can't link him to Bob unless you identify him."

She found her purse in a chair at the kitchen table. "Okay, let's go. Jay, can you watch the kids?"

"Of course."

As she headed toward the door, Zach stepped off the stairs. He'd clearly been listening. "Mom, I want to go."

Juliet slid her purse strap over her shoulder. "Kiddo, I'd rather you stayed here. Abe needs you."

"No," he said. "Mom, I'm twelve. I can do this. I want to go with you. I want to see this guy."

Juliet stared at her son for a moment. This was the first thing that had animated him since the shooting. Maybe it would do him good to see justice being served. She blew out a long breath. "All right," she said. "You can come."

As they rode in Michael's Trailblazer, Juliet's mind raced with memories of the night before. She tried to capture a snapshot in her mind of the man who had looked at her at the gas station then pulled up in the U-Haul lot and gunned her husband down. She hoped she could remember. What if none of the men in the lineup looked familiar? What if he was there, but he looked different now? What if she couldn't be sure?

Michael talked on the phone to Max as they drove. Juliet wondered who else they would put in the lineup. Would it be other police officers, people off the street, other inmates in jail? What if she chose wrong?

Zach was quiet as they rode. She patted his knee, hoping this wouldn't traumatize him. She had no idea if she was doing the right thing by including him.

At the police station, she followed Michael in, purpose quickening her stride. Zach trailed behind. Cathy was there, waiting in the lineup room with Max and his partner. "You okay?"

Juliet nodded. "Let's get this over with."

"Juliet, thanks for coming in," Max said. "I want you to look at the six men in the lineup and see if you can identify the shooter. Make sure you're absolutely certain before you ID anyone."

"Got it."

She felt Zach stiffening next to her, and she took his hand. His was cold, clammy.

The light came on in the small area behind the glass where the men would stand. A side door opened, and the first of the men walked in and turned toward the glass, followed slowly by the second.

"Can they see us?" Zach asked.

Max shook his head. "No, their side of the window looks like a mirror. Take your time, Juliet."

Juliet fixed her eyes on the first one.

"That him?" Zach asked.

"No," she said. The next one wasn't him either. The third and fourth came in. Neither of them looked familiar.

She felt Zach watching her. "Not yet?"

By now Juliet was disappointed, shaking her head. Finally the fifth, then the sixth man came in and turned to face her. Juliet sucked in a breath. "That's him! The last one."

"You sure?" Max asked.

"Yes, he's the one." An unexpected rage burst inside her, and tears blurred her vision. "I looked him right in the eye at the gas station. He shot Bob."

Max picked up a phone and spoke into it. "She made him," he said. "We have a positive ID. Put him in the interview room."

As the men filed out one by one on the other side of the glass, Juliet lunged for the window. Knowing the man couldn't see her, she hit the glass. He heard it and turned toward her.

"Why did you do it?" she shouted. "What did you want from him? Why did you kill my husband?"

Cathy touched her shoulder. "Juliet, he can't hear you."

Juliet turned back to her son, suddenly self-conscious, trying to catch her breath. Zach's face was twisted and wet. "I just want to know why," she said. "I want to be there. I want to hear what he says."

"You can't," Cathy said. "Honey, just be patient. They know how to get him to talk."

"But if he's the one who called and left that message . . . I want to know what they want."

Michael looked at Max. "Mind if I watch the interrogation?"

Max raised an eyebrow at Forbes.

Forbes shrugged. "Yeah, I guess that'll be okay."

"But why him and not me?" Juliet asked.

"It'll take hours," Max said. "We have to do it meticulously, without emotion."

Cathy put her arm around Juliet's shoulders. "They'll keep us informed. Michael and I will make sure."

Juliet wiped her face and turned back to Zach. He was still staring at the window behind which the killer had stood. She shook herself out of her thoughts and tried to focus on him. She put her arm around his shoulders. "Sweetie, this is a good thing."

He nodded. "I know."

"He's not going to get away with it. They have him now. And I'm sure all our questions will be answered soon."

"It doesn't even matter," Zach whispered.

"What?" Juliet asked.

"It doesn't matter," he said louder. "Dad's still dead."

She wilted next to him, dropping her face into his hair. "I know. It doesn't bring him back."

She could hardly breathe as she led Zach back to Cathy's car. Outside, humidity enveloped them. It smelled like rain, and the wind whipped their clothes and hair.

"What will they do to him?" Zach asked as he took his place in the backseat.

She tried to think. "They'll read him his rights. Then they'll charge him with murder."

"Will somebody bail him out?"

Juliet looked at Zach. How did he know about bail? Of course—he'd probably seen it in a hundred movies.

Cathy spoke up. "He'll be assigned an attorney if he can't afford one, and his attorney might request bail. But we'll make sure he doesn't get it. Or that it's so high he can't pay it."

"Then what?"

"Then we wait. He might realize how strong the case against him is and plead guilty. Maybe he'll talk and expose anyone else involved."

"Will they kill him?"

Cathy looked at Juliet, then back at Zach in her rearview mirror. "Florida is a death penalty state. He could be executed, or he'll get life in prison."

Juliet couldn't tell whether that comforted Zach or made things worse.

"Will they shoot him in the head like he shot Dad?"

Juliet felt as if she'd just turned a corner into a whole new tragedy. Why should her son be forced to think about things like this? "No, they don't do that, honey."

"They should." His mouth shook, and he struggled to hold back tears.

Several moments of silence ticked by. Then Zach spoke again. "Mom, I want to hear that tape."

"What tape?"

"The message they left on Dad's phone. I want to hear what they said."

"Why?"

"Because . . . I'm the man of the house now. I need to know what we're up against."

Juliet's heart plunged even further. "I gave the phone to the police. I don't have it."

He was quiet for the rest of the ride.

As Cathy turned into Jay's driveway, Juliet took a deep breath. "I so dread tomorrow night. The visitation . . . all those people. And the funeral the next day."

"I'm not going," Zach said.

Juliet closed her eyes. "Of course you are."

"No, I'm not. I'm staying home."

She turned toward him. His eyes glistened with unshed tears, and his lower lip trembled. "Honey, you have to honor your father. He deserves it."

"Why? You've told me before that funerals are for the family. What if the family doesn't want it? Then do they have to do it? I could stay at Uncle Jay's by myself."

"You'd regret it, Zach."

"No," he said, wiping his nose with his sleeve. "I don't want him to be dead. I don't want any of this to be true. I just want to be left alone."

Juliet didn't know what to say. "I'm sorry, honey. You're going to go. I need you there."

"But what about what *I* need?"

"We'll all need different things," Juliet said. "Whether you know it or not, you need your family. You're going, and you'll sit by me and hold my hand, and we'll honor your father's life."

Tears coursed down his red face. "You can't make me talk to anybody," he said. "I won't smile and laugh and pretend everything's okay. I'm not going to try to make people feel better when I'm the one who feels lousy. *Everybody* should feel lousy."

"That's fine."

"And I don't want to be in charge of Abe. I don't want to explain things to him or make him feel better."

"I'll do my best with that myself," Juliet said. "Cathy and Holly and Jay will help."

He looked at her as if she'd betrayed him. Then without speaking, he threw open his door and shot into the house.

Juliet sat staring after him.

"Are you going to be all right?" Cathy asked.

"No," she said. "I don't think I am."

CHAPTER 11

M ichael knew his place. He stood in the monitoring room at the police department, watching on the video screen as his brother questioned Jerome Henderson. He studied the man's slumped posture. He was wearing a white wife-beater shirt that looked as if he hadn't changed it in days, and his greasy hair hung over his eyes. Wired on whatever drug he'd used before his arrest, his knee jittered.

Max played it easy, leaned back, relaxed in his chair, his calf crossed over his knee, trying to look like a guy having a friendly conversation about murder. "So let's go back to Friday," he said. "You say you slept till noon. Then what did you do?"

"I don't know, man. Hung out with some friends."

"Smoke a little dope?" Max asked, as if it didn't matter one way or another.

"No, man. I don't use."

Max uncrossed his legs, shifted in his seat. "Well, that's

funny, because you flunked our drug test when we brought you in. Cannabis, cocaine, and opiates."

Henderson rubbed his dirty fingers across his lips. "I have a prescription for hydrocodone. Back problems."

"You have a script for crack?"

The man didn't answer.

"So what time did you leave your friends?"

"Midnight, maybe."

"Give us their names."

"No, man. I don't want to drag them into this."

"If you claim you were with them at the time of the murder, you know we have to verify it."

Henderson just rubbed his face and looked up at Max.

"So why don't you tell me how you wound up on Highway 57 that night."

"Man, I wasn't over there. I didn't have my car Friday. I let a friend drive it."

"What friend?"

"A guy named . . ." He glanced to the left. "Goes by the name of Cytrop. I don't know his real name."

The glances to the left alerted Michael. When right-handed people glanced to the left, it usually meant they were making the story up as they went along. They glanced to the right when they were remembering things that had actually happened. And knowing the guy only by his nickname was very convenient.

"Does he look like you?" Max asked.

The man slumped again, scratched the side of his nose with a thumbnail. "I don't know. Maybe. Yeah, a little, I guess."

"Why did he say he needed the car?"

Michael smiled. Max was letting Jerome talk on about the

friend borrowing the car so that, in court, they could prove he was a liar.

"He had a job interview, man. I'm trying to help him out. I don't know where he went."

"Job interview on Friday night?"

"Yeah, man. I don't know. Maybe he lied."

"When did you get it back?"

"Not till the next day."

Of course, Michael thought.

"This Cytrop guy," Max said. "Where does he live?"

"I don't know, man. I see him at my friend's house."

"You have his phone number?"

"No."

"Then how do you talk to him?"

"I told you, he comes over. He's a friend of a friend."

"But you trust him with your car. So give us the friend's name."

It went on like that for a while, Max letting Jerome drone on about this fictitious Cytrop who had taken his car, providing the alibi that supposedly made it impossible for him to have shot Bob.

Then Max threw in a twist. "You know, Jerome, we have video that shows you in your car that night, minutes before the murder."

He looked at Max now, straightening up and rubbing his mouth again. "No way."

"You went to the gas station before going to the U-Haul store. We have video of *you*, not some guy named Cytrop. You were alone. We have a witness who saw you there."

His Adam's apple bobbed. "I told you we look kind of alike."

"Well, you have to produce this guy so we can see that for ourselves."

Jerome said nothing.

Michael studied the suspect's posture on the screen, wishing the picture was sharper, that he could see his expressions more clearly, whether his top lip was sweating and his hands were shaking.

"We found the gun in your car," Max said. "Was it registered to you?" Max already knew the answer. It wasn't registered. But Michael knew that Max was trying to catch Jerome in more lies to impeach his testimony.

"No, it was his."

"He just left it in the car?"

"Guess so. I didn't even know it was there."

"You own a gun?" Max asked.

"No, man. I hate guns."

Michael shook his head. Henderson must have been high the night of the shooting if he'd forgotten to dispose of the murder weapon.

After a while, Forbes stood up and leaned against the wall, letting the guy know that he was getting impatient. His size was intimidating, and his age gave him a gravitas that Max's youth didn't convey. "We've got a few problems with your story, Jerome," he said. "We know it was you in the car, and your prints are all over that gun. And that's too bad for you, because that gun was the murder weapon."

The guy looked toward the door, as if calculating his escape path.

"How did you know Bob Cole?"

"I didn't know him. Man, you got the wrong guy."

Max gave a long-suffering sigh. "You were identified in

the lineup. At least one witness saw you shoot him. You had the murder weapon in your car."

"Are you charging me with murder? Because you ain't read me my rights."

"We read you your rights before we brought you in."

"Yeah, but that was for drug charges, not murder."

"Still applies."

Michael closed his eyes. He wished Al hadn't spelled that out yet. Now that Henderson realized he was about to be charged with murder, he would ask for a lawyer. Then the interrogation would end, and the only answers they'd get would be filtered through the attorney.

Michael rubbed his mouth and realized his own lip was perspiring. He pulled out his phone and texted his brother.

Max, play the good guy. Sympathize. Try to get him to say if somebody else paid him to do this.

He watched the screen as Max read the text. Max's lips tightened, and for a moment he was silent.

Henderson squirmed.

Max looked back up. "You need some water?"

Henderson nodded. "Yeah, I could use a smoke too."

"I'll get you some water," Max said and came out the door. In seconds the door where Michael stood flew open. "What do you think you're doing?" Max asked. "Texting me while I'm interviewing a witness! You know, I don't have to let you be here."

"I'm just saying, you're pushing too hard. He'll ask for an attorney before you find out who he's working with."

"I know how to do my job."

"I know you do. You remind me every time I suggest anything about a case. But we can't afford for you to screw this one up!"

"*I'm* not the one who screws them up."

Michael bit back his flaring anger and threw up his hands. "Okay, no more interference."

Without answering, Max left the room and closed the door. Seconds later, he reentered the room on the screen, a bottle of water in his hand. He tossed it to Henderson, sat down, and slid his chair up to the table across from him. Henderson guzzled the water.

Max sat down and leaned on the table. "Look, Jerome," he said after a short silence. "I can tell you're a good guy. And maybe this wasn't premeditated. If it wasn't, that's a huge difference in the charges we'll bring. We're talking the difference between life and death, and decades in prison."

Henderson stared at him through narrowed eyes.

"Did somebody ask you to do it? You had a bunch of cash in an envelope. Were you paid?"

Henderson sat back in his seat and looked down at the floor.

"Because I can understand how it would happen," Max said. "You need some drugs, you're low on money . . ."

Henderson looked up at him.

"Somebody offers you cash to do a hit. Easy money. Just follow him, hit him when he gets out of the car, get paid. It's all over. Maybe you didn't even know the guy."

Henderson shifted in his chair again, no doubt the one that Michael had used when he was a cop—the interview chair that had the front two legs a slight bit shorter than the back ones, so that the man had to lean forward and couldn't get comfortable. It always left the interviewees slightly off balance.

"If you gave us the name of the person who wanted Bob Cole dead, it would help your case a lot, man. Otherwise, it's going to be bad for you."

Henderson stared at Max as if thinking it through. Michael lowered himself slowly into the chair in front of the screen and locked in.

"Bob Cole was a prominent doctor, a good man. Had a wife and two young sons. It's going to be all over the news, and trust me, it won't look good."

"That's a crock. Dude wasn't as lily white as you think."

Michael went rigid and leaned forward, staring at the screen.

"So you admit you knew him?"

"No. I admit I heard of him. You think he was just an innocent victim. But he had dirty hands," Jerome said.

Michael sat stiffer, taking it in. Dirty hands? What did that mean?

"Define *dirty hands*," Max said.

"He was into some stuff. Made some people mad."

"What kind of stuff?"

"I don't know details, man. I just heard things."

"What people did he make mad?"

"I don't know. It's just rumors."

Max stayed calm, and Forbes sat back down. "So were you hired to execute him?" Forbes asked.

"No," Henderson said.

"Then what? Come on, I need specifics. You gotta help me out here if you don't want a capital murder charge."

Henderson jittered again.

"You started down this path," Max said. "Giving us information could help your situation. You're not stupid. You know how this works. What do you know about Bob Cole?"

Henderson sighed. "I know he wasn't the way he seemed. That's all I know. I never met the guy."

"So the first time you were ever close to him was when you shot him?"

"I've *never* been close to him."

"Then explain to me how your gun winds up being the murder weapon. How your prints were all over it. Why you just lied to us about whose gun it was and who had your car."

Now Michael could see the man's sweat. "Man, I'll take rehab. I got a problem. I need help."

Michael wanted to laugh. Drug charges often went away in favor of rehab. But not murder charges.

"Work with me and we'll see what we can do."

The man glanced to the door, as if assessing the possibility of escape. "I want a lawyer," he said suddenly.

Michael groaned.

Max sat still, staring at him. He looked up at Forbes. "All right. We'll get you one."

"You do that."

"You want to call your own or should I get you a public defender?"

"I'll call my own."

Max slid his chair back and stood up. "You can wait in the cell until he gets here."

Often, that was enough threat, but this guy wasn't afraid of jail. "I don't care if it takes a week," he said.

So it was over. Michael rubbed his aching temples. All they'd gotten from that was that Bob's hands might be dirty. They didn't even know for sure whether that was a lead in the case or just a red herring to distract them.

In a few minutes Max was back in the doorway. Michael looked up at him. "Guess that's that."

"Like you could do any better."

"I didn't say I could," Michael said. "So what do you think he meant about Bob Cole?"

"No idea, but it didn't sound good. What do you know about him?" Max asked.

"I haven't been around him that much," Michael said. "He's out of town a lot and usually if I go over there with Cathy, he's at work. Seems like a good dad, good husband, nice enough guy. I was with him helping Holly move yesterday. He seemed quiet, maybe a little distracted, but he got the job done."

"I need to look into this," Max said, "find out if he did have any shady dealings."

Michael shook his head. "I think Henderson was just blowing smoke."

"Could be," Max said. "So now that he's lawyered up, we'll have to dig for this ourselves. We won't get anything else out of him for a while."

Michael nodded. He stood up and let out a hard sigh. "Thanks for letting me listen, man."

"Sure."

Michael started to the door.

"I know it's tough for you, watching from the sidelines."

Michael hesitated and turned back. "Yeah, well. What can you do?"

It was the first compassionate thing his brother had said to him in a couple of years, but it helped.

CHAPTER 12

Juliet stood on her feet for hours the night of the visitation, as friends and colleagues and people she didn't know lined up in her church sanctuary to offer their condolences. Abe and Zach had long ago disappeared with their friends to somewhere else in the church. She hoped Jay was keeping an eye on them.

Cathy stood at her side, eager to get her water, help move the line along, or encourage her to sit. But these friends and family had come to offer their support, so Juliet wanted to greet them.

But when would this be over? The line snaked down the sanctuary aisles, out into the atrium, and down the stairs. She had no idea how long it was beyond that.

Bob had so many friends, so many colleagues. It shouldn't surprise her there was a crowd.

Earlier today, she'd had an anxiety attack and threatened

not to go. "Who came up with this stupid ritual? How come I have to get dressed, put on makeup, and stand there making conversation with strangers while my husband's dead body lies next to me in a coffin? Zach is right. I can't do it, either!"

"Don't, then," Holly had said. "We'll just cancel the whole thing."

"Juliet, you'll regret it if you don't," Cathy said. "When Joe died, I didn't want to stand there, either. I just wanted to fade into the Sheetrock. But people said such nice things about him, and somehow, when it was over, I felt good about it."

Juliet stared at the outfit they'd laid out for her. She'd never intended to wear the navy-blue dress for funeral clothes. "But do I have to open the coffin? I don't want the kids to see him like that. I told the funeral director to open it, but I've changed my mind."

"You don't have to do anything you don't want to do. We'll tell him to keep it closed. And if you get too tired to carry on, we'll end the visitation."

She had known they would all be there for her. Somehow, she would muddle through. Now she stood at the front of the church, next to Bob's closed coffin, and tried to be gracious to the people in the line, even those whose names she'd forgotten.

Gordon, one of Bob's colleagues reached the front of the line and pulled her into a hug. "Juliet, our hearts are breaking for you."

Juliet tried to smile. "Thank you for coming," she said for the thousandth time tonight.

"It's just so shocking," he said. "That this could happen to someone like him. Are you all right?"

"Yes," she said. "Thank you." Had she said that already?

His wife, Wanda, pulled her into another tight hug and

didn't let her go. Juliet told herself not to resent the intimacy; she didn't want to be rude. After all, she'd hung out with Wanda often when they traveled to conventions with their husbands. But Juliet's skin felt raw from all the hugs, and knots had twisted in her back.

Wanda finally let go, then took Juliet's hands and looked into her eyes. "I'll always remember going out to dinner with you guys on those crazy medical conference trips. Bob was so funny sometimes. He would crack me up . . . the things he'd say. And he was so caring. Why would anybody want to do this?"

"I know," was all Juliet could say.

"We missed you both at the Denver conference in May. It wasn't the same without you. And now . . . we're really going to miss him. We love you, girl."

Juliet returned the love, then turned to the next ones in line, two members from her church. As they muttered their condolences with tears in their eyes, her mind went back to Wanda's comment. *"We missed you both at the Denver conference in May."*

Wanda must have gotten confused. Bob *was* at that conference in May. It had been just a few months ago; Juliet's memory of it was clear.

Before she had time to think about it, she was bruised into another hug.

When the ordeal was finally over and she was back at Jay's house, she lay awake in bed, her feet and back aching, wondering how she would get through the funeral tomorrow. What would the kids wear? Did Abe have a clean dress shirt? Maybe she should do a load of laundry.

She got up and padded barefoot through Jay's house to the

laundry room. She sorted through the dirty clothes, threw a load of whites in, then stood staring at the washing machine.

That Denver comment came back to her again.

She closed her eyes and rubbed her temples, fighting the dull ache starting to take hold.

Bob *had* gone to the conference in May. He was gone for a whole week. Maybe Wanda had misspoken. Maybe she meant some other conference. Maybe her nerves and sorrow had gotten her confused.

Still, the question wouldn't leave her. She went back upstairs, found the suitcase where she'd put Bob's laptop computer and a few other things she'd brought from home. She turned on the lamp, sat on the bed, and opened the computer. The screen lit up with the file from Bob's last session on it. She closed the file, opened his calendar, and went back to May.

There it was. The Denver conference. He had it clearly entered on his calendar.

She opened his e-mail and found the folder he kept there for his electronic airline tickets. She scrolled through them until she found the one dated May of this year.

It wasn't to Denver. It was to Nassau.

She frowned. Had she gotten it wrong? Why would he have Denver on the calendar?

The door opened, and Cathy, who'd decided to sleep over at Jay's too, stepped into the room. "I saw your light under the door. What are you doing? It's 3:00 a.m."

"Close the door," Juliet said. "I don't want to wake the kids."

Cathy quietly closed it and came toward her, wearing a pair of shorts and a big T-shirt. "Juliet, what are you doing?"

"I couldn't sleep. Something Wanda said tonight was bugging me."

"Wanda who?"

"Wanda Bennet. Another doctor's wife."

"What did she say?"

Juliet looked at her sister. Did she want her to know that her husband might have lied to her? Maybe she should leave well enough alone. But since when had she been able to keep a secret from Cathy? "Wanda said they missed us at the medical conference in Denver back in May."

"Yeah?"

"Bob went. Or . . . he told me he did."

Cathy frowned. "You don't think he did? Maybe Wanda made a mistake, or maybe you heard her wrong."

"No, I just looked. He has Denver on his calendar, but his airline ticket was for Nassau."

Cathy came around the bed to look at the computer. "Are you sure?" Juliet showed her, and Cathy read it carefully.

"Maybe it doesn't mean anything. There was a lot going on in May. If he told you he'd changed his plans, you might have forgotten."

"No. I always have his itinerary. I thought he was in Denver. He told me he was. He said he was staying in a hotel near Mile High Stadium."

Cathy pulled up a chair next to her and scrolled through Bob's other airline tickets. "All this traveling. Where did he go?"

"To drug studies. You know, the pharmaceutical companies pay all their expenses so doctors can come and learn about their new drugs. Free vacations, really. I used to go with him, but when the kids are in school, I can't. That's why I didn't go in May."

"Well, I'm sure there's an explanation. Why don't you ask his travel agent or his secretary? See what they remember."

Juliet stared at the airline ticket. "Why would he lie? Cathy, do you think he was having an affair?"

Cathy stiffened. "No, I do not. Bob loved you. There's no way."

"But that guy . . . Jerome Henderson. Michael said he mentioned that Bob had dirty hands."

"Jerome is being accused of murder! He was trying to get the heat off himself. There's a perfectly reasonable explanation, and we'll find it. I think you should talk to Bob's office workers when you see them at the funeral tomorrow. Ask them to clear it up."

"But the phone call. Why were they threatening him?"

Cathy was quiet for a moment. "I don't know. But it isn't about another woman."

Juliet stared at the computer, numbness starting in her stomach and spreading up through her chest. "I'm just confused. I don't know what to think anymore."

"This is a little thing," Cathy said. "Don't blow it up in your mind."

"He was murdered. Not robbed, but murdered. Then the threatening call. Now I find out he lied to me. I need to know."

"Then we'll find out," Cathy said. "I'll get Michael on it. If Bob had a woman, we'll find her. And we'll figure out why he went to Nassau. But first let's get through this funeral. Come on. Go to bed."

Juliet just sat there, sorrow tightening her throat, rising to her eyes.

Cathy tried to hug her, but Juliet shook her off. "No, just stop."

"We'll get through this, Juliet."

"No, we won't! He's dead! He's not coming back."

Cathy had the grace to be quiet as Juliet wept. She tried to rub her back, but Juliet didn't want to be touched. She moved away and got under the covers. "Go to bed, Cathy."

Cathy closed the door quietly. Juliet buried her face in the pillow and wept until there were no more tears.

Sleep never came that night, but she forced herself to function. Her children needed her.

CHAPTER 13

Juliet kept her hand on Zach's knee during the funeral, wishing he would warm up to her, but he seemed angry. Truth be told, she was angry too. She had never envisioned herself sitting like this on the front row of the church, sandwiched between her two sons—one with tears rolling down his face, the other red-faced and sulking. The preacher droned on about Bob's character, his acts of grace and goodness, and what a good father and husband he had been. She tried to listen, tried to worship as they sang, tried to focus on God's goodness even when he allowed her to suffer.

They'd had a charmed life. From the time she met Bob, things had gone well. They'd gotten married just after he started his residency. She had worked as a secretary and paid the bills while he suffered through the long hours and no sleep. By the time the children began arriving, he was doing so well in his practice that they bought a house and she was able to be a stay-at-home mom, something she'd always wanted to be. Eventually they built the house they lived in now, a house too big and expensive for her tastes, but one that Bob had loved.

She would have preferred a much smaller property, smaller rooms, something cozier. But Bob liked things big, and he worked so hard for them. What would she do now? She'd never paid much attention to the finances, didn't even know how much she had in Bob's life insurance.

The thought of digging for all that information made her sick.

"It's hard to understand when things like this happen, when it seems the world is running crazy and Satan is having his way." As the pastor spoke, her thoughts drifted back to that threatening phone message. She closed her eyes and prayed that the guy she'd identified as his killer was already spilling his guts—confessing what he wanted, why he went after Bob, who else was in on it. *"Nervous people can be cruel to children."*

She heard her name and looked up again. The preacher had addressed her, but she didn't know what he'd said. She tried to pretend that she'd heard every word.

Later, as they stood at the grave site, she watched Zach standing back, away from the well-wishers. Finally, he went back to the van and sat there alone. Maybe she shouldn't have made him come. Maybe she should have let him stay in his room with his covers pulled over his head. Maybe that's what she should have done too.

She suffered through another hour of mourners' hugs and friends telling stories about Bob that she'd never heard before. Abe sat on a bench among his cousins on Bob's side who had arrived that morning. He seemed okay. But Zach never got back out of the van.

Finally, when she could appropriately get away, she took Abe's hand and they went to the van. They sat on the backseat together, the three silent as Jay got behind the wheel. Jackson sat quietly on the seat in front of them, probably remembering his mother's funeral.

Because other cars were blocking them, Jay idled the engine, watching for a chance to pull out.

"Finally that's over," Zach said. "I don't know why they do this. I think it's stupid."

"Why they do what?" Abe asked.

"Why they come all dressed up and tell funny stories and laugh."

"They didn't laugh that much," Abe muttered.

"The fact that they laughed at all is ridiculous," Zach said. "I didn't want to laugh today."

"It's okay," Juliet said. "I didn't want to, either."

"And they want to talk to you and hug you and drool all over you and tell you stuff that you don't want to hear." His chin was stiff with anger. "Dad would've hated it."

"Yes, he would have," Juliet said. "Your dad always did hate funerals."

He turned his face to look out the window. She knew he didn't want her to see his tears.

"They put him in the ground like he's nothing," he said.

Abe sucked in a sobbing breath, and Juliet took his hand.

"Honey, it's not like that," she told Zach. "You're upsetting your brother."

"It is like that," Zach said, pointing back toward the tent where his father's coffin lay. "As soon as we leave, they're going to put him in the ground."

"Are they, Mom?" Abe demanded.

She squeezed Abe's hand. "Honey, we bury the bodies, but your dad isn't in there. He's in heaven now. His body is just . . ." Her voice gave out, and she took a breath and tried again. "It's a shell."

"How do you even know that he's in heaven?" Zach asked.

The question was like a splash of ice water in her face. She tried to modulate her voice. "Because I believe your dad understood what Jesus did for him on the cross. He wiped away your dad's sins. That's how."

Zach looked out the window. "How do you know that's true?"

Juliet's mouth fell open. "I thought you believed that."

"I don't know what I believe," he said. "I'd never believe my dad would be shot, or that my family would be doing this."

Juliet glanced at Abe. He gaped at his older brother, his mouth hanging open as tears stained his face. "Zach, we'll talk about this later, okay?" She pulled Abe close. "Abe, don't listen to him."

"Don't listen to me?" Zach repeated. "My opinion doesn't matter?"

"It does!" Juliet bit out. "But you're not the only one in this car who's grieving today."

Jay looked back from the front seat. "Come on, buddy. Give your mom a break. Be mad at the guy who did this, not at your mother."

Juliet wanted to thank her brother, but instead she studied Zach's face, wishing she knew what he needed from her right now.

"Where are we going?" he asked as they pulled away.

"Our house. People are coming over and bringing food. After it's over, we'll go back to Jay's."

"Bringing food? Like a party?" Zach asked. "Why?"

She sighed. "They're coming to serve our family. It's traditional."

Now his face turned crimson, as if his skin couldn't contain his anger. "The funeral wasn't enough, but now we've got to have a party with them?"

"Just for a little while."

"I'm not doing it," Zach said. "I'm going upstairs."

"Me too," Abe said. "I'm not hungry."

"That's okay. If that's what you want."

When Jay pulled into the garage, Zach burst out of the van. Right behind him went Abe, wiping his tears on his sleeve.

Juliet just sat, shaken. Jay cut the car off and looked back over the seat. "You okay, Sis?"

She shook her head. "No."

"I know. Been there."

As Jackson got out of his seat belt, Abe came running back. "Mom, something's wrong. Somebody's been in the house!"

Fear coursed through her again. *"What?"* She got out of the van. "How do you know?"

"The back door is broken and open, and everything's a mess."

Her heart jolted. "Zach!" she called. "Get out of there!"

Zach came out, his face white. "Mom, call the police."

She turned back to Jay. He was already calling. "Stay here, both of you," she told the boys. She went to the door and stood at the threshold, looking in. The house had been ransacked. Bookshelves were turned over, couches slashed open, bar stools toppled onto the floor, drawer contents spilled out.

Nausea rose in her throat, and she stumbled to the mud sink in the garage and threw up. She could hardly breathe as she straightened. By now, Cathy, Michael, and Holly had arrived, and others were pulling up out front and getting out with casserole dishes in their hands.

She saw that Jay was telling her sisters what had happened, the phone still held to his ear. Then Cathy and Holly rushed out to the street to turn the mourners away. They wouldn't be taking meals today.

Juliet got a lawn chair that had been on a hook in the garage and sat down, her head hanging. These people . . . these killers . . . had broken into her house. It wasn't just Jerome Henderson. There were others, and they wanted something. But what?

Two police cars arrived and soon after, Max and Forbes drove up. Juliet went upstairs with them, assessing the damage.

The boys' rooms had been ransacked too. How could they violate her children's lives this way? What did they want in her house?

And what if she and the boys had been home?

Sheetrock was smashed in; insulation spilled out. Every bedroom was torn apart. Bedding on the floor, mattresses toppled, holes in the walls, mirrors broken, light fixtures pulled down and smashed on the floor.

"They were clearly looking for something," Max said. "But this is also a warning."

Juliet stared at him. "What kind of warning?"

"I'm not sure. But whatever they were looking for couldn't be found by breaking a mirror or the light fixtures. They were sending you a message."

She felt that nausea rising up again. "They said in the voice mail that nervous people can be brutal to children. But I have no idea what they want."

"They left the electronics—televisions, stereo," Cathy said. "The holes in the walls don't even make sense. It looks so random."

"Like a vandalizing mission," Michael said. "They may have been looking for something, but I think their main goal was to terrorize you. Maybe they didn't find what they wanted, so they want you to be scared into helping them find it. I'd be willing to bet they'll contact you soon."

She shivered and looked around. She suddenly felt so tired. When would this be over? If they were trying to terrorize her, it had worked. This crime ring knew what they were doing.

CHAPTER 14

Hours later, Juliet sat once again at the police station with Cathy and Michael, waiting to get information—*any* information—from Max. Jay had taken the boys to his house while the police finished photographing the mess and dusting for prints.

Max came in and sat down, his expression grim. "Juliet, we're trying to figure out what prompted this break-in, and we do think it was connected to Bob's murder. We've been tracing some of Bob's activities over the last few months. He was out of the office a lot, took a lot of trips."

Juliet felt a vice closing over her chest. "They were business trips. Medical conventions, speaking engagements, drug studies."

"The destinations were often out of the country."

Juliet straightened. "Wait a minute. You're making my husband out to be the bad guy, when he was the victim? That man walked up and shot him. I saw it. Why don't you ask *him* what they want?"

"We have. We've been interviewing Henderson with his attorney, and we monitored a call he made to Caleb Harper—one of the three brothers who may have made that first call. They were talking practically in code, pretty suspicious. But Caleb told him there were rumors that Bob owed a lot of money for some kind of shipment. That appears to be why he was executed."

"What?" Juliet shook her head. "No. That can't be. Caleb's probably the one who left the phone message! Why don't you arrest him?"

"I've already sent someone to bring him in for questioning. But we don't have grounds for arresting him yet."

Juliet shifted. "Did they say what kind of shipment? Shipment of what?"

Max met Michael's eyes, and Michael leaned forward, elbows on his knees, looking at the floor.

"Juliet," Max said in a softer voice, "Jerome Henderson is a junkie who supports his habit by dealing drugs. He's been arrested multiple times for armed robbery and drug distribution."

"Then why was he out on the street?"

"He was out on probation after serving three years. Drugs are his main focus. He lives in a rat hole. Yet he was able to hire one of the top attorneys in the area."

"How is he paying him?"

"That's just it. I think there are people behind him who are footing the bill. Taking care of him."

"So . . . you think someone paid him to kill Bob? Why?"

He shifted uncomfortably, as if he didn't want to tell her more.

"Max, tell me!" Juliet said.

He sighed. "Today I got a call from the Drug Enforcement Agency. I hate telling you this."

Juliet felt sick. "Just say it."

"The DEA has an open investigation on your husband. They've been watching him for a few months. They have reason to believe he was involved in drug trafficking."

She sprang to her feet. "*What?* No! That's not true. He was a prominent, well-respected surgeon. Patients came to him from all over. He was . . . he was a good man . . . a good father and husband. He would never do that!"

Cathy stood beside her. "Max, this is too much."

Max looked at Juliet. "You told us you wanted the truth."

"I do," Juliet said. "But this isn't the truth."

"We're not accusing him of anything yet, but the DEA agents have turned this over to the FBI. The FBI agents want to talk to you."

Juliet's head was beginning to throb. She brought her hands to her forehead. "Look, I don't know what's happening. All I know is that I trusted my husband. I know there are some things that aren't quite adding up, like that Denver medical conference he was supposed to be at. I don't understand it, but I believe in him. He would never be involved in the drug trade. Maybe some of his patients abused their medication and got addicted. That wasn't his fault. But you can't blow that out of proportion. He was a good doctor."

Max looked down at his hands. "Juliet, did you know about any bank accounts that Bob had, other than the one you paid your bills from?"

She hesitated. "We had a savings account at the same bank as our checking account. Stocks, bonds, a money market account, a 401K."

"The DEA has been tracking some other accounts with

quite a lot of money in them. They checked his paychecks against the deposits, and they don't match."

"What does that mean?" Cathy asked.

"The deposits were millions higher than his income from the practice. And we think there may have been more."

Juliet brought her hand to her chest. "Millions? Well . . . maybe he had investments that I didn't know about. I didn't keep up with that sort of thing."

"So you weren't aware of any other source of income?"

"No. I mean . . . he made a lot of money. And he got paid a good bit for speaking now and then. At medical conferences . . . about different procedures he had worked on. But he declared all of that on his tax returns. We always had more than enough, but I never really got involved with the record keeping." She shook her head hard. "I can't believe this. My husband's been murdered and here I am on the defensive?"

"We're not trying to put you on the defensive, Juliet. We just have to get to the truth."

She tried to think. "Well, do I have access to those accounts? Was I the beneficiary? If I was, maybe I should just hand those accounts over to these people so they'll leave me and my kids alone."

"No, Juliet," Michael said. "I wouldn't do that. It's real important that we find out what we're dealing with here."

Juliet didn't want to cry anymore. Her eyes felt raw. "This is like a nightmare. I buried my husband today!"

"You'll hear from those FBI agents in the next day or so," Max said. "One of them told me he knows Bob."

She tried to think. "Yes, that would be Darren Clement. Bob went to high school with him. They used to play golf, but I haven't seen him in years. I don't think Bob has, either."

"Well, he's on the case. He and his partner might even take the case over."

"I'll keep working on it myself," Michael said.

Cathy nodded. "We're on your team. We'll get through this."

Juliet wasn't that confident. "What was my husband involved in?"

"I know one thing for sure," Cathy said. "He loved you and the kids. Hang on to that."

But that was shallow reassurance, and it didn't ring true anymore. "I need to go home," Juliet said. "To my own house. I need to look through Bob's things."

"All right," Michael said. "We'll go with you."

CHAPTER 15

Juliet's house seemed like a foreign place to her. The mess the intruders had left looked even more ominous at night. Shadows were bigger, more jagged, and seemed deadlier. Everything had changed. The lighting, the silence, the pall of death hanging over the rooms. Funny that this house had always brought her joy. How could things have flipped so quickly?

She went into Bob's office, turned on the light. The contents of his bookshelves and drawers lay on the floor. She was grateful she'd had his laptop with her at Jay's, so they hadn't gotten that. She'd had Michael retrieve it from Jay's and turn it over to Max.

"If there was anything important here," Juliet said, "I think they would have taken it."

"Yeah, but we should look anyway," Michael said. "There might be something they didn't recognize, but it might mean something to you. I think your best bet is to go through his drawers and whatever files are left. And if you notice something missing, tell us about that too." He set his own laptop on Bob's desk and pulled his chair up to it. "I'll go through his computer files."

"How will you do that? I thought you gave his laptop to the police."

"Yeah, I did. But first I copied his hard drive."

Cathy high-fived him. "Nice."

"I'll work through his computer files and see what I can dig up about those airline tickets and trips out of town. Also, did you read through his e-mails?"

"No, not yet," Juliet said.

"I'll do that too. Do you have a file for your credit card statements? Did they get it?"

Juliet pointed to a drawer on the floor. "Well, that's the drawer. I think he kept those kinds of files there. He's a pretty organized person." She caught herself speaking in the present tense, but didn't have the heart to correct it. She lifted the drawer and slid it back into the desk. The files that had been in it were spilled across the floor. She stacked them on the table.

"Cathy and I could do a search of things in his closet," Holly added. "Check his pockets?"

Juliet nodded. "His clothes are all over the floor."

"I'll feel right at home," Holly said. "Okay, if there's anything we need to see, just come get us."

As Michael sat at the computer, Juliet put the rest of the drawers back into his desk—the desk she'd been so thrilled to find in an antique store. She had sent it out to be refinished before moving it into the office, and it had come back looking brand new and as opulent as Bob liked.

She stacked more of the messy files and papers on the desk and sorted through them. She studied a business card for a security alarm company—it wasn't the one they used for their home. She turned it over and found the name Sid Griffin in Bob's handwriting. She set it on the desk to show Michael, then flipped through more papers, finding the usual items— envelopes, prescription pads. She looked through each item, hoping for a clue, something that would tell her why Bob had other bank accounts and why these killers had been after him and invaded their home. There had to be a solid explanation, something that would relieve her pain and restore her memory of Bob as a good man.

She found nothing significant. She knelt and gathered up more papers. A map of the Bahamas stopped her. "This must have been for his trip to Nassau."

Michael rolled his chair to her, took the map, and unfolded it on the desk. Bob had jotted notes in the margin and circled an area on the map.

"I always wanted to go to the Bahamas," Juliet said. "Why wouldn't he have taken me?"

Michael shook his head. "I don't know."

She slid the business card to him. "I also found this. It's not the security company that monitors our alarm system here."

"'Sid Griffin, Owner,'" Michael read. "I know him. We were rookie cops together. His company usually does commercial security systems. Heavy-duty stuff. So maybe they wired Bob's office. Should be easy enough to find out."

Holly came back into the study. "Juliet, I just found something that's kind of interesting."

Juliet looked up with dread. "What is it?"

"I decided to look through your suitcases and see if Bob left anything inside. The small one on his side of the closet had this wallet in it."

"But his wallet with his license and credit cards was in his personal effects. I have it in the box the police gave me."

"This is a different one," Holly said. "And it has some credit cards in it. American Express and—"

"No," Juliet said again. "We don't have an American Express account. We only use my debit card, which is a Visa. I don't like debt, so we agreed not to run up credit cards. He had another debit card for his office account, but that's all."

Holly brought her the wallet. Juliet took it and looked through it. "I didn't know about any of these accounts."

"One more thing." Holly brandished a key on a small ring. "I found this key in his shaving kit. Did he keep an extra one there?"

Juliet took the key chain and looked at the key. "This isn't our house key. It's not even shaped the same. I don't know what this key goes to."

"Okay," Holly said. "Just thought I'd ask."

"Leave it here," Michael said. "We need to make note of it."

Feeling a twisting in her gut, Juliet turned back to the stacks of papers. The intruders had taken most of their financial papers. "Is there a way to access these accounts online?"

"Maybe." Michael turned back to his computer. "His computer had a key chain app that captures his password so he doesn't have to remember it every time. If he ever accessed it on his computer, it'll probably be here." His voice trailed off as he looked. "Score! He has passwords for American Express and Discover."

Juliet stood behind him as he pulled up the American Express account and opened the last statement. An itemized list of charges filled the screen. He scrolled to May.

"Ten charges in a row from the Bahamas," he said.

Juliet swallowed the knot in her throat. She studied the statement—restaurants, hotel, a rental car. All the week he was supposed to be in Denver.

She felt the blood draining from her face, and her head felt light.

Max had said the DEA suspected Bob was involved in the drug trade. Was it even possible?

She saw charges from a dress shop, a boutique, a hair salon. "What is all this? Why would he be buying stuff there? He didn't bring anything home for me. I would remember."

Cathy met Michael's eyes, and suddenly it hit Juliet. Clearly, he'd kept his secret activities confined to these accounts so she wouldn't see them. But who was buying things at those women's shops? She let out a broken sigh. "I told you, Cathy. Another woman."

"Honey," Cathy said in a weak voice. "I'm sure there's a perfectly good explanation."

"Or maybe there's not," Juliet said. "Maybe these cards are related to those bank accounts. I don't know what to think."

Cathy sighed. "Are you sure you're up to this? We could take you to Jay's and you could sleep. You need rest. We could come back and do this ourselves."

"No, I can't rest," she said. "I have to see this for myself. I have to know."

Her hands trembled as she trudged on, searching for clues. They searched until it was almost morning, and she realized she needed to get home to be with the boys. They would want to know where she had been all night.

She went back to Jay's, weary and shaken, sick over what her findings revealed about the man to whom she had committed her life.

CHAPTER 16

Holly took a four-hour nap, then dragged herself out of bed. There were a couple of conventions in town, and the taxi service needed all hands on deck. She needed the money, so she had no choice. She got a large cup of coffee from her favorite convenience store and drank it for breakfast. The baby didn't take it well. Hyped on caffeine, her child kicked like a martial artist all morning.

When things finally slowed, she went to her favorite hole-in-the-wall diner, where a lot of her friends hung out for lunch. She went in and spoke to some of them, scattered at tables, then headed to the counter.

"Holly!" her friend Deena cried from behind the counter. "Where have you been? I've been trying to call you."

Holly vaguely remembered seeing a missed call from Deena. She slipped onto a stool and dropped her purse on the one beside her. "Yeah, I've been busy."

"Well, you look like death warmed over."

"Tired. Haven't slept much. Hit me with some coffee, will you?"

Deena poured her a cup. "I wanted to see if you were going to Nate's party last night. It was fun but I left early because you weren't there. Why didn't you call me back?"

Holly took a long sip and felt the baby squirm again. Maybe she should have ordered decaf. "Had a death in the family. My brother-in-law was murdered."

Deena's mouth fell open, revealing her tongue ring. "You're kidding."

"Wish I was."

"Wasn't your sister-in-law murdered a few months ago?"

"Yeah. And my brother-in-law to be. Makes me glad I don't have a significant other. It's like a family curse or something."

"Are they connected?"

"No. Just a lovely coincidence, apparently. But it's weird, right?"

"Some coincidence." Deena drew in a deep breath. "What happened?"

"He was shot at the U-Haul place. He'd helped me move that day."

She gasped. "I heard about that. Dr. Cole?"

"Yeah, you know him?"

"He was my doctor. He was your brother-in-law?"

"Yep."

"Wow." She leaned over the counter. "I mean . . . Wow! Dr. Cole . . . he was my favorite person in the whole world."

Holly narrowed her eyes. "Why did you go to him? You don't have back problems."

Deena winked. "*He* thought I did. Is anybody taking over his practice?"

"I don't know yet." Holly shook her head. "Wait. Are you

telling me you liked to go to him because he'd prescribe you drugs?"

Deena looked from side to side, then lowered her voice even more. "Just so I'd have some when I need them."

Holly's eyebrows shot up. "Like what?" She'd known for years that Deena took painkillers recreationally, but lately Holly had seen her popping them more and more. Holly rarely mentioned it. It was none of her business. But now . . . "So how did it work?" she asked.

"I provided him with nice, neat medical records, and he took me at my word about my medical history and refilled my scripts without too many questions."

"Seriously? He didn't order new tests?"

"No. That's why so many of his patients loved him."

Holly tried not to look shocked. "So . . . you know other people who did this, then?"

Deena's boss walked by, and she snapped to attention. "So you want the usual?"

Holly tried to refocus. "Yeah, eating for two. And would you pour this out and give me decaf so my baby will stop tap-dancing on my bladder?"

"Right. Hamburger and fries. No onions. Best prenatal meal a baby could hope for."

"Lay off, will you? I eat healthy. I just need comfort food today."

Laughing, Deena put the order in and turned back to Holly. Holly lowered her voice. "So . . . you knew other people who went to him with the same MO?"

"Sure. He was known to be . . . kind of easy. He saw a different person about every five minutes, so he didn't take time to question us much. As long as we had paperwork, he took us at our word."

"For anything you wanted?"

"No, just painkillers."

"So . . . what did you get? Lortab? Oxycontin?"

"Yeah, and the new one. Opana."

Holly had never heard of Opana. "What is that?"

"Oh, you gotta try it, girl."

Holly had no idea that Deena's drug use had gotten that bad. "No thanks. I need all my brain cells."

Holly had been known to take pills when she was partying, but she had never gone far down that road. And she hadn't done it at all since she'd found out she was pregnant. From where she sat now, it seemed a little . . . sad.

So Bob was a favorite among drug seekers, but it didn't sound as if he had done anything illegal. At least, nothing anyone could pin him down for. But surely he would recognize fake records when he saw them.

She scarfed down her food, then hurried out and called Michael and Cathy on three-way to tell them what she'd learned.

"So what does this tell us?" Cathy asked.

"Not much," Michael said. "Just that Bob wasn't above all this. He relaxed his standards for more money."

"Could this be why the DEA was watching him?" Holly asked.

"Maybe, but if so, they wouldn't have gotten very far. Bob wasn't stupid. He would make sure he was covered legally. Really, this only tells us about where he was morally."

"Didn't his lies and secret bank accounts already tell us that?"

"Yeah. I think we need to get into his office, see what we can find. And talk to his nurse and secretary."

They agreed to meet at Jay's and talk to Juliet.

Holly hoped her sister had the strength to keep digging.

CHAPTER 17

Juliet had slept for a few hours while the boys played video games. Jay had taken Jackson to school, but she had let her own boys stay home. She didn't want them out in public with some lunatic threatening their lives. Besides, they were both still in mourning, and kids could be insensitive. Sending them back to fourth and seventh grades before they were ready could be like throwing them to the wolves.

Jay was working at home today so they didn't have to be alone. When the doorbell rang, she sprang up and ran to the staircase. "Don't answer that!" she yelled down to Zach, who was already in the foyer.

"Why not?" he asked.

"Just . . . let me."

She looked out the peephole and saw Cathy and Holly. Relieved, she opened the door. "Thank goodness it's you."

"We had a key, but I didn't want to scare you," Cathy said as they came in. "I tried texting, but you didn't answer."

"I was sleeping." Juliet raked her fingers through her short cropped hair, smoothing it down.

"Can we talk to you?" Holly asked.

Juliet tried to read her sister's expression. Something was wrong. She turned to Zach. "Zach, go play with your brother."

"Abe fell asleep on the couch," he said.

"You could probably use a nap too."

"I'm not tired."

Juliet blew out her frustration. "Then go take advantage of having the PlayStation all to yourself."

Muttering something under his breath, Zach headed back into the family room.

Juliet nodded toward the stairs. "Let's talk in the bedroom."

Her sisters followed her up the stairs and into the guest room where she'd been sleeping. She climbed back onto the bed and hugged her pillow to her chest, as if that would protect her from what she was about to hear.

Cathy sat on one corner, legs pulled beneath her. Holly took the other corner. Juliet wondered how long it had been since the three of them had sat like this on the same bed, telling secrets. Only this time she didn't want to know the secrets. "What did you find out?"

Holly told her of her conversation at the diner. When she finished, Juliet slid off the bed, went to the window, and looked out. The day was growing tired, but she didn't even know what time it was.

She fantasized about grabbing her purse and the kids, getting in the car, and driving as far as her gas would take her, never looking back. If she could just ignore all these revelations, she could grieve like an ordinary widow.

"We have to search his office," Cathy said. "We need to

call his secretary. His nurse. See what they can tell us. I'll do it if you want."

Juliet dragged her thoughts back and turned from the window. "No, I need to hear it for myself. And they're more likely to tell me things than you. They know me."

"Can you do it now?" Holly asked. "Because the sooner we figure all this out, the sooner we can track down the people making these threats."

Juliet stood there for a moment, her head swimming. She couldn't breathe, and she thought she might faint. She bent over, hands on her knees, and tried to draw in a long breath. Then she forced herself to straighten. "Okay. Yes, you're right. The sooner the better."

She sat back down on the bed and grabbed her phone. Did she still have the numbers of Bob's employees? She had entered them years ago when she'd planned a surprise birthday party for him and had to contact them at home. Her underarms felt wet as she found the name of his nurse, Tracy. Perspiration beaded on her lip.

The phone rang once, then someone picked up. "Hello?" Tracy sounded out of breath.

"Tracy? This is Juliet Cole."

Tracy let out a hard breath. "It said Bob Cole on the caller ID. Freaked me out."

Juliet glanced up at her sisters. "Yeah, our phones are under his name. I'm sorry."

"No, *I'm* sorry. Juliet, how are you?"

Juliet put it on speaker so Cathy and Holly could hear. "I'm doing okay. Thanks for asking. How about you and the rest of the staff?"

"We're all so upset. We don't know what to do. We realize

we can't go to work. But if you need us to wrap things up, box up the files, refer the patients to someone else, we're all happy to do that. We weren't expecting to have our jobs end so suddenly."

Juliet hadn't even considered that. "I . . . I don't really know how to handle that. But if I can, I'll try to make sure you get paychecks at least through the rest of the month. But I need to ask you some things about the office."

"Sure."

"I know Bob did surgery on Tuesday and Thursday mornings. He saw patients the rest of the time, right?"

"Yes."

"Were they referrals from other doctors?"

"Sometimes, but not always. We kept Wednesdays for Medicaid patients, and a lot of them didn't have referrals."

"So how did he know they weren't drug seekers?"

"They brought their records. Why do you ask?"

"I'm just wondering if he . . . if he ever did things that didn't seem right . . . like prescribing drugs to people who didn't really have back problems?"

Tracy hesitated. "Do you think that had something to do with his murder?"

Juliet looked at her sisters. "We're just trying to consider everything."

"But I thought they arrested the guy."

"They did. We just aren't sure he was acting alone."

Tracy seemed to be processing that. Her voice wobbled as she answered. "Juliet, we were a very busy office. But Bob was a good doctor. I don't think he'd ever do anything illegal."

Juliet touched her chest, and tears rimmed her eyes. "Thank you, Tracy. I needed to hear that."

When Juliet hung up, she stared at her sisters, her mouth trembling. "It's *something*."

Cathy came across the bed and pulled her into a hug. Holly joined them, and they sat in the middle of the bed. Juliet clung to them, unable to stand what she knew was coming.

Finally, Juliet said, "We should go look through his office."

"Won't the police do that?" Holly asked.

"Probably, but I don't want to wait until they do. I need to go now. They haven't told me it's off limits."

"I'll call Michael and ask him to meet us there," Cathy said.

CHAPTER 18

Juliet's hands trembled as she tried to use Bob's key to open the door of his medical clinic. Michael, who had met them there, took the keys from her hand. "Here, let me." He turned the key easily and the door opened.

Juliet stepped into the waiting room. It was clean, chairs lined up neatly, magazines stacked. She had helped decorate the room in a soft, pale gray, with black chairs and couches, art on the walls. She turned to the keypad on the wall. "Something's wrong. The security system isn't armed. It should beep when we come in until we type in the code."

"Maybe the staff forgot to arm it," Cathy said.

Frowning, Juliet crossed the room to the receptionist's desk.

She gasped. The office behind the desk looked like a tornado had hit it. File drawers were open, papers on the floor. The computer that had been on the receptionist's desk was missing, leaving only a tangle of cords.

"Someone beat us here," Michael said. "Stay back."

Juliet and her sisters waited, holding each other's hands as Michael went through the office, making sure that the thieves weren't still there.

After a moment, he came back. "It looks clear. But they've been all through the place."

Juliet felt sick. Of course the people who'd killed her husband had been here. They had invaded her home. She should have expected this.

Cathy pointed. "What was there, in the wall?"

Juliet looked and saw a large rectangular hole in the wall. "There was a safe there, hidden behind a picture. They gutted it right out."

"What did he keep in there?"

She shrugged. "The proceeds from each day, if they couldn't get to the bank."

"Where was his drug supply closet?"

Juliet headed down the hall to the closet she knew was there. "He kept samples from the pharmaceutical reps here."

She opened the walk-in closet. The shelves were empty. "They got everything. I haven't been this far into the office in a few months. When I've come here, I never go past his office." She stepped into Bob's office and saw that it had been ransacked too. Drawers open, files strewn on the desk, others left on the floor.

She took each blow calmly, like an abuse victim who expected nothing less.

They went through each examining room until they reached the last two on the left. Juliet opened one of the doors and saw that the room had been turned into someone's office. A picture of a woman and child sat on the credenza. "Whose office is this?" Cathy asked.

The woman was pretty and blonde, and the child . . .

"Why does she have a picture of Abe?" Everyone turned to the picture Holly was studying.

Juliet took the picture off the shelf. "Wait. That's not Abe. That must be her baby."

"Looks a lot like him, though, right? Spitting image." Holly's voice trailed off as she realized what she was saying.

Juliet turned to her, stricken. Her heart raced, and she put the picture back.

"Her name's Amber Williams," Cathy said, pointing to a nameplate on a file cabinet.

Juliet tried to think. "I know he hired a new financial secretary about a year ago. He never talked about her."

Michael picked up a framed picture of the woman from her file cabinet. She was on a sailboat in a bikini, posing in front of a sign that said "Nassau Marina."

"The Bahamas," Cathy whispered.

Juliet took the picture, then turned back to the one with the baby. Her stomach plunged, and her heart slammed.

"What did they take in here?" Michael asked, as though to shift her attention. "Looks like another computer," he said, pointing to unplugged cords. "Possibly more files. Did Bob have security cameras?"

"I think so," Juliet whispered, putting the pictures back.

Michael disappeared up the hall and quickly returned. "They got the hard drive of the security system. Whoever came in here knew how to disarm it. They covered their tracks, but maybe we'll get lucky. They might have left prints or other evidence."

"How would you be able to tell the intruders' prints from the patients'?" Holly asked.

Michael shook his head. "The police can run prints on the security keypad or the computer cords or the areas around the safe and the security system."

"I'll call," Cathy said.

They all seemed to turn to Juliet, waiting. But she couldn't think. Bob may have taken this woman to the Bahamas . . . He may have had an affair that lasted months. The baby . . .

She couldn't let her mind follow that path. Not yet.

"Okay," she said finally. "Yes, call the police."

CHAPTER 19

The more Juliet knew, the darker she felt. She had always been one to find joy in every situation. Depression didn't often find a resting place in her heart. Even when tragedy struck their family and grief wound its way around her soul, her brain's need for happiness quickly moved her along. Whether it was wiring or faith, she didn't know. But that trait that others found so admirable in her had now fled. She wondered if she'd ever feel joy again.

The boys were brooding when they arrived back at Jay's house. Juliet went inside, keenly aware that, at a time when they needed her most, she had been pulled away to deal with her dead husband's mess. It seemed like betrayal. They needed to remember their father's goodness, and here she was helping dismantle his reputation.

She was thankful Jay had taken another day off work, so at least they weren't really alone. Both boys slouched on the couch, looking utterly miserable as *Karate Kid* played on TV. Abe clung to her after she hugged him, but Zach recoiled from her touch.

"I'm sorry I've been gone for so long." Her voice sounded distant, foreign, inadequate. "We had to go to your dad's office to get some things. Then we had to talk to the police again."

"Will you stay now?" Abe asked.

"Yes, honey. I don't expect to have to go out again today. But I'm going to be in Uncle Jay's study talking to Michael about some things."

Abe whined and asked to come with her, but she put him off. When she, Michael, and her siblings were closed into Jay's study, she set her hands on her hips. "Michael, I need to look at Bob's e-mail. Can you access his computer hard drive from here?"

"No," he said. "I have it at the office. I've already gone through a lot of his office e-mails, but he had a Gmail account for other e-mail. I haven't made it through those yet. You could get that from here."

Juliet sat down at Jay's computer and opened the Google home page. "Yeah, I know that account. I used it sometimes to send him personal e-mails."

She typed in Bob's e-mail address, and the log-in screen popped up. "If he used the password he used to use . . ." She typed it in, but an "invalid password" message came up. She tried another of his old favorites, but it didn't work either. She tried to think. Bob didn't like remembering passwords, so he tended to use the same ones over and over. He'd once used Two2kids, but that was years ago. She tried that one. The ball began spinning, and the messages came up.

"You got it," Cathy said, standing beside her.

"Let's see what he has from Amber." She typed the name into the search box. After a few seconds, dozens of e-mails came up in a list. Her throat grew dry. She paused to prepare herself, then scrolled down to the e-mails in May and opened one from Amber after the dates he'd been in the Bahamas.

Her heart stopped as she read.

Had a wonderful time last week. You're spoiling me. Sure you can't see us this weekend? Robbie misses his daddy.

Juliet sprang up, knocking over Jay's penholder.

Cathy leaned closer and read it out loud.

Holly's chin set. "That dirty cheating skunk."

Juliet's heart pounded in her ears. The veins in her temples felt as though they would burst. "'Robbie misses his daddy'?" she rasped out. "He had another child! No wonder that baby looked like Abe. And she named him after Bob!"

She was falling apart, bit by bit, and she couldn't seem to catch the pieces. She tried to keep her voice down, but she couldn't stop the sobs tearing from her throat. "My life was . . . nothing but a lie. All these years . . . he lied to me . . . about *everything*!"

Holly tried to put her arms around her, but Juliet shook free.

Suddenly the doorbell rang. It barely registered. She couldn't see anybody. Not now.

"I'll get it," Jay said in a soft voice. "Don't worry. Whoever it is, I'll tell them it's not a good time."

She stood there, her hands covering her face, as Michael read over the e-mail. "He had another woman," she said. "He took her to the Bahamas and who knows where else. They had a *baby*. No wonder he was gone so much! He had another whole *family*!"

Cathy and Holly had no words of comfort. They just looked at her, tears in their own eyes. She knew they felt her pain, but they couldn't understand. No one could.

Jay came back in. "Juliet, it's the FBI. Two agents. They want to talk to you."

She wanted to scream, put her fist through the wall, smash that computer into a million pieces. But she couldn't say no to the FBI. She drew in a deep, shaky breath and wiped her face. Cathy handed her a tissue and she blew her nose. "I'll be okay."

"Are you sure?" Jay asked. "Maybe we could ask them to come back a little later."

"No, let's just get this over with." She said a desperate, silent, angry prayer for strength, then stepped out of the study.

CHAPTER 20

Two agents stood in the foyer, waiting to talk to her. One of them was Darren Clement, the one Juliet knew had gone to high school with Bob. He smiled sadly and reached out to hug her. "Juliet, I'm so sorry about Bob."

She hadn't seen Darren in a couple of years—she couldn't remember whether he'd been at the funeral—but she gave him a hug and accepted his kiss on her cheek. "Are you on the case, Darren?"

"Yes," he said. "This is my partner, Special Agent Blue."

Juliet turned to the woman and shook her hand. She was smaller than Juliet, but she had a hard edge and a cool look of professionalism. "Nice to meet you," Juliet said, though it really wasn't. She turned back to Darren. "I'm surprised they let you work on this case, since you knew Bob. It's not a conflict of interest?"

He shook his head. "I haven't seen him in years, so it's not a problem. I'm bureau chief of our Panama City office, and this is an important case, so I took it."

She wasn't sure she agreed. An old friend wouldn't be as likely to assume Bob was a criminal based on the facts they'd uncovered. Part of her was relieved to see a familiar face, but the other part—the part that needed to know the truth—felt slightly uneasy. But she knew Darren to be a professional, and he had been with the FBI for twenty years or more. "Well, it'll be a little easier to talk to you." She introduced him to Cathy, making sure he understood that she was her attorney, then introduced Michael, Jay, and Holly. He agreed to allow them to stay for the questioning and to add anything they'd like to.

But Cathy said, "I'd rather it was just my client and me in the room. You can talk to the others later if you'd like."

Juliet nodded and glanced at her siblings and Michael.

"I'll just go back to work," Holly said. "I'll see you guys later."

Michael nodded. "I'll walk you out. I have things to take care of too."

Jay disappeared into the house, and Juliet followed Cathy back into the study. The fact that Cathy was trying to control the situation made her uneasy. Did she fear they were going to arrest her? Or that one of her siblings might say something to implicate her?

No, of course not. Cathy was just doing what attorneys do—trying to make sure that Juliet's rights weren't violated. But Juliet had nothing to hide. She was happy to tell them every single thing she knew. Maybe they could make sense of it. Maybe they would tell her that Bob wasn't really involved in anything illegal, that it was all a terrible mistake . . .

But the FBI wouldn't have taken over the case if it wasn't big.

As the agents walked into the study, Juliet started to close the door, but Agent Blue stopped her. "Leave it open, please," she said.

Juliet swallowed. Of course. Law enforcement people were paranoid. Closing them into a room would rob them of a little control, wouldn't it? She just hoped the kids were still playing video games. She'd have to keep her voice low.

Zach hated being left out. He wasn't a little kid who would hide under the bed at the thought of danger, like Abe might. He was twelve and he could take it. But the whole family had been talking in code language and locking themselves behind doors to whisper and plan. His mom, who was a wreck, wouldn't have been gone so much when her kids had just buried their dad unless something even worse than his murder was happening.

But what could possibly be worse?

He had tried to listen through doors and walls, but he could never hear more than mumbling. Now there were FBI agents in Uncle Jay's study, and they were questioning his mom.

What was up with that?

Wasn't the FBI only called in on special cases? Big ones? Maybe they were here now because his dad was an important man. Someone people looked up to. Maybe they knew that he wasn't just some ordinary dude gunned down on the street, so the big guys were called in.

But Zach had been there himself when his mother identified the shooter. She had been sure. So why wasn't the case over? Why couldn't his family just be left alone?

He knew the house had been broken into. He had seen the mess and the damage. His family had been destroyed, and now his home had too. They could never go back to the way things were before; they couldn't even pretend. And now, before they could move back into their house, they'd have to patch walls and floors and replace furniture . . .

It would be a long time before anything was normal again.

Even his dad's office. He'd heard his mom talking about that. She had cut off her words when she saw him, but he was pretty sure that someone had broken in there too. So if that Jerome Henderson guy had done the shooting, and he was in jail, who was doing all these break-ins? And what did they want?

The whole thing made him sick, but he had to know what was going on.

Zach went down the stairs and into the foyer. He heard Uncle Jay in the kitchen, and the sounds of Abe's video game in the den. He stole up the hall toward the study, hoping Abe and Jackson didn't come looking for him.

He pressed his back against the wall. He could tell that his mother was crying.

"Max said that Bob was being investigated by the DEA," she said. "That he might have been involved in the drug trade. I didn't think that was possible. I still don't. But things aren't adding up, and I can't explain what was going on."

The drug trade? Zach caught his breath. His dad involved with drugs? No way. How stupid was that? Heat rushed to his face, and his hands closed into fists. How could his mother say things like that? She knew Dad was a good man, that he would never do anything to hurt anybody. He *helped* people!

Zach fought the urge to bust in and defend his dad. He wanted to hear everything.

"Your husband traveled a lot," the lady said. "Did you ever go with him?"

"Not much, not in the last year." Zach heard a long moment of silence. "But I don't think he was going alone." Her voice seemed to crack. "I found e-mails between him and . . . a woman named Amber Williams." Her voice dropped lower, and Zach strained to hear. "She worked in his office. I think the e-mails indicate that she . . . that he . . ." She couldn't seem to get the words out.

Now Cathy spoke up. "The e-mails indicate that they might have had an extramarital relationship. They may have had a child together."

Zach pushed off from the wall, almost showing himself through the open doorway. He wasn't sure what he'd just heard. He didn't know what an "extramarigold" relationship was. He'd have to google it. But the thing about the child?

He couldn't have heard that right.

"We're aware of Miss Williams," the man said.

"Did you know, Darren? Did you know he had another woman?"

"No, Juliet, I didn't. I told you. It's been a long time since I've talked to him."

Zach heard his mother blowing her nose, then she said, "Just because he was . . . cheating on me . . . doesn't mean he was a criminal. That he was involved in something terrible."

Cheating? Now Zach understood. Tears burned in his eyes, and his heart thudded against his chest. No way. His father wouldn't do that. They were liars, all of them, even Mom.

What was she trying to do to their family?

He wiped his tears on his sleeve. His shirt stuck to him from a cold, clammy sweat. He wanted to run upstairs and get into bed and cover his head with his pillow so he wouldn't hear any more. But he *had* to hear. He had to know what other lies they were telling about his dad.

He stayed where he was, desperate to hear everything, but dreading every word.

CHAPTER 21

Special Agents Clement and Blue seemed to be aware of most of what Juliet told them, but they still wanted her to repeat it. When she was finished, Agent Blue said, "Mrs. Cole, did you have any inkling that your husband was involved in the drug trade?"

She sucked in a breath. "No, of course not. This is shocking to me. I never had any reason to believe anything was out of the ordinary. Even after he was shot, I thought it was a random shooting. That he was an innocent victim."

"Did you know about the investigation the DEA had under way regarding your husband?"

"Absolutely not. Nobody ever questioned me before the shooting. I've told you everything I know."

Darren got to his feet and walked around the room, looking at framed family photos on Jay's shelves. They weren't even hers; Juliet felt like shouting that Jay's pictures had nothing to do with her husband. He slid his hands into his pockets and turned back to her. "Juliet, we have reason to believe that Bob was brokering shipments of cocaine from Colombia."

"Brokering? What does that mean?"

"Brokers arrange the purchase and transport of drugs from other countries, then get them into the hands of distributors when they arrive."

"No, that's not possible. He's never been to Colombia. He doesn't know anyone there."

"We think his shipments were coming via one of the Caribbean islands," Blue said. "Customs officials usually stop boats coming from Colombia, so the traffickers often route them to some other point and ship from there."

"Somewhere like the Bahamas?" she whispered.

"Yes, maybe the Bahamas. We're aware that he traveled there this year. He may have set up a contact to receive the shipment and then ship it again to the US, with Bahamian papers."

Juliet got up and crossed her arms. "I still can't understand . . . why would he do this? And why cocaine? Painkillers he prescribed regularly, but cocaine wasn't even related to what he does. Why would someone like Bob do something so dangerous? He made plenty of money. He would never join some Colombian drug cartel. That's ridiculous."

Darren sat down, set his elbows on his knees, and leaned toward Juliet. "Cartels are a thing of the past, Juliet. Now the drug trade is made up of people who don't know each other but who perform certain functions in the chain. Farmers who grow the drugs in Colombia, someone else who processes it into cocaine, brokers who set up the purchase, someone involved in transport, someone to receive the shipment, the distributors who supply local dealers."

"And the money laundering," Blue said. "We think Bob may have started out that way—handling the money and sending it through several other companies, then paying off Colombian sources."

"Money laundering? He was a doctor, not a banker! How would he know anything about that?"

"We're not sure," Darren said. "But it would have been a clean way to make a lot of cash. He never touches the drugs, never meets or talks to the transporters or distributors, never gets his hands dirty. But he makes a *lot* of money."

Juliet sat back down, her head throbbing. "This is just too crazy. I can't even picture him doing something so evil. He was my *husband*. I lived with him for fifteen years! I knew him."

Cathy seemed unruffled. "You said he was a broker. Now you're saying he laundered the money?"

"We believe he might have taken a bigger role after he was successful with several deliveries. There was even more money to be made if he brokered the deal."

Special Agent Blue turned her sharp eyes to Juliet. "Did you know of any accounts that your husband had overseas? Any businesses he owned, other than his medical practice?"

"No. He wasn't a businessman. He was a surgeon. A busy surgeon. He wouldn't have time to run businesses."

"Yet we've been able to find at least three businesses that he owned—in St. John, in Mexico City, and in the Dominican Republic."

Juliet didn't know how much more she could take. "That's impossible. What kind of businesses?"

"An auto parts wholesaler, a consulting firm of some kind . . . things that don't have lots of customers coming and going. But we don't think they were legitimate businesses.

They were most likely dummy corporations created for the purpose of laundering the drug money."

"It feels like we're talking about two different people."

"Juliet," Blue said, "did you and Bob own any other property here, other than your house and the medical practice?"

"No. We helped my sister Holly buy her house, but our name isn't on the deed. We just gave her some money for the down payment. But no, no other property. Why?"

"Because the drug shipments were delivered somewhere. We need to find out where, and who else was involved."

Juliet felt sick again. "Well, I can't help you. I have no idea."

"Breaking this ring will significantly affect the amount of cocaine on the streets of Panama City and northern Florida," Darren said.

Juliet looked at him. "I can imagine. If I knew, I'd tell you. I want to get drugs off the streets. I have two boys, and the threat of their getting drugs at school or anywhere is terrifying to me."

"Then we'd like you to help us," Blue said.

Exhaustion—both emotional and physical—took hold. "What do you mean? Help you how?"

Darren's eyes were sympathetic. "We've interviewed Amber Williams already, but we didn't get much. I really hate to ask you this, Juliet, but we need you to make contact with her."

Juliet's blood drained from her face. "I can't do that."

"We believe she was involved in this drug ring. She may have even been the one who got Bob involved in the first place. We need to find out what she knows and what she has access to. She might be able to lead us to the others involved."

Cathy touched Juliet's hand, as if to guard her. "What could Juliet find out from her that the DEA and the FBI don't already know?"

"We're thinking that she might reveal something to Juliet inadvertently, out of some kind of emotional reaction," Darren said. "It was a tight ring, and Bob covered his bases in every way imaginable. Amber Williams is our only clear doorway. She has a police record. She's been to prison for mail fraud under another name. She's a pro. She's not going to give us anything now. There's too much money at stake here."

"Why would she tell me anything?" Juliet asked.

"We think she may be colluding with the people threatening you, because otherwise they'd be threatening her instead of you. Through her, you could send a message to these people. Tell them you're ready to hear what they want."

"But if she's involved, wouldn't she already have access to whatever he had? Surely she knows more about all of it than I do."

"Clearly not," Blue said. "She isn't hiding, and her house hasn't been invaded like yours has."

Juliet sighed. The thought of coming face-to-face with that woman made her nauseous.

"Just let her know that you want to make contact with the others so they'll leave you and your kids alone."

How would Juliet manage to get through a conversation like that? She would cry in front of that home wrecker. She didn't want to give her that satisfaction. This was asking too much. "What if I say no?"

Darren rubbed his face. "Juliet, if you say yes, we'll give you immunity from any prosecution that may come."

"Prosecution?" Juliet cried. "I don't need immunity. I haven't done anything wrong."

"Your husband has been implicated in a series of crimes,"

Blue said. "You are connected to him. You could be implicated, your bank accounts could be frozen—"

"Now wait a minute," Cathy said. "My client has been forthcoming with you about everything."

"Immunity would be very helpful to you, Juliet. We can't tell you what the DOJ might do. But this is a federal crime, and the people who are involved will face years in federal prison."

"But not me," Juliet said. "Darren, you know I'm not involved!"

"Your helping us is the only way to be certain that you're not blamed."

Tears burst into her eyes. "It was one thing to try to find answers for myself, so I could protect my boys. But this?"

Cathy tried again. "If she agrees, how will you protect her?"

"We'll be seconds away at all times. We'll wire her, and if anything at all goes wrong, we'll move right in."

"Move right in and do what?" Juliet asked, terrified at the prospect.

"Protect you. Make an arrest if it's warranted."

Juliet looked at Cathy, seeking an answer. Cathy seemed as uncertain as she. "I don't want to help you prove Bob was a criminal. This is all out of control. My children are going to find out."

Darren spoke again. "The boys might find out their dad wasn't what they thought, but their mother will be a hero."

"I don't *want* to be a hero," Juliet cried. "I just want to be left alone."

Cathy asked the agents a few questions about the immunity they were offering and what exactly they were asking Juliet to do. But Juliet couldn't hear any of it. Her head was pounding and she felt sick.

Finally, Cathy took Juliet's hand. "Honey, I think you should do it. Take the immunity, just in case. We don't know where this will lead, or what Bob might have done. You're tangled up in this just by being his wife, like it or not."

"You want me to wire up and go visit my husband's mistress?"

"I don't want you to have to do any of this. But as your lawyer, I recommend that you take the immunity."

Finally, Juliet did the only thing she could. "All right. I'll help you."

"Not until we have the immunity agreement in writing," Cathy said. "Signed by Department of Justice officials."

Blue met Clement's eyes, and he nodded. "All right. We'll get the paperwork right away."

CHAPTER 22

As they waited for the paperwork for Juliet to sign, giving her the immunity that she was sure she didn't need, Juliet sat on the bed in her dark guest room and tried to sort this out.

Fifteen years. Her marriage had lasted almost half her life. She had met Bob in college, when she'd been a sophomore studying communications, and he had been a medical student. She'd worked in the library for her work/study program, and he came in each day to bury his head in his books. She'd been smitten since the first day he asked her for help. Though she knew less about the workings of the library than he did, even though she worked there, she faked it until she found what he needed.

"Saved my life," he said. "If you ever need a tumor removed . . ."

"You're going to be a surgeon?" she asked, impressed.

"If things go like I hope. It all depends on whether I can

get a residency where I want. It's not always up to us what specialty we can go into."

"I'll bet you can do anything you want."

He basked in her admiration, and sometime over the next few weeks, he began to return it. He asked her out the day of his third-year finals. He took her to the lab where cadavers lay in cold storage and showed her a real brain.

She managed to put the gross factor out of her mind and fell in love with his enthusiasm for his subject. And he fell in love with her adoration.

Over the next year, they grew to be a couple, spending more and more time together. He studied most of the time, so she did too. But they came to depend on each other. She had never been more comfortable with anyone.

He served his orthopedic residency out of state at Duke University in North Carolina. They said temporary good-byes until she could finish her senior year. But the night after her last final, he showed up at her house with a ring and a question.

She said yes, and they married quickly. She joined him in North Carolina, where she supported him by working for a newspaper. She missed her mother and siblings terribly and felt as though she had somehow betrayed them. They needed her, and she wasn't there.

But as soon as he finished his residency, they returned to Panama City and she stepped back into her role of substitute mother to her younger siblings. Once he was in practice for himself, she was able to quit working and start having children. They found a church where the people embraced them as family, and he served as a deacon.

One day, after they'd attended a funeral for a friend who'd died suddenly, Juliet cried on the way home. When they pulled into the driveway of their home, Bob sat there with her. "You know, it's almost impossible to get out of this life without suffering," he said. "There'll be bad days and good days for all of us." He leaned over and pressed a kiss on her lips, whispering, "But for us, right now, these are the good days."

That became a phrase they exchanged often, when gratitude found its way into their hearts. But had they really been good days? Or distorted illusions?

The life she had known wasn't just over. That would have been somewhat bearable. Instead, it had been erased. Her memories seemed like holograms, transparent and foggy. How would she sort through it all?

She heard a knock on the door and called, "Come in."

Zach opened it, and light spilled in from the hallway. "Why are you in the dark?" His tone suggested he was battling anger and disgust.

She hadn't even realized it. "Am I? You can turn on the light."

He flicked on a lamp, and she saw his puffy, red eyes. "Honey, come here."

He shook his head and closed the door. "I don't want to. I want to talk."

She sat up and leaned back on the headboard. "Okay, we can do that."

His chin was shaking. "I want to know why you're trying to ruin Dad."

"What?"

"I heard some of what was going on today. You talking to . . . all of them. The police or FBI or whoever they were."

She closed her eyes. She should have known. "How much did you hear?"

"Enough to know that you're trashing Dad and telling lies about him."

"No, honey. That's not what I'm doing. You don't understand."

"I understand enough. You're making him out to be some kind of drug dealer. Why would he do that? He was a doctor! He took that oath."

"The Hippocratic Oath. You're right."

"He said he wouldn't hurt anybody. I don't believe any of what you told them."

Tears assaulted her again. This wasn't fair. *God, what are you doing?* "It's okay if you don't. Just . . . remember your dad the way you need to."

"I can't! Because if you're going around telling police and people that Dad was a criminal, how do you think that will make us look?" He lost control of his emotions, and tears ran down his face. "Dad was a good man. He would never do what you said. *They* murdered *him*. How come now he's the bad guy?"

"I know it's complicated, baby. I'm sure there's a reasonable explanation for all of it. But right now, the FBI is investigating, and they've told me that if I don't help, I could be implicated."

"What does that mean?"

"It means that I could wind up going to jail for whatever your dad was suspected of doing. They would think I was doing it too."

Zach backed against the wall. "Mom, he wouldn't lie to us. I know he wouldn't. He was a truth-teller. He taught us not to lie."

How could she explain that his father had lied anyway? That he'd had another family . . . a secret life? "Honey, there are things that have come out. Things he wasn't honest about. The people who killed him said that he had something of theirs. Something he was hiding from them."

Had he heard about the mistress and the baby? Why hadn't she taken the conversation outside or insisted on doing the interview somewhere else? What had she been thinking? Of course Zach would have listened.

"But that doesn't mean he was a criminal," she said. "If he just had a chance to explain, I bet it would all make sense. But he can't. He's not here."

"Mom, quit looking for dirt on Dad!"

"We're not looking for dirt. We're trying to protect you from these crazy people . . ." Her voice broke off. "Honey, trust me. I want even more than you do to find a good explanation and . . . *rescue* all our memories. I don't want to believe that your dad lied to us." Her words trailed off, and she buried her face in her pillow, hiding it from her son.

Zach just stood silently, waiting. Finally, she felt him climb onto the bed next to her. Juliet lowered the pillow and put her arms around him, wishing he didn't have to grow up so fast.

CHAPTER 23

Juliet read through the paperwork the FBI agents had brought her to sign, the pen trembling in her hand. Cathy sat next to her. She had already reviewed the documents and agreed to them. Juliet would have to trust her sister, because right now she couldn't even think. A slow burn had started in her stomach, and acid filled her chest. She was having trouble breathing and her head felt light.

Had she really agreed to go visit her husband's mistress, to look her in the eye? *What have you done to me, Bob?* How had she gotten to this point?

"You can do this," Cathy whispered.

Juliet shook her thoughts back to the form in front of her. She had helped Michael solve at least a dozen cases. She had helped solve her sister-in-law's murder. Yes, she could do this.

She just didn't want to.

She shook the pen, retracting the ink, then clicked it again.

She signed the document and looked up at Darren and his partner. "So when do I visit her?"

"The sooner the better. Today."

Juliet wanted to beg for another day, another year, another life, but another part of her longed to get this over with.

"When we questioned her," Blue said, "she didn't admit to the affair or any involvement outside the office. Let her know you're not in the dark about what Bob was doing. Tell her you want to give them what they want so they'll leave you alone."

At least that was true, Juliet thought.

"Remember she's probably connected to some pretty scary people," Blue said. "Don't say anything that might make them think of you as a danger. Tipping her off that you're working with us would be dangerous."

"Great. Just what I wanted to hear."

"But if anything goes wrong, we'll move in. We'll be listening to all of it, only seconds away."

"Just remember," Juliet said, "there's a baby in that house. I don't want to do anything that hurts the baby."

"We don't expect anything to go wrong," Darren said. "The baby will be safe."

CHAPTER 24

Amber Williams had a patio home with a French-style courtyard at the front, closed off by a decorative iron gate that probably stood open all the time. Plants in colorful pots dotted the stained concrete surrounding a wrought-iron table.

Juliet stood at the front door, staring at the brass knocker, trying to decide if she was doing the right thing. She glanced back toward her car. She had driven Bob's BMW, so that if she had to follow Amber later, her van wouldn't be recognized. Somewhere nearby, FBI agents waited to rush in if she ran into trouble. She hoped they wouldn't let her down.

Gritting her teeth, she knocked hard on the door, then rang the bell twice. A dog barked, and she heard a woman's voice, then the lock being unbolted.

The door came open. Their eyes met. Juliet forgot to breathe.

Amber looked startled at first, but quickly seemed to get

her bearings. The little dog kept yapping, staying back as if afraid of her. Juliet's lips felt dry.

"Hello," Amber said, her voice low, raspy, seductive even now. She raked her fingers through her platinum hair. Of course it was platinum. The woman was a walking cliché. Size zero designer jeans, four-inch heels, enhanced cheekbones, plumped lips, caked eyelashes. Her grief hadn't put a dent in her personal grooming.

"I'm Juliet Cole."

Amber lifted her chin. "I know who you are."

"Bob Cole's wife of fifteen years." She had to say it, had to let the woman know that he had chosen to stay with her all these years.

"Got it. What do you want?"

"I want to talk to you about your relationship with my husband."

The woman stood frozen for a moment, then she exhaled loudly and stepped back from the door. "Might as well come in," she said.

Juliet stepped over the threshold. As Amber closed the door, Juliet glanced back at it, realizing that she was committing to this. The dog sniffed around her feet, tail wagging, as she entered the living area. Funny thing. Her family had a Yorkie too. Bob had been in love with the breed and had insisted on one for the kids. Brody was now a member of their family. Of course he would choose one for his other family as well.

A baby sat in a Pack 'n Play in the living area, chattering and banging on a toy. Juliet stepped closer. The child looked about nine months old, and yes, he was the spitting image of Abe, who was the spitting image of Bob.

She felt suddenly dizzy. "Can I sit down?"

"Sure," Amber said in a dull voice. "Whatever." She picked the baby up out of the play yard.

Juliet fought the rabid feelings escalating about her husband. "How old is he?"

"Nine months."

She counted back. Where was Bob nine months ago? Nine months before that?

"I don't guess I need to ask . . ."

Amber's face grew tighter. "He's Bob's." The words were delivered with a knife's edge. "Bob was with me when he was born. He was a great father."

Juliet couldn't speak.

"So you were with him when he died?" Amber asked.

Juliet's chin stiffened. "When he was murdered."

Amber bit her lip and pressed her forehead against her baby's head. "So . . . how did you know about me?"

"I know a lot of things." Juliet wanted to wilt, to run out, to burst into tears. But she wouldn't show this woman any weakness.

Amber set the baby down, stood slowly back up, and crossed her arms. "What kind of things?"

"All sorts of things," Juliet said. "But I'm not here to tell you what I know. I'm here for you to tell me what *you* know."

Amber's eyes narrowed, as if surprised at her tone and her attitude. Had Bob told her that she was a wimp? A weeping willow? A doormat? "I don't know what you're talking about."

"Oh, I think you do."

Amber stared at her for a long moment. When she didn't speak, Juliet tried again.

"I want to give them what they want so they'll leave me and my kids alone. Tell me what it is they want."

Amber's plump lips parted. Juliet wondered if Bob had

paid for the filler. "Again . . . I don't know what you're talking about."

Juliet's heart pounded so hard her sternum hurt. Of course Amber wasn't going to spill her guts, but all the feds needed was proof that she'd lied to them. "So . . . just tell me. His trip to the Bahamas. Was it with you, or was that someone else?"

Amber breathed a laugh. "No, no one else. There was only me."

"And me." Juliet tried to focus on the satisfaction of knowing she'd opened a crack, rather than the rage at Amber's amazing arrogance. She hoped her admission was enough for the feds, but Amber's attitude still stung.

"True," Amber said. "Too bad that wasn't resolved before he died. He was going to ask you for a divorce."

Again, it was the Fourth of July in Juliet's brain. Shock and awe. Bombs bursting in air. "How many years did that keep you hanging on?"

Amber didn't like that. She pulled her chin up and stiffened her lower lip. "You should have seen him in the Bahamas with me," she said. "He was so relaxed. We spent every minute together when we went away. It was great for him to have a break from the mediocrity. And the noise."

Juliet let out a slow, controlled breath. How dare she refer to the noise? Did she mean her children? *Bob's* children?

As if Amber had summoned that noise, the baby began to cry. Amber didn't respond right away. Juliet looked uncomfortably at the child, wishing his mother would pick him up. Finally, Amber clomped over to him and swept him back up. "I need to change his diaper. I'll be right back."

Juliet waited, wondering if she was going into the back to call someone. Would Amber's cohorts sweep in and execute

Juliet—the same way they'd had Bob executed—before the FBI could respond?

Her heart racing, she looked around the room. Her gaze fell on the pictures on the mantel. Amber and the baby. Amber alone, striking a Kardashian pose. Bob and the baby. He was smiling like a proud daddy.

Juliet wanted to throw up, but she forced herself to take a deep breath.

On the coffee table in front of her lay a photo album. Leaning forward, she opened it and flipped quickly through.

Toward the back of the album, she found a picture of Bob and Amber at a party somewhere, Amber's shoulder thrust forward as if she'd taken the picture herself with her phone. On the next page, Amber again in a group of people, wearing the same outfit. No Bob this time. She scanned the faces, looking for anyone she knew. Who else knew about this affair?

And then she saw another familiar face.

Leonard Miller.

Juliet sucked in a breath so hard that she coughed. Rallying, she pulled out her phone and snapped shots of both pictures, then stuffed her phone away and studied it again. No, it *couldn't* be Miller. Bob would never have been at a party with that man—or if he had, he'd have told Michael. He knew that Miller was a murderer and drug dealer. That he had killed Joe—Cathy's fiancé. That they had been searching for him since he vanished after his acquittal.

She heard Amber's heels clicking on the hardwood, so she closed the album and sat back. Amber came back in, this time without the baby. "It's time for you to go."

Juliet couldn't wait to get out. "Tell them I want to work with them. I'll give them whatever they want."

Amber straightened, and her eyebrows lifted. Juliet would have bet money that the woman couldn't move her forehead. She waited for Amber to say something else . . . anything that the FBI could use.

But Amber said nothing. Juliet's mind raced, searching for some comment that would needle her, make her talk. But that picture hammered in her mind. She couldn't think of anything else.

"Will you tell them?"

Amber didn't answer. She just wet her puffed lips and headed for the door. Juliet followed her. Did the woman always wear heels when she was at home alone, taking care of her child? Did she dress up like this when she was in grief?

Maybe she did. Maybe that was why Bob was attracted to her. Suddenly Juliet felt frumpy and abandoned.

Amber opened the door, and Juliet stepped out.

"Thanks for coming by. I'd always wondered if you were like he said. Glad I had the chance to see for myself."

"You were exactly what I expected too." Unflinching, Juliet met her eyes, noting the strain of deep insecurities and failed expectations, the biting misery. Juliet reached to the back of her heart for forgiveness, because she knew it was required of her. But she couldn't quite grasp it. She turned and walked away.

CHAPTER 25

Tears blurred Juliet's vision, but she managed to drive to the convenience store parking lot where the agents had told her to meet them. Their van wasn't there yet, so she sat for a moment, waiting. People walked in and out of the store, and an employee stood outside smoking. She didn't want them to see her fall apart, so she went inside, cut through the store, and hurried to the restroom.

She locked the door and stood at the mirror. No wonder Bob had sought out someone else. She hadn't been taking care of herself. She was getting old. She didn't look twenty-five anymore. After two kids, her body wasn't as tight and fit as it had once been. She'd been way too consumed with busyness and church work, and she hadn't given her husband the attention and adoration he needed.

She ripped the wire off her back and untangled the microphone cord. Gripping it in her hand, she backed against the

wall and slid down it as grief overtook her. How had Bob justified cheating on his wife? Had he told himself that she didn't
understand him? That they had grown apart?

If they had, it was because of his frequent trips away, trips
that hadn't been what he'd told Juliet they were.

And now his possible connection with Leonard Miller,
who'd murdered her sister's fiancé, Michael's brother. Leonard
Miller, the archenemy of their entire family. Had Bob known
where he was all this time?

Oh, God, what are you doing?

On the bathroom wall, someone had written in a black
Sharpie "Romans 8:28." Ironic, she thought, that someone
who wanted to spread God's Word had used vandalism to do it.

But the words of that verse were written on her heart:
*"And we know that in all things God works for the good of
those who love him, who have been called according to his
purpose."*

All things. She certainly qualified as someone who loved
the Lord and was called according to his purpose. But how was
God going to pull anything good out of a cheating, murdered
husband with a criminal history and underworld connections?
Out of killers who were bearing down on them? How would
she protect her children when she could barely think?

*He cheated on me. He lied about everything. I don't even
know who this man was.*

Had some part of her known that there was someone
else? She searched through the dark chambers of her mind
and heart, looking for any sign. But there wasn't one. She had
trusted him because she believed him to be a man of God.

Was anything how it seemed? Was everything a lie?

She pulled her knees to her chest and buried her face in her arms, letting out her grief. What was she going to do? How would she survive this?

After a long while, someone knocked on the bathroom door. "Just a minute!" she called out. She got up, pulled in a breath, bent over the sink, and washed her face. She wiped it on a paper towel, then opened the door.

Special Agent Blue stood there, her gray eyes sharp. "I thought you might be in here. Are you okay?"

The humane question struck Juliet as funny, but she couldn't manage to laugh. "Yeah, I'm fine. Here." She thrust the microphone pack into Blue's hands. "We need to talk privately. I know it sounds like I didn't get much, but I saw something important."

Blue glanced back into the store. "All right."

"Let's meet at Michael Hogan's office." Juliet gave her the address. "I'll head there now."

"We're right behind you. And, Juliet? You did fine. It helped."

Juliet got back into her car and tried to pull herself together. Before turning the ignition, she texted Cathy and copied Michael on it.

Important news. Meet me @ office ASAP.

As she drove, her mind worked the puzzle. Was it possible Bob had been at a party with Leonard Miller and not recognized him? Miller had a shaved head with a tattoo on his skull when he was arrested for Joe's murder. Maybe Bob hadn't recognized him with hair. But Bob wasn't stupid. Miller's face had been all over the local news for months during the trial. If Bob was at a party where Miller was present, he had to know it was him.

She thought back to that time after Joe's murder two years before, when she had worried incessantly about her sister. Bob had seemed detached and disinterested as always, but she'd told herself that he was just busy, that it wasn't his immediate family and that he was doing the best he could.

But maybe that hadn't been it at all. Maybe Bob had seemed detached because he was involved in the whole mess.

The idea nauseated her. How could he have been close to that scum? How could he have stayed quiet all these months? If Bob knew where Leonard Miller was, and knew that he was still involved in drug trafficking and distribution, Joe's murderer could have been arrested and finally taken off the streets.

What did it all mean?

Terror hammered in her chest, and she slammed her hands on the steering wheel as she drove. "God, are you listening? Are you watching? Do you see this? Do you care?"

She had served him faithfully, even when her pastor father had abandoned their family to run off with his secretary when she was just a teen. The church that had previously been like family to them had evicted Juliet and her mother and siblings from the parsonage, leaving them homeless. During all that, she had been the one to remind her brother and sisters that God hadn't changed. That Jesus was still faithful even when his people had forsaken them. That they couldn't let their circumstances dictate their beliefs.

For so long, she'd counted herself among the blessed, among those who had been granted peace for obedience, mercy for service, prosperity for generosity. God had rewarded her for serving him. But now the family curses seemed to be rearing their heads, and those blessings seemed as fragile as children's bubbles. Maybe they weren't blessings at all.

For Bob's crimes, he'd faced a bullet. Now his sins were being exposed. The consequences were sure to fall on his wife and children. Once again, the man she'd believed to be godly and faithful had turned out to be a traitor.

"It's not fair, Lord. My boys didn't do anything to deserve this."

With that thought, she parked next to one of the defunct gas pumps in front of Michael's converted office. Cathy's car was already there, and the unmarked FBI van pulled in behind her. Juliet tried to rein in her anger and grief. There was work to be done. She had to focus on facts, not emotion.

Special Agent Blue got out of the van as Juliet locked her door. "Who else is here?"

"Cathy, my attorney," Juliet said. "And Michael Hogan. I want them both to hear this. What I learned impacts Michael too."

Blue didn't comment, but she didn't look happy as she and Darren followed Juliet in.

CHAPTER 26

Cathy could see that her sister was distraught, and it made her livid. They'd forced Juliet to do the unthinkable—face her husband's mistress. Juliet was going to have a nervous breakdown if Cathy didn't intervene. Immunity or not, enough was enough.

But Juliet seemed stronger than Cathy had expected. "As you heard," she was saying to Special Agents Blue and Clement, "I didn't get much out of Amber. She didn't concede to any of the trafficking."

"Then the trip was wasted?" Cathy bit out. "You had to suffer through that for nothing?"

"It wasn't for nothing," Agent Clement said. "She admitted to the affair and the trip to the Bahamas. That proves she lied to us when we questioned her."

"She took the baby to change his diaper," Juliet said, "and when she did, I looked through a photo album on her coffee table." She looked at Cathy, then Michael, her eyes round with sorrow. "I saw a photo of her and Bob at a party, and another one taken at the same party. Bob wasn't in that second one, but you won't believe who was."

Cathy frowned. "Who?"

Juliet swallowed hard, and her eyes welled. "Leonard Miller."

Michael sucked in a breath, and Cathy came out of her seat. "What?"

"Yes. They weren't together in the picture, but they were at the same party. Miller had hair covering that hideous tattoo on the back of his head, so he looked different, but I'd know that face anywhere."

Blue looked at Clement. "Hold on here," she said. "You all clearly know who Leonard Miller is, but you need to clue us in."

"I remember who he is," Darren Clement said.

Cathy started to answer, but couldn't. At the flood of memory, she felt that tear-surge pressure in her nose, her eyes, and she didn't want to cry in front of these people. She bit her lip and let Michael answer.

"Leonard Miller murdered my brother." His voice shook. "Joe was a cop in the Major Crimes Unit for the Panama City Police Department—I worked there too—and he was working on a drug-trafficking ring. They had a sting operation scheduled, and when Joe's team went to make the bust, Leonard Miller shot him."

Clement nodded. "We considered taking that case, but it wasn't clearly a case that crossed state lines, and the PCPD really wanted to take him down for murder one. Cop killer and all."

"Yeah, only they didn't. He got acquitted."

That jogged Blue's memory. "Oh, right. Because of the cop who lied on the stand."

Michael slapped his chest. "That would be me."

The memories sent a tremor through Cathy's body, and she found her voice. "Michael didn't lie. He had an affidavit by a woman who clearly had dementia, and she claimed she saw someone else shoot Joe. But all the other witnesses saw Miller do it."

"I just forgot about her affidavit and didn't think to give it to the detectives working the case. She wasn't a credible witness."

"Right. So they claimed you suppressed evidence," Blue said.

"And the bad cop narrative turned the jury. Miller got off scot-free." Michael swallowed hard. "So you're telling us that Miller is involved in all this?"

It was too much. Cathy couldn't process it. "And . . . you're saying *Bob* was involved with Miller?"

Juliet couldn't hold her tears back. "I don't know if he was *involved* with him. They were just in the same room. Bob may not have noticed him. It could be a coincidence." She pulled out her phone and showed them the pictures she'd taken.

As they all studied them, Juliet wiped her tears. "I feel like I'm in an episode of *The Twilight Zone*. Like Bob isn't really Bob . . . he's some person I don't know." She reached out to take Cathy's hand. "Honey, I'm so sorry to tell you this."

Cathy's mind still raced to make the right connections. "Then let me get this straight," she said, a little breathless. "Could Bob have been involved in all this as far back as Joe's death? If he was . . ." Her voice faded off.

Juliet stared up at her. "Maybe . . . maybe he just found out after it happened. I can't believe he was involved in Joe's death in any way."

Cathy shook her head. "But he did all this other stuff. Had a secret life, secret bank accounts, a secret family. If Bob was involved with Miller, and Joe was getting close to bringing them all down—Bob's whole secret world was at risk."

Juliet sucked in a sob and wilted, covering her face. "I know. But he wouldn't . . . he couldn't be connected to that."

"At the very least, he probably knew where Miller was all that time," Michael said in a low voice. Cathy looked at him and saw the stiffness in the set of his chin, the suppressed anger in his eyes. "He knew Miller was still tangled up in crimes that could have gotten him sent away for years. He knew I was looking for Miller, hoping to nail him for something else . . . *anything* that would get him put away so he'd finally face justice. If Bob knew where he was and kept it quiet, he *must* have been connected to Miller."

Michael turned to the agents. "How far back do you think Bob's drug activities go?"

Clement spoke now. "One of the dummy corporations Bob used for laundering money was set up three years ago."

Cathy felt the blood draining from her face.

"The question is," Blue said, "what does all this tell us about why Bob was murdered?"

Juliet wiped her wet face and looked at them. "Amber didn't even look that heartbroken. Maybe she turned on him."

"Maybe. We need to know who else is involved," Blue said.

Juliet straightened, new determination filling her eyes. "Tell me what to do to help find out. I'll do whatever you say."

CHAPTER 27

Juliet felt as though high blood pressure, a pounding heart, and trembling hands were her normal state these days. When the FBI agents left and Cathy walked Juliet to her car, Juliet realized that her own pain had now bled right into her sister. Cathy's nose was red and her eyes were pink, and she had that distant look that she'd had in those first months after Joe's death.

"Honey, are you all right?" Juliet asked.

Cathy met her eyes. "You're asking me? You're the one going through this."

"You're going through it too. I didn't want to tell you about Bob and Leonard Miller, but in some ways, it gives us hope that we'll be able to bring him to justice." She opened her door, and Cathy went around and got in on the passenger side. Juliet knew she didn't want a ride. Cathy's car was just feet from hers. She let her sit there in silence, staring out the windshield.

"Michael's calling Max. He'll be as upset as we are."

Juliet looked toward Michael's office window. "Yeah, he will."

"It's just so wrong," Cathy whispered. "If Joe were still here, we would have been married for almost two years by now. We'd probably have a baby. Joe would have been a great father."

"Michael will be too."

Cathy sighed. "I don't know if we'll ever get that far. We both feel so much guilt about our relationship. Like we're both cheating on Joe. We seem a little stuck."

"Life's short, honey. Don't waste time. You deserve to be happy, and Joe would want that for both of you."

Cathy chafed her arms as though she were cold, even though it was balmy outside. "I get jealous of Holly sometimes, you know? That she's the one pregnant. I know it's not rational. She's not even married . . . it'll be so hard for her. But I feel my biological clock ticking, and instead of thinking of Michael, I always just go back to Joe and all those feelings of what might have been. I think Michael senses that."

"He has the same feelings, Cathy. The what-might-have-beens. Maybe if we find Leonard Miller you two will get unstuck."

"Yeah, maybe." But Cathy seemed far away.

Juliet's mind wandered too, images rolling like nightmare sequences through her mind. Bob with Leonard, discussing the plan that would take Joe down . . . his seeming compassion at the funeral . . . his out-loud prayers with her that justice would be done.

She wanted to drive into a tunnel somewhere and scream until her vocal cords shredded.

Cathy grabbed a tissue out of the box on Juliet's console and wiped her nose.

Juliet looked at her. "Maybe . . . maybe Bob didn't have anything to do with Joe's murder. Maybe it was a shock to him too. I don't know how I could live with a man and not know he's capable of the things he was doing."

"He was a good actor."

"But I've always thought I was a good judge of character. You liked Bob, didn't you?"

Cathy hesitated. "I would never have questioned his love for you or the kids. But he irked me sometimes."

"How?"

"The way he took you for granted. He was gone so much, leaving you to do everything. Always distracted. And he seemed a little . . . full of himself."

Juliet's mouth fell open. "You never said that."

"I knew you loved him. What was I going to say? I liked him in the early years."

Juliet thought that over. "I was happy. I trusted him and believed in him. I know a little now about how Jesus felt when Judas betrayed him. When Jesus said someone would betray him, none of the disciples pointed to Judas and asked if it was him. But Jesus wasn't fooled. I shouldn't have been either."

"Jesus could see into Judas's heart, but you couldn't see into Bob's."

Juliet was surprised that Cathy hadn't changed the subject. She usually ran from spiritual conversations. "I did get irritated sometimes," she said. "But I tried to live by the love chapter."

"First Corinthians 13," Cathy said. They both managed a smile. Their father had forced them to memorize it as children—even though, as they discovered later, he hadn't followed it himself.

"The part that says 'love does not seek its own, is not provoked, does not take into account a wrong suffered . . .'"

Cathy nodded. "'Bears all things, believes all things, hopes all things, endures all things.' That's how you were in your marriage."

Juliet's throat felt so tight she couldn't speak. She had loved Bob, so if there were clues that he was cold and deceptive, she had deliberately chosen not to see them. She didn't keep score and always tried to see the best in him, as she wanted him to do in her.

Was she just a stupid fool?

"If I could just understand . . . when did he decide to do this? What prompted it? At what point did he start to lie? What part of our lives was true?"

"It wasn't all a lie," Cathy said. "I remember your wedding. He was so happy, and so in love with you. I remember watching you two dance, and I prayed I would have someone love me that way someday. Somewhere along the way . . . he just fell."

"But which came first? The affair or the crime ring? Sounds to me like the crime came first. That baby is only nine months old."

Juliet looked out the window, wishing she could go back to being oblivious. Just a normal grieving widow, remembering her husband fondly. She could have kept loving him.

But now her love was edged with razor-sharp facts that left her bloody. Now Cathy and Michael were bloody too.

It was too much, all these revelations. Too many blows to the head, the heart.

Night was falling. The streetlights cast lovely circles of light on the street, and the homes in the neighborhood across the road were lit up, families busy inside. She imagined them laughing, talking, arguing . . . unaware how quickly their lives could run off a cliff.

She wished she had enjoyed the good days more.

CHAPTER 28

Michael stood at his office window, watching Cathy's car pull away into the night. The news of Bob's possible involvement with Leonard Miller had shaken her, and he hadn't been able to erase the deep lines of grief etched on her face.

His own grief mirrored hers. Two years hadn't been enough time to forget the pain of losing his brother, and now it seemed fresh, as if it had happened yesterday.

Headlights turned into his parking lot and stopped at the defunct gas pumps, left over from when this building had been a convenience store. As the door opened and the car lit up, he recognized Max.

Max leaned into the backseat, retrieved a box, and headed inside. Michael went back to the chair behind his desk and dropped into it, waiting.

His brother came into the front room, then seconds later appeared at Michael's office doorway. "Hey."

Michael glanced at the box. "Whatcha got?"

Max came in and set the box on the desk. He lowered himself into the chair in front of Michael's desk. "All the files related to Joe's death. Everything we had on Leonard Miller, plus the files having to do with the drug-trafficking case Joe was working on. I thought we could look over them now that we have this new information about Bob and Leonard Miller."

Michael sat up, stunned that his brother would share this with him. Max opened the box, began unloading folders. "I know you were still at the department during the investigation. You know all this as well as I do. But it's worth a review, right?"

"Right." Michael rolled closer to the desk and sorted through the folders.

Max pulled out a bound one over a foot thick. "Here's all of Joe's notes about the case leading up to the drug bust, where Miller was waiting for him. If you and I spend some time going over all this, and we find out what he knew, we might be able to locate Miller through the network Joe's investigation uncovered."

Michael sat back in his chair. He met his brother's eyes. Max's eyes had misted over, and Michael's stung as well. Michael rubbed the corners of his trembling mouth. "Have I ever told you you're a genius?"

Max looked away. "No. No, you haven't."

"Well, I should have."

Max didn't answer. He just dove into the files, pointing out the things Joe had uncovered about the drug-trafficking operation in northern Florida—a trafficking operation that could intersect with Bob's activities.

"Miller wasn't high up in the drug ring," Max said. "He wasn't a broker, probably just a low-level transporter. I've been all through this, and Miller wasn't even on the horizon until he ambushed Joe. Someone had tipped these guys off about the bust, and Miller was probably low enough on the totem pole to be tasked with ending it."

"That probably earned him the trust of the higher-ups."

"Right. The whole network reorganized after the bust. There was heat on all of them—I think most of them left the area. That left positions to be filled. If Miller stayed, he could have gotten a higher position and a bigger cut of the pie."

"But we were convinced he'd left," Michael said. "I've turned this town upside down looking for him. The only time I've seen him back was when his mother died a few months ago."

"But I got Juliet to send me a copy of the picture she took at Amber's, even though I'm not on the case anymore. I studied it. That was taken at Mal's Irish Pub here in Panama City. Miller's hair was longer than when you saw him last. And I asked Juliet about what Bob was wearing in the picture. She bought the shirt for his birthday, about three months ago. So we can date the picture to sometime in the last three months." Max leaned forward and locked his gaze on Michael. "Think about it. If he had the chance to stay here and fill a vacuum in this drug ring, and make a ton of cash, I think he'd do it. The guy thought he'd get away with it. He did last time."

Michael's heart began to race. "We're going to find him. And this time, we'll send him away for a very long time."

"If anybody can find him, you can," Max said.

That was the kindest thing Max had said in two years, and Michael realized then how much he had missed his younger brother. He swallowed the knot in his throat and threw himself into reviewing the files.

CHAPTER 29

As Juliet drove back to Jay's house, her grief hit her again, and she gave in to deep, ugly, wet sobs that seemed to rip out every belief she'd once held dear. *God, how will I survive this? How will I protect my kids?*

Closed off in the car, she didn't muffle her wails. No one could hear her, and in the dark, they couldn't see her either.

Just strike me dead, Lord. Just kill me now. I want to go Home.

She wanted to just pull over and fall asleep right here and be done with it. But her kids . . . they needed her. They had been betrayed too. Zach already knew so much about it. Had Bob ever considered what it would do to his sons if the truth came out? Had it kept him awake nights?

At least one of their parents had to be there for them. She had to go on. She had no choice. It wasn't about her. It was about them.

"Lord," she said through her teeth, "I believe Romans 8:28 is true. But I can't imagine how all of this is going to work for good, because all I see is tragedy and heartache, and shock after shock. We need some real miracles here."

Her tears left her battered, but her prayer gave her a bittersweet, soft warmth that fell over her like a hot shower, as though God wept with her. She wept until she was dry, until she had no more energy to shoulder the pain. A divine numbness set in, one that would help her to take another breath, and then another. She felt the warmth of divine arms around her. His love renewed her strength, as impossible as that was. The miracle of that startled her, then settled into her heart.

She would learn to do this, taking steps like a baby learning the power of his legs. And she knew that God would have his hands out for her, waiting to catch her when she fell.

Bled dry emotionally by the time she got back to Jay's, Juliet went into the TV room where Zach and Abe sat sprawled on the couch. After hugs and apologies again for being gone so long, she sank into a club chair and stared, unseeing, at the TV screen.

Jackson, who'd been playing on the floor, looked up at her with his sweet eyes. She smiled at him, hoping he wouldn't ask her to come play with him.

Instead, he got up and climbed onto her lap.

She kissed his cheek and put her arms around him, and he laid his head against her chest. No words were needed, and her heart filled to overflowing. Little Jackson, who'd lost his mother just months earlier, understood her sorrow. Only five years old, he seemed to understand that she had nothing to give. But he did.

She held him that way for a long time, wiping her tears

before they hit her cheeks and saddened her boys. She hoped the TV distracted them from their pain.

Later, when Jay had taken Jackson upstairs to bathe him and get him ready for bed, Juliet went to the guest room and lay on the bed, staring at the ceiling.

Abe came to the doorway. "Mom, I want to go back to school tomorrow."

Juliet sat up and saw Zach in the hall behind him. "I'll have to think about it. I don't know if it's a good idea yet."

"Well, the only reason I should stay home is if it makes me feel better, right? But it's boring here. Uncle Jay wouldn't have to work at home to watch us. So if it doesn't make me feel better to stay home, why can't I go back and be with my friends?"

"Don't listen to him," Zach said. "I don't want to go back to school. I don't want to hear any questions. I don't want to be stared at by people who feel sorry for me."

Juliet wished she could save this for another day. "Come on in here, guys."

They came into the room, and Abe got onto her bed. Zach sat on the floor and leaned back against the wall.

"Your eyes are all puffy," Abe said.

"Yeah, I know." She looked at her younger son. "So are yours."

He nodded.

"It just stinks," she said. "Losing your dad, having to deal with all this."

Abe wiped his nose. "I dreamed about him last night."

Zach looked at him. Abe's face turned red and twisted as if he tried hard to hold back the emotion, but couldn't keep it in.

"You did?" she asked. "Tell me about it."

"I dreamed I saw him. He was just standing there, but he

wouldn't look at me. It was like he was ignoring me. I called out, 'Dad! Dad!' But he didn't answer."

Juliet closed her eyes. Even in their son's dreams, Bob was hurting him. "Just remember . . . it was a dream. I'm sure Dad wouldn't have ignored you."

"I just can't picture him gone," he said. "I keep thinking he's going to come home, that he's just on a trip somewhere. He's going to come back and we'll all sit down and have tacos."

"I know," she said. "I keep thinking things like that too."

"I wish you wouldn't be gone all the time. I wish you would stay here with me. I don't have anybody to talk to. Zach doesn't want to talk."

Zach rolled his eyes, as if he resented the guilt trip.

But that same guilt crushed her. "Sweetheart, you know what I'd love to do is be here with you 24/7, and make you and Zach my main focus as we get through this. But things have happened . . . and I've had no choice about where I'm spending my time."

"Yeah," Abe said. "But that's why I want to go to school."

She sighed. She would need to talk to the principal about security. "I'll think about it. You know, if you need to talk to somebody besides me, I can get you a counselor."

"I don't want to talk to anybody else," he said.

She slid her arms around Abe and held him close. How would she tell him about his father? When would she tell him? She could keep as much of it from him as possible, but soon it would be all over the news. Kids would mock the boys at school. Parents wouldn't let their kids hang out with hers. They would think this family had too many secrets. She couldn't stand the thought.

But she couldn't worry about that yet. One step at a time.

First she had to feed her kids, then she could spend time with them. Then, when she got them to bed tonight, Michael, Cathy, and Holly were coming over for a strategy session. She wished it could wait, but it couldn't. Too much was at stake. Too many dangers lurking.

The only way to get to the other side was to plow through. Time could be running out for her and her kids.

CHAPTER 30

While Juliet was upstairs with the kids, Cathy, Michael, Holly, and Jay gathered on the back patio to go over the events of the day. It made Cathy sick to rehash it, but her siblings needed to know.

"I can't believe you left me out of this whole thing," Holly spouted.

Cathy didn't want to fight. "Holly, I'm her attorney. We met at Michael's. The FBI didn't want a crowd there. But Juliet wanted Michael to hear it because it was about Leonard Miller."

"Just sayin' . . ."

"Hey, I'm left out of everything," Jay said. "I hear everything after the fact."

"You're watching the kids," Cathy said. "That's important. What do you guys want? It's not about you. It's about Juliet. She's the one suffering."

"You don't have to get huffy." Holly sat in the rocking chair, her hand stroking her swollen belly. "I'm the one who's supposed to get moody."

"You're updated now, so get over it."

Always the peacemaker, Jay got to his feet. "Holly, come in and help me get some nachos together, will you?"

Holly got up and followed him in, a pinched look on her face, as if she was disgusted with her sister.

Cathy looked at Michael. "You believe her?"

Michael shrugged. "She doesn't realize how important this news was to us. Jay's probably straightening her out." He turned his chair to face her and leaned forward, touched her chin. "Sure you're okay?"

She met his eyes. "Okay, no. I'm not okay. Are you?"

He drew in a deep breath. "Not really."

"The monster who killed Joe is out there, still doing what he was doing, partying and having a big time. And everything about both of our lives has changed."

A golden light danced on one side of Michael's face, light cast by the flames in the fire pit. "We're going to find him."

Cathy just looked away.

With gentle fingers, he turned her face back and leaned closer. "Do you believe me?"

She thought about that, then nodded. "Yeah, I do. It just . . . dredged it all back up, you know? I thought we were digging for one thing, and all of a sudden, we find something else. Leonard Miller seems to intrude into every area of our lives. So much would be different if Joe hadn't been killed."

"But then we wouldn't be here."

She knew he didn't mean sitting on Jay's patio. The two of them . . . the relationship that seemed unspoken, yet was so intense. And filled with so much guilt.

"I'm not saying this is better or worse," he added. "Just

that it's where we are. And I'm kind of tired of analyzing it and finding reasons to kick myself for it."

She felt her hard edges softening. "I know. I'm tired of it too."

"Maybe by finding Miller we can move on. Get over that barricade."

"And if we don't? Then we don't move on?"

He smiled and kissed her, stroked her face. "No, we still move on. I'm not going anywhere until you tell me to get lost."

She managed to smile now. "That won't happen." She pressed her forehead against his, touched the stubble on his jaw, breathed in the scent that was so uniquely his. When their lips touched, she closed her eyes and savored the feeling. Hope . . . love . . .

But the barricade still existed. Leonard Miller—the unfinished business that bound them together but kept them apart. Maybe if he could be extricated from their lives, instead of remaining a constant regret hanging over them like a thundercloud that hadn't yet burst . . .

When their kiss ended, they kept their foreheads together, Michael's fingers laced through her hair. "I thank God for you."

Cathy let that sink in. "God. I still have issues with him. He takes so much away from us."

"But he gives us so much. Don't miss what he's given you."

She swallowed hard, wishing she could change her thinking. But loss still hung so heavy in her mind.

But in spite of it all, she missed her relationship with her Creator. Her thoughts wandered to him often, and she found herself talking to him when she didn't even plan to. She didn't call it prayer. Prayer was too intentional. But those conversations she had with him were still wrought with sorrow and blame. She didn't know if that would ever change.

CHAPTER 31

When the kids were finally in bed asleep, Juliet went downstairs and met her siblings and Michael on the patio. They sat in a circle around the fire pit—Cathy and Michael on the rattan love seat, Jay in a rocking chair, Holly with her feet curled up beneath her on a cushioned chair, her hands crossed over her small round belly—all of them lit in a pretty yellow glow.

It reminded her of camping as a child, back when their father was still with the family. They'd roast marshmallows and make s'mores, until their faces and hands were sticky and soot-covered from the smoke that stuck to their sugar-coated skin.

But these weren't good times. Jay had made it as pleasant as he could, but they spoke outside so Zach wouldn't wake up and sneak down the stairs to hear them. And there was nothing pleasant about this subject. She'd rather be in bed with the covers pulled over her head.

"They're asleep, finally," she said, dropping into a chair. "So what are we going to do?"

Michael had laid out equipment at the center of a patio table next to the fire pit—several cameras, binoculars, and a few things Juliet hadn't seen before. "First, we talk to the security company we found on that card in Bob's office and see if they can give us an address. I checked, and the security companies that wired your house and the clinic were different. So there must have been another property. I'm guessing it was where they received and held the drugs when deliveries came."

"Right," Juliet said. "I'd forgotten about that card."

"Second, we'll follow Amber and hope she'll lead us to Miller or her other contacts."

"But don't you think the feds are following her already?" Jay asked.

Michael shrugged. "If they are, that's fine, but it won't hurt for us to do it too."

Juliet looked at the equipment, studying each item.

"You know how to use some of this," Michael said.

Juliet nodded. She had learned through trial and error over the last few months as she'd followed Michael's cases. She was glad he'd started paying them. She was going to need that money even more now. She'd never dreamed she'd have to use those skills to uncover her own husband's crimes or to follow his mistress.

She reached for a camera. "This is the one I've used?"

"Probably," Michael said. "It's all set up. The zoom lens will come in handy."

"We need to be constantly armed," Cathy said, "except for Michael, of course."

Juliet nodded. "Totally agree."

"The cartridges and clips are right here," Michael said, pointing but not touching them. He wasn't allowed to be in possession of firearms or ammo, so Juliet assumed Cathy had provided these. "Juliet, you've had shooting practice. You know what to do."

"I just don't want to do it," she said.

Jay got up, put his hands into his jeans pockets, and paced across the concrete. "Look, I know what you guys are doing really works. You helped solve Annalee's murder. But I'm worried about this. I don't like having my sisters in danger."

Juliet regarded her younger brother. "I know, Jay. That's exactly what I said a few months ago when we were working on Annalee's case. I didn't want to moonlight as a private investigator. I didn't want Holly doing it, and I didn't want Cathy doing it. But if we hadn't, you would be in prison right now, and Jackson might be dead."

She saw the color drain from his face. "I know," he said. "It's important. I just wish the feds would solve all this so you guys wouldn't have to."

"Maybe they will," Juliet said. "But I don't have a choice. I have to help get to the bottom of all this. My children's lives could be in danger. We'll never get our lives back to normal until all this is resolved. I can't even begin trying."

Michael spoke again. "Remember, things got this far even though the feds were watching Bob. Now Bob is dead, someone is threatening Juliet, her house is torn up . . . Believe me, the more people we have working on this, the better."

Juliet nodded. "And whatever we find we'll share with the feds. They'll just be a phone call away. We won't keep anything from them."

Jay turned back to Michael. "I'm worried about you too, dude."

"Why?" Michael asked.

"Because of this gun thing. You can't shoot. I don't want you dead, and I also don't want you to go to prison."

"Don't worry. I'm careful. I know the rules."

"But you're the one I would've trusted most to take care of my sisters, and now you can't."

Juliet looked at Michael, wishing Jay hadn't brought that up. Michael looked down at his feet.

"Michael takes care of us in a lot of ways," Cathy said. "He's taught us everything we need to know. We can do this."

"So when do we start?" Juliet asked.

"I think pretty early tomorrow morning," Michael said. "Whoever's watching Amber's house needs to be there at six thirty or so, to make sure that if she leaves, we can follow her. She's probably unemployed since Bob's clinic has closed. But if we follow her she may lead us to the others. Juliet and Holly, you start out watching her. Cathy and I are going to go hunting for Leonard Miller."

"Do you have any leads?" Juliet asked.

"No, not yet. But we can ask old neighbors, stake out his mother's old house. I think his sister lives there."

By the end of the meeting, Juliet had a plan and a strategy that made her feel a little more confident. Anything could happen tomorrow—the people tormenting her could do something even more tragic to her family. Or the feds could make a dozen arrests and put the case to bed.

As she went back up to get a few hours' sleep, she prayed that God would intervene in this mess and protect them all.

CHAPTER 32

Wednesday morning Cathy read back over the blog she'd just written, conflicted about whether to upload it or delete it. For the last two and a half years, she'd written about murder cases that interested her. But this one . . . this murder of her brother-in-law that seemed related to the murder of her fiancé . . . *interest* wasn't the word that described it. She was inescapably tangled up in this case, and her passion just might lead her to say something that would tip off the killers.

Two and a half years ago, when my fiancé was gunned down by a man who later walked away scot-free, I started this blog in the hope of making sure murderers paid for their crimes. Along the way, some have and some haven't. But I've done my share of investigative journalism. I've discovered evidence that prosecutors had missed, and in some cases that has led to a conviction.

But once again my family has been rocked by murder.

My sister is a grieving widow now because a man gunned her husband down in a parking lot. Her children will grow up without their father. To make matters worse, her husband had secrets that reach back to my Joe's death. But we're uncovering those secrets, and the killers should take note. We are coming for them. They will not get away with it this time.

No, she couldn't write that. She couldn't let Leonard Miller know they were closing in on him. She couldn't let him know they had linked him to Bob, and she couldn't yet reveal Bob's criminal bent to the world.

So far, to Juliet's great relief, the local media hadn't gotten wind of Bob's criminal life. Cathy wouldn't be the one to reveal it. She deleted the last part and stared at the computer screen again. What was there to write, if not the truth? Always before, she had dived in without much thought to her family's comfort. She was never part of the case—defense or prosecution—so her opinions were considered nothing more than speculation. But this was different.

This case left an acid burn in her stomach. She wanted to write about it but couldn't.

Sighing, she deleted the rest of the blog post and decided to wait a while longer to write about this family tragedy. The moment the media connected her with Bob, they would do exactly what she would have ordinarily done. They'd barrage her with interview requests. That would instantly elevate the story to national news. She could hear it now: *Popular blogger Cathy Cramer, whose fiancé was murdered two years ago, is now dealing with another family murder—her sister's husband, Dr. Bob Cole . . .*

No, none of them could handle having the news blood-hounds sniffing around this case. Not yet.

Her phone rang, and the caller ID said Michael Hogan. She clicked it on.

"Cathy, you busy?"

"No, just banging my head against my computer screen. Did you talk to the security company guy?"

He sighed. "No. I called his office, but he's been on vacation in Colorado. They told me they'd have him call me, and they gave me his cell number, but I can't reach him. I'll keep trying him."

"Did you ask them if we could get an address?"

"Yes, and they said it would be up to Sid."

"Can Juliet get access to Bob's account now that he's dead?"

"Again, up to Sid. They said he'd probably need to see evidence that she's his next of kin. So all we can do is wait. But start getting the paperwork together for her. Marriage license, his death certificate, that sort of thing."

"Okay, but I thought we were going to hunt Miller," Cathy said.

"I decided I should watch the Harper brothers."

"Who?"

"The guys who made that first phone call to Juliet," Michael said. "They led us to Jerome Henderson. They might also lead us to Miller."

"I could help you after I get my blog done," Cathy said. "My advertisers are breathing down my neck for new content. I haven't blogged since the shooting."

"You talking about Bob?"

"Not yet. I've decided it's not wise to say more than I've already said."

"Good. They might follow your blog to see what you say."

"I'll write about some other case, if I can just focus."

"Okay. Give me a call when you finish and I'll tell you where I am."

She hung up and stared down at Michael's picture on her phone. Ironic that she'd cropped his face out of a photo that included him, Max, and Joe. He was laughing and looked carefree. She didn't think his eyes had carried that much joy since before Joe's death.

If only they could get Leonard Miller put away this time. If only they could take down the crime ring that Joe had died trying to bust. If only they could get to the bottom of Bob's role in all of this.

Then maybe they could help Juliet deal with it and get on with her grief. Cathy knew about unhealed wounds, and she wanted better for her sister.

CHAPTER 33

Juliet parked on the street that ran parallel to Amber's. From their vantage point, she and Holly could see straight past the houses between them to Amber's front door and driveway on the next street over. With her camera's zoom lens she could look through the window to see movement inside the house.

Though Michael had balked about her buying this mini-van with blacked-out back windows, she'd bought it anyway. It was great for transporting her kids, along with their soccer gear and a million other things that moms were required to load into their cars, and it also made surveillance easier. But Michael claimed that the best vehicle for PI work was a small nondescript car, not a clichéd van that he feared would attract suspicion. He alternated between his gray Trailblazer and an old Chevy Caprice. He usually made Holly drive the Caprice instead of her taxi when he sent her to do surveillance.

It didn't matter, usually, because most of the PI work Juliet did was in an office on a computer. But she was glad to do this one on the street. Following her husband's mistress, the mother of his baby, might uncover more secrets about the people who had made her a widow. But there was more. Revenge pulsed through her in a way that shamed her. She had never hated anyone before, and had never sought revenge for anything in her life. Vengeance was God's, and she trusted him with it. This sudden thirst for vengeance was foreign to her, and she knew it needed prayer.

She sat in the backseat, her zoom lens trained on the house. Holly sat on the bench seat behind her, watching through binoculars.

They sat there for the next hour, listening to the radio and trying to keep their minds occupied. It was 9:00 a.m. now, and Amber hadn't come out of the house.

"This could be a really boring day," Holly said. "If she doesn't do something soon, I'm going to have to find a bathroom."

Through the zoom lens, Juliet saw the garage door going up. She caught her breath. "She's coming out!"

Juliet zoomed in closer and saw Amber with the baby on her hip. She was decked out in a business suit, a short blazer, and a skirt with high heels. The baby wore a onesie, and his feet were bare.

She snapped pictures, just in case they needed them later, then clicked on her digital voice recorder. "Subject leaving residence at 955 Anchor Boulevard at 9:03 a.m., with baby." She watched Amber buckle the baby into his car seat in the back then go around to the driver's side.

"Why is she so dressed up?" Holly asked, ignoring the tape. "Maybe she has a new job."

"If she did, I think the FBI would have mentioned it."

"A job interview, then? She could be dropping the baby off at daycare along the way."

Amber started her car and backed out, so Juliet handed the camera to Holly and, pulling her baseball cap low over her forehead, got into the driver's seat. She started the van and turned it around in a driveway, then slowly drove up the street, not wanting to hit the stop sign until Amber had turned and passed them. Then she quickly got to the stop sign, turned left, and followed at a distance behind Amber, dictating every turn as she went.

"Did you see the baby?" Juliet asked as she drove.

"Yeah," Holly said. "Weird. He looks exactly like Abe."

"Who looks like Bob." Tears stung Juliet's eyes again, but she forced them back. She didn't have time for that now. Amber turned off the main road, cut across to another highway, turned left. Juliet followed her, allowing two or three cars to get between them. Finally Amber turned into a bank parking lot, the same bank where Juliet and Bob had accounts—Centennial Bank. But Juliet had never used this branch.

"Quick, just pull over here on the road," Holly said. "We have a good view without going into the parking lot."

Juliet pulled over and slid into the rear seat again. She took the camera from Holly and zoomed in. Amber was out of the car with the back door open, talking to the baby. She closed the door without getting him out and high-heeled in.

"She's leaving the baby in the car!" Juliet said. "It's too hot for that."

Holly's hand went to her stomach. "I wonder if she left the car on for the AC."

Juliet looked up at the bank sign that had the temperature. "It's ninety-five degrees. The baby could bake in there."

"What do you think she's doing?"

"Maybe she's got an account."

"She could have driven through if she wants to make a withdrawal or deposit. She'd only go in if she had to talk to a loan officer. I'm going in."

Juliet glanced back at her. Holly grabbed the bag she always carried on surveillance and pulled out a blonde wig. Pink hair didn't blend in well, but usually it didn't matter. She rarely needed to cover it up.

She pulled the wig on over her ponytail.

Juliet gave her a worried look. "Cover your tattoos."

Holly unrolled her sleeves, covered them. "Anything showing?"

"No, you're good. Be careful."

"Here we go." Holly shoved on sunglasses, got out of the car, and trotted through the parking lot and into the bank. As she waited, Juliet prayed that Amber wouldn't recognize her. She didn't think Amber had ever seen Holly, but she couldn't be sure.

Juliet began to get hot, and that was with her air conditioner running. Her gaze strayed to Amber's car and she watched it through her zoom lens. The sun was beating down on the car's windows. That poor baby was probably right in the sunlight.

What if Amber had underestimated the heat? What if something happened to the child?

Juliet knew she should stay here, out of sight, but she couldn't. She had to check on the baby.

She shoved on her sunglasses and adjusted her cap. Too bad she didn't have a wig.

She got out of the car, stuffing the camera into her big purse. She went around the back of the parking lot, the camera making her bag feel like it weighed a ton. She came up behind Amber's car on the side away from the bank. She looked in the window. The baby was crying and kicking, his red little face shining with sweat.

At least Amber could've cracked the window a little to allow some air to get in or the hot air to get out. She could've parked at an angle where there was shade for the baby, or left the car running with the air on. Or she could have taken the baby in with her. What kind of mother was she?

The bank doors opened and a customer came out. This was dangerous, but Juliet couldn't just leave the baby. She tried the handle on the car's back door.

It was unlocked. Amber hadn't even bothered to lock her child in! She opened the door and tried to lower the power windows, but couldn't without the key. "It's okay, sweetie," she said to the screaming baby. He had a bottle with water, but he had dropped it on the seat. She handed it to him, and he took it greedily and began sucking.

She touched his forehead. He was burning up with fever. Snot crusted under his nose. "You're going to be all right," she said. She glanced around inside the car and saw a cell phone sitting on the console. Amber's phone!

She thought of taking it, but she hadn't turned into a thief overnight. No, she could watch her, but she wasn't going to steal from her. Heart pounding, she straightened up and shut the car door, praying that the child would be all right, and quickly went back the long way around to her van. She got into the backseat and put the camera to her eye.

Holly came out the side of the bank, strolling slowly. She made her way back to the van and jumped in. "She's talking to a loan officer," she said.

"You think she's trying to get a loan?"

"Either that or she's trying to get access to one of Bob's accounts. You bank here, right?"

"Yes. You couldn't hear what she was saying?"

"No, I tried to get close, but they were inside a glass office."

Juliet's gaze drifted back to Amber's car. "I went over to the car."

Holly gasped. "Juliet, you didn't!"

"I had to. That baby's in the sun. She didn't leave the window cracked. He's crying and kicking and screaming, and he's burning with fever."

"You got that close?"

"Yes. The door was unlocked. I got in the car and tried to calm him down."

"Juliet, that was unbelievably stupid!"

"I know, but she's a sorry mother, leaving her child in the car like that. She could've taken him in with her or gotten a babysitter. She probably couldn't take him to daycare, because he's sick." She swept her lens back to the bank door. "Her phone was sitting on the console. I thought about taking it."

"Wait a minute. You saw her phone and didn't grab it?"

"I'm not a thief, Holly."

Holly breathed a laugh. "Well, I am." She got out of the car and cut through the parking lot, came up behind Amber's car. Juliet watched through the camera, making sure no one was watching.

Was Holly seriously going to steal Amber's phone?

She watched Holly open the car door, lean in, then quickly back out. She walked back rapidly but nonchalantly. She jumped into the van with a victorious smile. "Got it."

"I'm going to kill you," Juliet said. "You cannot do that!"

"I'll bet she's in there right now trying to steal from you."

"I don't care. It's not right."

"Deal with it. I can't put it back now," Holly said.

The bank door opened, and Amber strutted out. "There she is." Juliet couldn't breathe. She put the camera back to her eye and watched as Amber opened her car door, tossed her purse in, then opened the back door to soothe the baby.

Juliet hoped she would turn the air conditioner on quickly. "Cool your baby off, lady," she muttered. "Better yet, take him to the doctor!"

Holly clicked Amber's phone on. A picture of Bob holding the baby popped up as Amber's wallpaper. Juliet turned away.

"I'm writing down her phone numbers and contacts to see who she's talked to lately. Then I'll read her e-mails. This thing is a gold mine."

"Holly, this is wrong!"

"*You* didn't do anything wrong. Get over it. It was a gift. She left her door unlocked. It was sitting on the console in plain sight."

"Just because something is accessible doesn't mean we're supposed to take it! You weren't raised by wolves!"

"You want to solve this or not? I might get some valuable information that will crack this whole case wide open."

Juliet could do nothing about it now—Amber was pulling out of the parking lot, and she had no choice but to follow. She quickly slipped back into the driver's seat, waited for Amber to get a couple of blocks up the road before pulling into traffic. Holly was already going through the phone, taking notes on the back of a drugstore bag.

Juliet whispered a prayer that the phone would lead to Leonard Miller, or anyone else involved in Bob's crimes. But they would have to give it back at the next opportunity. Taking it broke one of Michael's biggest rules: "Never commit your own crime to investigate another one."

Not to mention the whole "Do Not Steal" rule in the Bible.

She brooded as she followed Amber, more nervous now than she'd been before.

CHAPTER 34

Juliet glanced in her rearview mirror at Holly in the backseat, writing feverishly. "Holly, it won't take her long to figure out it's missing," she said. "And not having it could interfere with everything she does."

Suddenly Amber's phone rang, and Juliet caught her breath.

"Answer it," Holly said, thrusting it at her. "Act like you're Amber."

Juliet couldn't do it. She looked at the screen. Only a number showed on the caller ID.

"Answer it!" Holly cried.

Juliet didn't, and the phone quit ringing.

Holly let out a loud grunt. "Juliet, *think* about this. Amber's in on all this. She's communicating with the others. That could have been a call from one of them."

"Then why didn't *you* answer it?"

"Because . . . you talked to her. You know how she sounds."

"I can't believe you got us into this position!"

The phone rang again, and the caller ID showed it was from the same person as before.

Holly just about came out of her seat. "Answer it, Juliet! Come on!"

Juliet's heart almost exploded, but she banished her guilt and clicked it on. "Hello?"

"Amber, this is Jack. I know I'm only supposed to e-mail you in code, but you weren't answering."

"Sorry," she said. "Go ahead."

"I need to know if we can fish at the same dock."

"Yes," Juliet said, trying to give her voice the same haughty edge as Amber's.

"You're sure the sharks aren't circling there?"

It was code. And whatever they were talking about, Juliet *wanted* the sharks to bite.

"It's fine. The place is still clear." She squeezed her eyes shut. Had she just given herself away?

"Great. Tomorrow, twenty-three thirty. We'll need to bring the fish right in to clean them. You're sure we can do that?"

Juliet's throat almost closed up. She looked at Holly in the mirror, terror in her eyes. Ahead, she could see Amber turning. *Where* were they talking about?

Holly sent her a prodding look. *What fish?*

Juliet swallowed. "I told you. We're clear."

"Okay. Give me a heads-up immediately if anything changes."

Juliet hung up and let out a pent-up breath. "I'm sweating."

Holly handed her the voice recorder. "Before you forget, dictate every single thing he said."

"It was code. Fish, dock, twenty-three thirty. Could that be an address?"

"Exact words, Juliet. Start with Hello."

Juliet followed Amber to another turnoff. She dictated the conversation into the recorder as she drove, praying she hadn't left anything out.

When she was finished, Holly almost came over the seat. "Twenty-three thirty. That's eleven thirty tomorrow night. It has to be a delivery."

"But where? What dock? I couldn't ask without giving myself away."

"We'll figure it out. Maybe Amber will lead us there."

Juliet turned the AC up and directed the vent to blow on her. Amber was turning again. "Where is she going? We're backtracking."

Holly winced. "She's probably realized her phone is gone. Going back to look for it?"

"Great. Now what do we do? I can't call the FBI and tell them we stole her phone."

"They'll understand why we took it," Holly said.

"Are you crazy? They have to go by the law, Holly!"

"So what do we do? We have critical information they need to know. We wouldn't have it if I hadn't done that."

"I don't know. But I don't want to do this!" Juliet slammed the steering wheel. "Look at me! I'm following my husband's mistress and talking to drug traffickers and stealing phones. I won't be like them!"

"PIs have to be deceptive sometimes."

Juliet let a car get in front of her, hoping Amber still hadn't seen her. She had to focus. "It's not the same. I uncover lies by following the rules. But you . . . you never follow rules, Holly! That's why this whole PI thing is too much temptation for you."

"Juliet, we have a time for a delivery now! We have her entire contact list. You're totally missing that."

Juliet didn't know what to do. If they put the phone back in Amber's car, would that be enough?

And it wasn't just Holly. She had gotten into Amber's car and touched her baby. She had pretended to be Amber on the phone. Darren and his partner would be livid. But how could the FBI help her if she lied to them?

"I'm calling Michael," she said. "He'll know what to do." She pressed speed dial for him as she followed Amber. The woman turned into another bank parking lot. "She's not looking for her phone. She's turning in there. Here, tell Michael what you did."

Holly took the phone and put it on speaker.

"Maybe she hasn't realized the phone is gone yet," Juliet whispered.

Juliet heard Michael answering. "What's up?"

"We got something big," Holly said. "We're following Amber, and we got her phone."

"She stole it out of her car!" Juliet called out so Michael would hear.

"We'll deal with my criminal behavior later," Holly said. "For now, you need to know that we just intercepted a call from someone who talked about a delivery tomorrow night at eleven thirty." She repeated the call to him.

"Okay," he said, "we have to figure out where it's going to be. Maybe it's the place wired by the security company I've been trying to get in touch with. If Sid, the owner, calls, maybe I can convince him to give us the address. Did you see a listing for Miller on her phone?"

"No, nothing. Not under L or M."

Juliet could hear the disappointment in Michael's voice. "Too bad."

"It could still be here. She has a lot of nicknames and initials in here, but nothing that sounds like him."

Juliet watched Amber pull into a handicapped space. "So what do we do now, Michael? Do I call the FBI and confess that we took the phone? Call Max? What should I do?"

"Let me handle it," Michael said. "I'll call the feds and let them know. They already have a wiretap on that phone, so they probably already know."

Juliet sucked in a breath. "So you think they heard the call?"

"Probably. But they might not have realized you were the one talking."

"How come they can do that and I can't do what I did?" Holly asked.

"Because they have a court order from a US judge. They don't give those to PIs. Where are you now?"

"We're watching Amber go into the Bay Bank and Trust on Krieger Avenue," Juliet said. "Ironic name, huh?"

"Yes, kind of."

"I just pulled into the parking lot at the Zaxby's. Two parking lots away." Juliet pulled her camera to her eye and through the lens saw that Amber had left the baby in the car again and was heading inside.

"I'm about to call the police on her for leaving that baby in a hot car," Juliet said. "We have a tiny window where we can put the phone back."

"Yeah, you should probably put it back before she realizes it's gone. And Holly . . . never do that again."

Holly blew out a heavy sigh. "Okay."

"But don't put it where you found it," Michael said. "Put

it under the seat so she'll think she dropped it, in case she's already noticed it's missing. Take the battery out. She'll think it fell out when she dropped it."

Juliet hoped Holly was paying attention.

"Let's hang up and I'll call the feds," Michael said. "I'll get back to you. Be careful, Holly."

Juliet watched Holly check her wig in the mirror. Her gaze fell to her sister's round belly. Even with the wig, Holly stood out too much. What if someone noticed her getting into Amber's car? She sighed. "Give me the phone. I'll put it back."

"What? No. I'm doing it."

"I don't want you to do it. It's dangerous. I'll take it."

Holly frowned. "Juliet, I got us into this mess. I'll get us out."

Time was running out. Juliet grabbed Amber's phone out of Holly's hand and pulled her cap low over her hair, then opened the door and got out.

"Juliet!" Holly whispered harshly.

Juliet ignored her and walked through the Zaxby's parking lot, crossed the Enterprise Rent-A-Car lot, and reached the bank. As she passed parked cars, she checked to see if anyone was in them. No one waited there.

But could Amber be watching through the bank windows?

As Juliet approached Amber's car, she heard the baby crying. Her heart melted. She went closer, pretending to get into the car next to Amber, then acted as if she'd dropped something. Stooping, she opened the back door and looked in at the baby. His little face glistened with tears. He looked at her, his feet kicking, his fists punching the air.

"It's okay, Robbie," she said, setting the phone and battery on the floorboard in front of him.

What kind of mother was this woman? What had Bob seen in her?

She forced herself to close the door and kept stooping as she crossed behind the cars on that row. Then she stood and headed back to her van.

She had to do something. She couldn't let the baby stay in that hot car.

When she got back to the van, Holly looked ready to jump out of her skin. "Where'd you put it?"

"On the floorboard in the backseat. Give me your phone, Holly. I'm calling the police, but I don't want them to see my name on their caller ID."

"So you're letting them see mine?"

"You weren't married to their most recent murder victim!"

Holly handed Juliet her phone. Juliet called 911.

"Bay County 911, what's your emergency?"

Juliet cleared her throat. "I'm at the Bay Bank and Trust on Krieger Avenue, and there's a baby that someone left in a white Lexus. It's crying and sweating, and it must be over a hundred degrees in that car."

They asked her name, and she said she'd rather not give it. They would get Holly's number and think it was Holly, but that was all right. The last name of Cramer wouldn't raise red flags like Cole would.

Juliet and Holly waited in the car, watching. Within minutes, a police cruiser pulled into the parking lot—just as Amber came out the back door of the bank.

"Uh-oh. She's going back to her car."

The cop got out and met Amber at the car, looked at the baby through the window, and seemed to be giving Amber a lecture. She got into the car and turned the ignition, probably turning the air conditioner on. She was smiling, flipping her hair, explaining, and the cop seemed to be listening. Finally, he turned and went back to his car.

"Oh man," Holly said. "He's just giving her a warning."

"Well, maybe it'll make her quit doing it. That poor baby."

Amber pulled out of the parking lot, and Juliet gave her a head start, then tailed her again.

"Thanks for putting the phone back," Holly muttered. "I could have done it myself."

"I didn't want you doing it."

"You're not my mother."

Juliet didn't answer. She just tried to concentrate on Amber's car.

CHAPTER 35

Amber tried not to panic. Where was her phone? She had just realized that it hadn't rung in a long time, and when she reached for it, it was gone. She racked her brain, trying to think back.

Had she left it at the first bank? The second?

Robbie wouldn't stop crying, and she looked back, found the pacifier, and stuck it into his mouth. He spat it out and kept screaming. "Hold on!" she said. "Just wait! Mommy will feed you when we get home. I have to think!"

But her voice and tone only made Robbie cry harder. She turned the air conditioner on high, hoping the cool air would calm him down. Could she have dropped her phone? What if someone had picked it up at the bank? She was supposed to hear from the transporters. If they couldn't reach her, they might get spooked and not make the delivery. Her heart pounded. What was she going to do?

She pulled over into a parking lot, unfastened her seat belt, and looked on her floorboard and under her feet. Nothing. She searched between the two front seats, then went around the car and looked on the floorboard of the passenger seat. No, she hadn't dropped it.

Why hadn't she locked her car?

Robbie kept screaming. She got into the backseat and dug through the diaper bag for a bottle. She found a half bottle of formula from earlier that morning. Hoping it hadn't soured, she stuck it in his mouth. He hushed and took the bottle in his own hands, sucking desperately.

Think! Trembling, she got back into the driver's seat, trying to decide what to do. She'd just have to retrace her steps. When was the last time she'd seen it? She tried to remember. Lenny had called before she went into the first bank, and he'd told her he was going to call back. What was he thinking now?

They had never fully accepted her. But hadn't she proven herself, setting up Bob's murder? She had told them where he would be and when. Still, if anything went wrong, they would question her loyalty, or her competence. It was a terrible day to lose her phone.

As she drove back to the first bank, she turned the air conditioner vents on herself. She was sweating.

Had she taken the phone in with her? Why was this such a hard thing to remember? She was always misplacing her keys too. She just had too much on her mind. Bob always chided her for that, and for not locking her car door when there were valuables inside.

He'd noticed that one time when the baby was in the car. "Anyone could kidnap him," he'd told her. "When our kids were babies, Juliet would never have left them alone in a car."

That had enraged her. "I don't care what Juliet would do, so stop throwing her up to me."

"You've got to do better than this, Amber. You're a mother now."

Grudgingly, she had promised him that she wouldn't leave Robbie in the car anymore without at least the air conditioner running, and she would lock the car. But she often forgot.

That was probably why he'd never given her access to the bank accounts.

She pulled into the lot of a convenience store, looking for a pay phone, but there wasn't one. Had the phone company taken them all out? Frantic, she drove up the long, busy road until she spotted one. She got out and hurried to it, but she didn't know how to use it. Then she found the slot for her debit card, slid it in, and waited for the dial tone. When she got it, she dialed Lenny Miller's number. He didn't pick up, probably because he didn't recognize the number, so she left a message: "Lenny, it's me, Amber. I've misplaced my phone. I don't know what happened to it, but I need you to call me at this number. I'm on a pay phone. I'll wait a few minutes until I hear from you."

She hung up, waited, hoping he didn't ignore his messages. If he was trying to get in touch with her, maybe he would listen. She paced in front of the car until Robbie started crying again. Why had she brought him with her? He was driving her nuts. She should have taken him to the daycare center in spite of his fever, or gotten a babysitter. She had too much on her mind—she couldn't worry about him too.

She opened the car door and leaned in. "What is it? What do you want?"

Vomit dribbled down his chin. She cursed and reached into the diaper bag for a wipe, scrubbed the mess off his face and chest. She would need to change his clothes now. This was getting ridiculous.

And his incessant crying was like a sledgehammer on her skull.

She unhooked his safety strap and pulled him out, trying to avoid getting vomit on her clothes. Suddenly the pay phone rang. She carried Robbie with her to answer it, but he wouldn't stop crying.

What a nightmare. What was she going to do?

She couldn't risk missing the call, so she picked up the receiver and tried to hear over the wailing. "Hello?"

"Amber?"

"Lenny! Finally!"

"What's going on with you? What do you mean, you lost your phone? On a day like today, when we have to communicate?"

"Don't lecture me!" she said. "I don't know what happened to it. I was going to the banks and somewhere along the way my phone disappeared."

"I've been trying to call you for an hour. Have you looked in your car?"

"Yes, and it's not there."

"Well, look again."

The baby was screaming; she bounced him, trying to distract him. "Why were you calling?"

"I wanted to know if you'd heard from them yet. Apparently you haven't, since you lost your phone like some ditzy teenager."

"I've had a lot on my mind!" she bit out. "I doubt you could do better. I'm on top of things."

"Really?" he asked. "You got the baby with you, I can hear him. How could you be on top of things?"

"He's sick," she said. "I couldn't take him to daycare. He's throwing up—they just would have sent him back home."

"Then get somebody else to take care of him. You need your head in the game."

"You don't have to tell me that," Amber said. "I know what I'm doing."

"Well, if you don't find the phone in the next few minutes, come by my place. I have some extra Go Phones. You can use one of those."

"All right, I will."

"What about the accounts? Any luck?"

"No. They want all sorts of paperwork to prove I'm his wife. I need to forge some documents before I go back."

"This isn't going well, Amber. You led me to believe you could get into those accounts. I went out on a limb for you."

"I never told you for sure I could. I told you I'd try."

"I'm losing faith in you."

She squeezed her eyes shut. "Lenny, I think I've proven myself. I just need a little more time. Work with me here."

"We can't mess this up. And you have to communicate with the transporter. You're the only one he knows to contact. We have to change the delivery point. The feds will be looking for properties Bob owned. We can't use that place again."

"I know," she said. "You don't have to remind me. Just calm down. I doubt they've tried to call yet."

She hung up and put Robbie back in his car seat, vomit and all. She didn't have time to change him. She got back in behind the wheel, searched her purse and the front floorboard again, and then gave up. She would just have to go to Lenny's and get one of his prepaid phones. Then she'd work on getting another phone from her cell company so her regular number would be running again.

At least her voice mail would still be working, even if she couldn't access it yet. But would they dare leave a message?

They probably wouldn't, for fear of being caught. The whole operation was so segmented and compartmentalized that none of the major operators even knew who the others were.

She knew the transporter only because Bob sometimes couldn't take calls, so he set her up as a secondary source. And she knew only first names. Lenny was the only one she knew personally, because he had recruited her.

If she messed this up, she could wind up like Bob. She had to come through today so they wouldn't distrust her.

Except that in this line of work, nobody trusted anybody. Results were all they cared about. She had to make sure she got them.

CHAPTER 36

Michael checked his watch. So far, his surveillance of the Harper brothers had been a waste.

His income-producing work was piling up, and here he was doing virtually nothing. But this was one of the few leads he had.

His phone vibrated, and he touched the Bluetooth in his ear. "Michael Hogan."

"Michael, Sid Griffin here. How's it going, man?"

Relief flooded through him. The owner of the security company he'd been trying to get in touch with. He took a few minutes to catch up with the man he'd been a cop with in their younger days, before Sid had left to start his company. Then Michael told him what they needed.

"Yeah, I remember that. Kind of a weird job, but it's none of my business. He paid a pretty penny for it."

"So what do we need to do to get his wife access?"

"When I get back, I'll sit down with her. I'll need proof

she's his next of kin, but once I have it, I'll reconfigure the codes and scans so she can get in."

"Any way we could e-mail you the proof and get the codes over the phone?"

"No, won't work. This place has fingerprint and retina scans. I'll have to scan hers and put them into the computer so his system will recognize her. It has to be done in person. I can't get any of my staff to do it because I'm the only other one with access. But I'll be traveling back tomorrow."

Michael let out a sigh, but he knew Sid wouldn't budge. "Okay, but can you at least give us the address?"

Sid paused. "You don't know the address? How'd you know about the place?"

"We found a business card with your info on it. When I called your office, they confirmed that they had wired something for Bob. But we need to see the place."

"Sure. It's 542 Court Boulevard."

Michael frowned as he jotted it down. Court Boulevard. That was a residential neighborhood. Not what he'd expected.

When he got off the phone, he put the address into his phone's GPS. Just as he thought—it was in North Bay, near the Hathaway Bridge and Pretty Bayou.

He drove across town and found the subdivision. It was called King's Point. The homes were on the bay, with boat slips and private docks. They must be seven-figure homes.

He counted down the numbers on the mailboxes, slowing as he grew closer. It was an even number, so it would be on the water side.

He finally came to 542. The house wasn't visible from the street. It hid behind painted block walls with an iron gate at the entrance. He pulled up to the curb, got out, and peered through the black bars. The house was Spanish ranch style, not as attractive as the others in the neighborhood. Past the house, he could see a canal behind it, an offshoot of the bay. From where he stood, he didn't see a boat.

He shook the gate. It was solid, unmoving. Probably remote-controlled by whomever lived here. There was a button to push to communicate with the house. He thought of ringing it, coming up with some pretense for being here, but then decided to do a little more homework first.

He got back into his car and pulled away, checking out the rest of the area. Why would Bob have a seven-figure home that Juliet didn't know about? It wasn't for Amber. She lived in a patio home. Did he have *another* woman?

But the security system was far more sophisticated than a normal home would have.

He drove to the nearest Starbucks, sat in the parking lot, and used his laptop to look up the real estate records for that property. Bob wasn't listed as the owner. The title holder was D&B Properties. He did a quick search—D&B had a business license, but nothing else he could find. That was unusual. Most businesses had a paper trail of some kind.

Michael knew Sid well enough to know that he wouldn't have installed a security system without knowing he was dealing with the owner. Bob must have proven to him that he was the owner of D&B.

So if Bob owned this house that was wired like Fort Knox and a company called D&B with no paper trail . . . this house wasn't your run-of-the-mill residence. Bob was using it for his extracurricular activities.

Satisfied that he'd made some progress, he headed back across town to get Cathy.

CHAPTER 37

After a couple more stops, Amber led Juliet and Holly to an apartment complex. Juliet pulled into a space across the parking lot and climbed into the back of the van. She had a clear view out her rear window, and through her camera's zoom she watched as Amber got the baby out of the backseat and carried him into the building with her.

"Write down this address," Juliet told Holly as she snapped Amber going in.

They waited, silent, for Amber to come out. "Keep your camera pointed at the door she went in," Holly said. "Whoever she's visiting may be visible when she comes out."

Juliet already had the lens zoomed in on the door.

"I need to eat something," Holly said. "My stomach is growling so much it's scaring the baby."

"You knew we were doing surveillance. You should have packed some granola bars or something."

"Well, I didn't."

"So what do you want to do? Lose this trail so we can go get you a burger?"

Holly grunted. "Of course not."

"Look in my purse. I have some protein bars in there."

Holly moved to the front and dug into Juliet's purse. "You carry these all the time?"

"Usually, for my kids. You qualify."

"You don't have to get snippy." Holly tore open the wrapper and got back into position. "I thank you and the baby thanks you."

The baby. Juliet wished Holly had a name picked out. But she hadn't been able to afford an ultrasound yet. She would get one, though, on her next doctor's visit. Juliet had promised to help her pay, since Holly had no insurance. Then they would know the sex of the baby.

"Door's opening," Holly said. "You got a good view?"

"Yes." Juliet snapped a few pictures as Amber came out. "She's turning back. Somebody's in the doorway." She zoomed in more, trying to see who was inside. It looked like a man. He was tall, over six feet, but the inside of the apartment was too dark to see more. She took pictures anyway, hoping something would come out. Then she got lucky—he stepped outside and walked with Amber toward the parking lot, his door still open behind him.

As he stepped out of the shadows, Holly gasped. "No way!"

Juliet's mouth fell open as she locked onto his face and snapped. "Leonard Miller." She would recognize that face anywhere. "Call Michael."

Juliet took one picture after another as Holly got Michael on the phone again. "We've got Leonard Miller," she blurted when he answered.

Juliet could hear Michael's excited response: "Are you sure?"

Holly gave him the address and apartment number. "Want us to stay with him or follow Amber?"

"Stay with him until I get there," Michael said.

As Amber got into her car and drove out of the parking lot, Miller closed himself back into his dark apartment. Juliet lowered her camera and drew in a deep breath.

"Man, are we good or what?" Holly asked.

Juliet couldn't help smiling and giving her a high five.

CHAPTER 38

Where are you going?" Cathy asked Michael as he turned his car around.

"I'm taking you home before I go to Miller's apartment."

"No, I want to go!"

His jaw muscle was clenched tight, and she could see the intense anger on his face. "Cathy, I'd rather you didn't."

"I don't care what you'd rather. I'm as invested in this as you are."

"But it might get dangerous."

She stared at him for a moment. "What are you going to do? Go in there and beat the daylights out of him?"

"No, of course not."

"Then I'm coming. You'll need me. Between the two of us, we can gather a lot of information about him. We're not letting him disappear this time."

Michael still hadn't turned back around—he was taking her home. "Michael, Miller lives that way. Turn the car around."

Michael let out a great sigh and turned into a parking lot.

As he circled it and came out, Cathy sulked. But Michael was quiet too.

"I know how you feel," she said in a softer voice. "I feel the same way. I dream about Miller suffering. Tortured. Locked behind bars. I could hurt him."

Michael didn't answer.

"But, Michael, we have to keep our heads. We have to do this right."

Michael's eyes had taken on a steely determination as he drove. "We'll do it right, don't worry about that. Leonard Miller is about to get what's coming to him."

CHAPTER 39

School was the last place Zach wanted to be today, but when his mother had given him the choice, he'd decided to go. Uncle Jay had a password on his computer, so Zach couldn't get on it without telling him why. The password was mainly to keep Jackson from getting on the computer when he wasn't supposed to, and since his cousin was only five, Zach got that. But he didn't want every Google search to turn into some big hairy deal. At school, he could search in peace.

The first few teachers who'd greeted him with hugs had made him mad, and he'd locked into brooding mode, practically daring anyone to talk to him. Some of the girls ventured too close and told him how sorry they were about his dad, but he pretended not to hear. What was wrong with them? Couldn't they see when somebody didn't want to talk?

He thought of putting a sign around his neck that said, "Yes, I'm fine. Leave me alone." But that would just draw more attention.

He bided his time, paying no attention in class, counting down the minutes until he had computer lab. Finally, fifth period came. By now, most of his classmates were giving him his space, but the teachers hadn't got the memo.

Mrs. March greeted him at the door. "Zach, I didn't expect you back so soon." She touched her chest as if she was about to cry. He hoped he didn't get stuck having to comfort her. "I know this has been a hard week for you."

"I'm okay," he managed to say around the knot in his throat.

"I won't make you take the test today since you've been out for a few days. You can make it up next week."

Zach didn't even know there was a test. "Okay, thanks."

Good. Now he'd have time to get on the Internet and see what was going on with his dad's case.

He waited until the test started and his classmates were working, then he signed onto the computer and got online. He googled "Dr. Bob Cole Murder Panama City" and waited as the list of related articles came up.

He clicked on the first one. It only outlined what had happened the night his father was shot. Nothing new. The next one was pretty much the same, but told about the arrest of Jerome Henderson in his father's shooting.

He made a mental note to find out everything he could about Henderson. But first he clicked on the third link, which took him to the *News Herald*, Panama City's local newspaper. Today's news links came up, but he saw nothing about his father. He typed "Bob Cole" into the search box, and several headlines came up. He skimmed them, looking for the most recent one.

There it was—an article posted two hours ago. "Bob Cole Murder—Drug Deal Gone Bad?"

He clicked on the article and saw a photo of his dad that he hadn't seen before. His pulse throbbed in his temples as he leaned forward and read.

Panama City Police Department spokesman Horace Gerrison told the *News Herald* today that the investigation into the murder of Dr. Bob Cole was turned over to the FBI, after Drug Enforcement Agency officials in Florida alerted police that the prominent spine surgeon had been on a watch list for the past year.

Sources say that Dr. Cole was suspected of money laundering and drug trafficking, though officials at the DEA and the FBI declined to comment. However, anonymous sources at the PCPD confirmed that the murder may have been drug-related.

Cole was gunned down in front of his wife in the U-Haul store parking lot on Highway 57. Dr. Cole's wife identified Jerome Henderson in a lineup, and he was arrested. FBI agents have confirmed that the investigation continues and that Henderson may have been part of a larger conspiracy.

Zach wanted to put his fist through the computer. What did they mean, drug trafficking? And money laundering . . . what was that?

He read the article again. Were they implying that his dad was to blame for his own murder? That he'd made drug dealers mad or something?

Those were lies! His dad was a good man. Tears sprang to his eyes, and he blinked them back and looked around. His classmates were focused on their tests, but if he lost it, all eyes would be on him. No, he couldn't do this. Not here in front of everybody.

Heat flushed his cheeks; his chest grew tight. He closed the computer window so no one else would see the article, and got up. He slipped between desks to where the teacher sat. "Mrs. March, I don't feel good. I need to go home."

She gave him a long, sympathetic look, which didn't help. "It's okay, Zach." She wrote out a hall pass. "Maybe it's too soon to be back?"

He grabbed the yellow slip and rushed out of class and into the bathroom across the hall. He stood at the sink and let the tears go.

Why had his dad been on a drug watch list? What did that mean? He was a surgeon—a great one—and people respected him. Now he'd been shot dead in the middle of a parking lot, and they were twisting this around and trying to make him the bad guy?

No way.

He went into a stall and sat down, pressing his face into his palms as he wept. The sound of footsteps made him cover his mouth to muffle his sobs until the boy left. He couldn't let people see him like this . . . hear him like this.

He had to talk to his mom.

He went to the sink and threw water on his face, then wiped it off with a paper towel. Taking a deep breath, he headed for the office.

Two student workers stood at the front desk and looked up at him as he came in.

He looked past them to the secretary beyond. "I need to go home," he told her.

"Zach, are you okay?" the girl at the desk asked.

"No. I have to call my mom."

The secretary came to the desk and handed him the school's landline with that stupid look of sympathy. He hated that look. "Sure, go ahead, honey."

Zach punched in the number and turned his back to them, not wanting them to see him if he fell apart again.

CHAPTER 40

Juliet's phone rang as she waited with Holly in the van for Michael to arrive at Leonard Miller's apartment complex. She recognized the number that came up—Zach's school. Quickly, she clicked it on. "Hello?"

"Mom, it's me." Zach sounded hollow, stopped up.

"Honey, are you okay?"

"No," he said simply. "Come get me. I don't want to be here."

"What's the matter?"

"Just come get me. I can't be here." His voice was muffled, low.

She closed her eyes, hurting for him. "Okay, but I can't come right this second. It'll be a few minutes before I can leave."

"No, Mom! I can't go back to class. Please just come."

She frowned at the urgency. "Did something happen?"

"Yes." His voice flattened to a whisper. "I read what they're saying in the paper, okay? Everybody's going to think he's . . ." His whisper faded out.

Alarmed, Juliet met Holly's eyes. "Zach, what did it say?"

"We can talk about it when you get here. Just hurry. Will you ask her to let me wait in the office?"

Juliet sighed. "Yes, put Miss Carol on the phone."

In a moment, the secretary's voice came on. "Hi, Juliet," she said. "I'm really sorry he's so upset. What you must be going through."

Juliet didn't know what to say. "Look, I can't get there for a few minutes. Can you let him sit in your office until I do? Just don't make him go back to class. I think I needed to give him the rest of the week. He's really grieving."

"I can see that," she said. "I'll get him a drink and let him cool off."

Juliet ended the call and leaned her head back on the seat. "I can't believe this. Did you hear that? The newspaper is onto Bob's past. Now it's going to be all over the news."

"I'm looking this up." Holly was already on the Internet on her phone. She found the article recently posted on the newspaper site, skimmed it quickly. "Okay, it really doesn't go into any detail about the trafficking and stuff. It just says there are rumors that the murder had a possible drug connection and that Bob had been on a DEA watch list."

Juliet took the phone and read. "How did they find out?"

"People talk. At the DEA, the police department . . . any-time humans are involved, you know somebody's going to spill it."

Juliet didn't know how much more she could take. "What am I going to tell people? And now the kids have to deal with it."

"Maybe it's not so bad. For now, let the kids think it's just a rumor. People who knew Bob won't think it's true."

"But it *is* true," she said weakly. "And the kids will have to know the truth soon enough. Zach is too adept at googling and researching things on his own. There's no way to keep him in the dark." She put her hand over her mouth. "I never thought I'd feel this way about my own husband."

Holly nodded. "I know."

"He's not even here and he's hurting our kids. It was bad enough when it was just me who was crushed, but now Zach and Abe . . . How did he think he'd keep getting away with it?"

Holly had the grace to stay quiet.

Soon Juliet saw Michael's Caprice pulling into the parking lot. "There they are. Call them and tell them which apartment."

When Michael had positioned his car to watch Miller's apartment, Holly called him. "Can you take it from here? Juliet needs to leave." She listened to Michael for a moment, then said to Juliet, "He wants to talk to you." She put it on speaker. "She's on."

"Juliet," Michael said, "I got a call from Sid Griffin who owns Griffin Security. He gave me the address of the place he wired for Bob."

Juliet sucked in a breath. "What is it?"

"It's 542 Court Boulevard, in King's Point subdivision. I just went by there. It's a gated house on North Bay."

"A *house*?" she asked. "Why would he have *another* house?"

"No idea. We can't get in until Sid gets back to town and gives us the codes, and he'll have to scan your eye and fingerprints and put them in the computer instead of Bob's. Apparently, it's locked down like Fort Knox."

"Why?"

"We'll find out soon."

When Juliet hung up, she wiped her tears and pulled out of

the parking lot. Somehow she'd have to swing by that address. She had to see what other secrets Bob had kept from her.

———

Zach had little to say when Juliet checked him out of school. His eyes were puffy, his nose red, and he didn't meet her eyes as the two of them walked out to the car.

Juliet climbed into the driver's seat just as Zach opened the van's sliding door—where Holly was already sitting. She looked up from her camera screen. "Hey, kiddo. You can sit up front with your mom."

He didn't answer, just got into the front next to Juliet and slammed the door, eyes straight ahead.

During the entire trip to Holly's house to drop her off, he just stared silently out the window. When they were finally alone, Juliet set her hands on the steering wheel. "Son, tell me what you're thinking."

His face turned crimson and twisted. "I'm thinking that they're telling lies about Dad, and you don't care. He was murdered, and you're back to work like nothing even happened."

"That's not true, Zach. I'm working on finding everyone involved in killing him."

"Great," he said. "You're still helping them make Dad out to be a criminal. It's not right."

"Honey, I'm trying to protect you and Abe, trying to get to the bottom of this so we can be safe and go back to our house."

"How can they accuse him of stuff when he isn't here to defend himself? He was a good man."

She sat there a moment as he smeared the tears across his

face. "Zach, your dad wasn't honest with me about things. We already talked about this. You know he had secrets."

"I don't want to hear that."

"Then why were you googling him?"

Zach wiped a tear rolling down his face. "Because I thought they'd be saying things about the dude who shot him. I wanted to see what you were keeping from me. I didn't expect them to accuse him of things."

"I know, Zach. The whole thing is like a nightmare."

"Whatever you're doing, I want you to stop. I don't want you looking for more reasons for people to talk about Dad. Why can't we just remember him the way we knew him?"

The tragedy of Bob's choices cut through her. "I wish we could, honey. But we're in it, and I don't know a way out of it. Your dad exposed us to danger, and somehow I have to get us out."

"My dad would never hurt people with drugs or anything else! He took care of people! He saved lives! They're getting everything wrong." He wept for a moment, wiping his face on his sleeves. Finally, he looked at her. "What else haven't you told me?"

She stared at him, wanting to say there was nothing else. But what about tomorrow, or the next day, when the local media's investigative teams went snooping for dirt in what could be the year's biggest local story? Zach was sure to see that too.

"There is something else."

"What?" he asked.

"Your dad . . . he had a girlfriend."

"I heard you say that to the FBI people. But it's not true!" He paused. "Who was she?"

"Somebody who worked in his office. Her name is Amber. And she had a baby."

His mouth fell open. "A baby?"

She nodded. Zach had known where babies came from for years, so she watched his face, heartbroken, as he puzzled it together. "Did she have a husband?"

Juliet shook her head. "No."

"Then Dad . . . ?"

Juliet nodded. "He's nine months old."

"A boy? Like . . . my stepbrother?"

Her heart sank further. "No . . . your half brother."

A fresh flush of crimson reddened his face and his ears. He shook his head and leaned his forehead against the window. "This is so messed up."

"I didn't want you to know. But it might come out, and you might as well be ready. But let's not make Abe deal with it yet, okay?"

Face pinched and twisted, he nodded agreement.

"Just remember that I'm trying to help the FBI find anybody who had anything to do with Dad's death. I want this behind us."

Zach seemed to consider that. Finally, he managed to speak again. "Can't they just let all this go? It's not like they can arrest him or something. He's not here."

"But the others connected to this drug ring are, honey."

"But I don't care about them. I don't want you to help them ruin Dad's reputation. Can't you just leave it alone?"

Juliet didn't tell him that she wanted nothing more.

CHAPTER 41

Michael had parked two buildings over from Miller's, his car facing Miller's apartment. He squinted into the setting sun. Though it was hard on his eyes, he hoped it put a glare on the windshield that would keep Miller from seeing through it.

Cathy was in the backseat, digging through a duffel bag.

"What are you doing?"

"Disguising myself," she said. "I'm going to walk behind his building and see what I can see."

He watched in the rearview mirror as she pulled her hair into a high ponytail and tied a bandana into a do-rag, covering most of her hair.

"Cathy, I'll go. You stay here."

"No," she said. "I know what I'm doing. I'll go through one of those passages between the apartments and get to the back. I'll just get close enough to take a few pictures of the back of his apartment so we'll know if he has a back door or back windows. You wait here in case he comes out."

She was out the door before he could stop her. What *was* this? Cathy acting like the boss, telling him what to do?

She was a piece of work, and she clearly thought he'd kill the guy with his bare hands if he got the chance.

He watched her walk across the parking lot. There were three two-story buildings, each one made up of four units—two up and two down. According to Juliet, Miller was on the first floor of Building C, his door facing the stairs between the two bottom apartments.

Cathy walked through the passage in Building A and disappeared out the back of the building. He had gotten the lay of the land as he'd come in. Behind Building A was a small plot of grass and another building. He wasn't sure what was behind Buildings B and C. Probably woods, from what he could tell.

He checked out the windows on the upper floors. Some of the blinds were closed, some open. He prayed no one would spot Cathy sneaking around back.

Cathy pulled out her phone and pretended to be texting. She walked purposefully through one of the apartment buildings, came out on grass, and checked out the upper windows on the back of the buildings. The first-floor apartments had privacy fences around patios that were about twelve feet square. The upstairs units had balconies.

Since Miller was in a downstairs apartment, Cathy took a picture of the privacy fence closest to her, still pretending to be texting. Though it wasn't his unit, it would give them an idea of what his looked like, if she couldn't get close enough.

She crossed the grass to Building B, glanced up. All the

blinds were closed, and no one seemed to be looking out. From here she could see behind Building C. She saw Miller's privacy fence but couldn't see inside it without going closer.

She angled her phone and took a quick picture inside the opening of the privacy fence in Building B. It had a waist-high iron gate. This tenant had a grill, a small table and chairs, and a sliding glass door. Leonard Miller would have the same square footage on his patio.

She backed away, looking through her dark lenses at Miller's windows. One on the back of the house, one on the side, and one on the front. His blinds were closed, too. She stepped back beside one of the privacy fences, where he wouldn't be able to see her if he did happen to look out, and took a picture of the wooded area behind his building. If the feds ever found a reason to make an arrest, they'd have to guard the back door or he'd be able to escape this way.

She hurried back the way she had come and cut across the parking lot to Michael's Caprice. She got in and pulled the pictures up on her phone. "Here's the back. There's woods there, a sliding glass door, privacy fence."

Michael studied the pictures. "Good work. We may be here awhile."

"That's okay," Cathy said. "I have nowhere to be. Can't think of a single thing that's more important."

Michael looked over at Cathy as she leaned back in the seat, her bandana still covering her hair. She was beautiful, even when she tried to hide it. Even with the scarf on, she would turn heads.

A look of deep reflection darkened her eyes. Was she

remembering the pain of the trial, with Miller sitting smugly as the defendant? Was she remembering how he'd high-fived his attorneys after he was acquitted?

Or had her memory taken her further back, to that day when she'd gotten word that Joe was dead? That the man in that apartment had murdered him?

Suddenly the door opened, and Michael snapped to attention. "He's coming out. Be ready to write his tag down when we see which car is his."

Yes, it was Miller . . . about twenty pounds heavier, with longer hair than the last time Michael had seen him when Miller's mother died. He looked less threatening, not like someone you would automatically assume to be a thug. He stepped out of his building and crossed the grass to a white cargo van. Cathy brought the binoculars to her eyes. "Got it," she said, then wrote the tag number down.

Miller pulled out of his space and passed them without glancing their way as he left the complex. Michael gave him a few seconds, then followed. As he did, Cathy opened her laptop, signed onto one of their databases, and typed in the tag number.

A couple of minutes later, she had what she was looking for. "The car is registered to a Miller Arden."

"See what else that name brings up," Michael said as he drove.

She typed on the laptop and waited. "Okay, the apartment lease is in that name. I have a landline phone number. And a cell phone. Utility bills."

"Driver's license?"

She typed again. "Yep, he has a Florida driver's license in that name. That's his picture, all right."

"Okay," Michael said as he watched Miller up ahead. "This is it. His luck is about to run out."

CHAPTER 42

"Where are we going? I want to go home."

Juliet wasn't sure how to answer Zach. She was headed to King's Point to see the house Michael had told her about, but she didn't want to tell him that his dad owned it. He'd had all the revelations he could take today.

"Mom?"

She sighed. "I have to pick up Abe in forty-five minutes, so I'm going to use that time to run by an address that Michael wanted me to check."

"No!" he said. "Please, Mom. Take me to Uncle Jay's."

"I don't want you staying by yourself."

"I'm twelve years old!"

"I know, but these are not normal times for us. Uncle Jay isn't working at home today, so you're going to stay with me until we pick up Abe. Then Aunt Holly is going to stay with you."

He let out an exaggerated sigh, slumped in his seat, and

pulled his DS out of his backpack. Good. Maybe he'd get engrossed in his video game and not demand to know why she was driving by that particular house.

King's Point was a ritzy neighborhood across town, where millionaires lived. When they were shopping for a house a few years ago, Bob had wanted to live there. But it wasn't in Zach and Abe's school district, so Juliet had insisted they avoid that area. Secretly, she'd worried about the money they'd be spending. At the time, Bob hadn't been earning enough to comfortably afford that. But appearances were everything to him.

She drove down Beach Drive, turned to get to King's Point, and crossed Pretty Bayou. As she reached Court Street, an eerie feeling came over her. The layers of deception in Bob's life were astonishing. Now to learn that he owned one of these homes? Did he spend time here? Did he have another girlfriend and more children?

She counted down the houses, a knot in her throat, and slowed as she came to a wall blocking the view of the house. She passed the gate, peering through the iron bars, trying to see the house through the opening.

Zach looked up. "Who lives here?"

"I don't know," she said.

"Then why are we here?"

"Michael thinks this address might have something to do with people involved in your dad's case. But I don't know what yet."

Now she had Zach's attention. He strained to look back.

"Maybe it's the wrong address," she said.

"Well, he must have told you who lives there."

"He didn't. He's working on finding out."

Zach slumped back in his seat. "I hate this," he muttered.

"Yeah, me too. You have no idea."

By the time she got to the pick-up line at Abe's school, she had almost convinced herself to tell Michael, Cathy, and Holly that she was done. Zach sat in the seat next to her, his thumbs moving across his DS, a look of grim determination on his face as he tried to lose himself in the video game.

But without her help, they might never break up this drug-trafficking ring. Amber, Miller, and the others would get away with it.

But that wasn't her problem, was it? She could just get those codes from the security company, give them to the FBI, and be done with it.

She would busy herself cleaning and repairing her house, getting it ready to sell. She didn't think she wanted to live there anymore. Besides, how would she be able to afford it?

She could work full-time for Michael. He needed someone. The pay wouldn't be stellar, but after being a stay-at-home mom for years, her resume wouldn't be impressive, and working for Michael might be the best she could do. Besides, it would be flexible enough that she could be there for the kids.

She heard the bell ring, and children began spilling out of the school. As she watched for Abe, she noticed a teenager standing across the grass near the portable buildings. He had a T-shirt with the sleeves cut off, and tattoos adorned his biceps. Was he someone's older brother?

She watched as three boys who looked to be about Abe's age went over to him and handed him something. He glanced from side to side, then pulled something out of his pocket that he handed to each of the boys.

Juliet sat up straighter. Was she witnessing a drug deal at her fourth-grade son's school?

She nudged Zach. "Zach, see that guy over there?"

He followed her stare. "Yeah."

"Do you know him?"

"No, but I see him sometimes. He comes to my school too."

"Do you know why?"

Zach didn't answer for a minute. He went back to playing his game.

"Zach, answer me. Why does he come?"

"He's selling stuff."

"What kind of stuff?"

Zach looked up at the boy. "Crack or weed, probably."

Her jaw fell open. So this was what they had come to? Drug dealers at her son's elementary school? Stalking Zach's middle school? And could his supplier be someone in the chain whose links went back to Bob?

Would the person who'd called Amber today be bringing more drugs for this boy to sell? Would his "fish" go into the hands of children?

Her heart pounded and her mouth went dry. She grabbed her camera from the floor behind her seat, zoomed in, and waited until the guy turned toward her.

"What are you doing?"

"I'm taking his picture," she said.

"Why?"

"So I can give it to the police."

Zach pushed the camera down. "Mom, don't let him see you!"

Juliet lifted the camera and snapped more pictures. Satisfied that she'd gotten the shots she needed, she lowered the camera. Then she made a quick call to the police station, told them about the boy at the school, and e-mailed them his picture.

When she hung up, Zach stared at her. "Mom, if he finds out you reported him, Abe and I will be toast."

"Then don't tell anybody. Zach, there are times when you have to do the right thing even when it costs you something." She looked out at the boy again. "I can't imagine why he hasn't been reported before. I couldn't be the only one who realizes what he's doing."

"Mom, he's at my school almost every day. You probably only noticed today because of all this stuff with dad. Most of the parents just think he's picking up his kid brother or something."

"Well, why haven't you told me?"

"Because I don't want to get my face smashed in, okay?"

She saw Abe coming out of the school, grim and pale. He headed for her van, saw his brother in the front, and opened the sliding door. "Why are you here?" he asked Zach. "Your school's not out yet."

Zach looked down at his game. "Came home early."

"Why?"

"Because I wanted to, okay?"

"Zach was having a bad day," Juliet said. "What about you?"

He shrugged. "It was like I was famous. Everybody felt sorry for me. Everybody was real nice."

"Yeah, well, wait till tomorrow," Zach muttered.

Juliet shot Zach a withering look. There was no reason to upset Abe.

"Can we go home now?" Abe asked. "I'm tired of being at Uncle Jay's. I want my room."

"No, honey. Not yet."

He let out a long sigh and turned on the DVD player in the backseat. He shoved his ear buds into his ears.

As Juliet pulled away, she saw a police car turning into the school's circular driveway. She prayed they'd catch the dealer.

Driving back to Jay's, Juliet thought about that drug dealer at the school. The local police weren't naive. They probably already knew about him. He might even have a criminal record already.

They pulled one off the street, and more popped up. It was like a game of Whac-A-Mole. But the children were the losers. In fact, everyone lost, except those who made money on them.

Those like Bob.

Rage rose in her chest. Would Bob have been involved in this if he'd known it would trickle down to their sons' schools? Or would he have cared?

She really knew nothing about the man she had lived with for fifteen years. She would have to recalibrate every emotion she had for him. Reset every memory in light of what she now knew.

Was he really the greedy coward that he seemed to be? Had drug money paid for their house? Her car?

Her heart ached for her children, who would have to learn the hard way that their father wasn't a man of integrity. He wasn't brave. He wasn't noble.

But *she* could still be.

Resolve rose within her, filling her with the courage her husband had lacked. And suddenly she knew that she had to stay the course. She couldn't back out of helping the FBI with the case, no matter what Zach wanted. She had to make sure they were all caught, from Leonard Miller and anyone above him, right down to that kid in the schoolyard.

She would not shrink back or give up. Lives depended on her following through.

CHAPTER 43

The baby had vomited again, and now the smell was getting to Amber. She pulled into a parking lot. She'd have to change Robbie's clothes before she went in. Furious, she got into the backseat and pulled him out of his car seat. Setting him on her lap, she wiped his face again.

"I know you don't realize this, but you're putting us in serious danger today. I *so* don't need for you to be sick."

She pulled off his onesie and stuffed it into a garbage bag she carried for dirty diapers. She'd just throw the thing away so she wouldn't have to smell it all the way home.

She wiped off his chest, making sure she got all the vomit, then laid him down on the seat and quickly changed his diaper. As she stuffed the dirty diaper into the garbage bag, something caught her eye.

She looked closer. On the floorboard in front of the car seat lay the phone battery.

What was it doing there?

She closed the diaper and pulled a T-shirt over Robbie's head. She reached for the battery. If it was here, maybe the phone . . .

She looked under the seat. Yes! There it was—her phone!

Had she dropped it hard enough to knock the battery out? She wasn't sure how that could have happened without her realizing it, but apparently it had. She'd looked on the floorboard of the front seat, not the back—and it had been here all along.

Thankful, she snapped the battery back in and pressed the power button. The phone came to life.

She'd had thirteen missed calls, most from Lenny Miller earlier today. But the transporters had also called. She hoped their failure to get ahold of her hadn't changed their plans about making the delivery tomorrow night.

Taking Robbie with her, she got back into the driver's seat and called them.

"Hello?"

"Hey, this is Amber."

There was a pause. "Yeah?"

"I'm sorry I missed your call." She didn't want to tell him she'd misplaced her phone, so she said, "My battery died. I just saw that you tried me."

Again, silence.

"Can you hear me? Hello?"

"I talked to somebody. They said they were you."

"What?" She'd startled the baby and he began to cry. "No! What number did you call?"

"The number you're calling from. I talked to a woman and she said to make the delivery, that the delivery point was the same and was still secure. Is that a baby crying?"

"Yes, it's my baby." She tried to grasp what he'd said, but she didn't understand. She sat there staring out the windshield, trying to think over Robbie's screaming. "That's impossible. No one's had my phone."

"Have you been drinking?"

She breathed a frustrated laugh. "No! This woman. Did she sound like me?"

"How would I know? I've never talked to you in person."

"What did you tell her?"

"Nothing that she didn't already know. What's going on?"

Amber closed her eyes. "Tell me you didn't give her an address."

"No, I didn't say where it was. She sounded like she knew."

Amber groaned, bouncing her son. "This can't be true!"

"Amber, that could have been the feds or the police. They could be setting us up. If it's not safe to deliver there, we need to set up another place or call this off right now."

She shook her head, trying to figure it out. Had her phone really been in her backseat all along? Or had someone taken it and then put it back there? "I don't know. Let me talk to my contact. I'll get back to you. But we need that load!"

"I'm not dropping it anywhere until I hear from you, and if I'm not absolutely sure that things are secure, I'll contact another broker. We'll have to abort this delivery."

"No, that won't be necessary. It'll be fine."

"I don't think it will. I'm going to talk to my contacts and decide. You can contact me later and if I don't answer, then it's off. If you do get me, we need a code word so I'll know it's really you."

All she could think about was her crying baby. "How about *babysitter*? I'll say, 'I got a babysitter,' and you'll know it's me."

The man breathed a disgusted laugh, then clicked off the phone.

Amber fought the urge to throw hers as hard as she could. The baby screamed an octave higher. She held him out in front of her and screamed, "Will you shut up?"

Robbie's cries pierced her ears. She couldn't think. She had to get a babysitter. What time was it?

Maybe her go-to babysitter was home by now. The middle school got out around three, didn't it? She pulled out of the parking lot. She couldn't call Lenny until she got the baby quiet or found someone to watch him. Meanwhile, she had to make a plan.

CHAPTER 44

Miller hadn't led them anywhere significant, but Michael and Cathy kept watching him. Thursday morning he finally took off in his van. They had followed him discreetly for miles.

"Come on, Miller," Cathy whispered. "Go round up all your friends."

Two blocks ahead of them, he turned right. Cathy glanced at Michael's GPS map. "The street he turned on was Frankford Avenue."

Michael nodded. "This is the area where the King's Point house is."

They grew quiet. Instead of turning off with him, Michael zoomed out on his GPS to see the nearby streets and turned on the next street over. "We need a plan. I don't want to drive up Court Street if he's trying to get in the gate. He'd see us for sure, and if he sees me, he'll recognize me."

Cathy opened Google Earth on her phone and clicked on the satellite icon so she could see a bird's-eye view of the houses on the street. "Bob's house has a canal behind it. But the houses on the other side of Court Street don't. It's on a peninsula, and the street forms a U. The two middle rows of houses are backed up to each other, no water. If we park on the other side of the U, maybe there's a way to see between the houses." She tapped one of the houses lined up with 542 Court Street. The address popped up. "So there are two turns for Court Street. Take a right, go two blocks, and take the *second* Court Street turn."

He followed her directions. As he passed the first Court Street turn, he glanced down the street and saw Miller's car halfway down. He drove past and took the next turn, also Court Street.

"Go to 914. It looks like it's backed up to the house directly across the street from 542."

"Smart lady."

"Smart *phone*."

He slowed as he got closer, glancing between houses, hoping there was no one outside at 914 and that there wouldn't be privacy walls or shrubbery obstructing their view.

He reached the house, but it was massive and provided no visibility through to the houses behind it. He scanned the street. There was a house for sale three doors up, and the grass was a little higher than the neighbors'. Maybe it was vacant.

He pulled up to the curb. "Stay here," he said. "I'll be right back."

He got out and walked up to the house like he was going to knock on the door. As he passed a front window, he looked inside. Vacant. Perfect.

He rounded the house to the backyard. He couldn't see 542 from here, so he walked between the yards backed up to each other until he reached the house across from Bob's property. An oak tree stood between that house and the one next to it. He stood behind the trunk and peered across.

Miller was trying to get the gate to open, but when it wouldn't budge, he gave up and went around the wall. It was probably open at the canal. The wall looked as if it was more for privacy than protection—it probably wasn't completely secure.

It didn't appear that anyone was waiting in the car. Miller was alone. Michael checked to make sure there were no dog walkers or yard workers within sight, then he crossed the street, went to the opposite wall, and crept down toward the canal. When he reached the water, he looked around the wall. Miller was in the yard. He watched as Miller went to the back door of Bob's house and tried to get in. He didn't have a key, but he had a crowbar.

Michael stayed hidden behind the wall, watching as Miller tried to pry the door open. It was metal, and it wasn't budging. Miller backed up and kicked, then kicked again harder.

Nothing. It was Fort Knox.

Michael took a quick look at the canal behind the house. There was a boat dock and a landing there. It looked as if there had once been a pool in the yard, but it had been filled in. The square border of the pool was still there in brick pavers, but the rest had been filled in with rocks.

Miller kicked the door hard enough to risk breaking his foot, but the door never budged. Michael heard him curse, then watched as he went to a window. The shutters were closed. He used the crowbar to pry one open.

But instead of glass, there was nothing but steel plates. Amazing.

Miller went to each window, splintered open the shutters with his crowbar, cursing each time when the window turned out to be steel. Finally, he backed up to the rocks and looked at the roof tiles. Was he thinking about trying to beat his way in through the clay tiles and decking?

Michael peered across the canal. There were houses on the other side, probably less than 800 feet away. If Miller tried to beat his way into the roof, the neighbors across the water would notice. He doubted Miller would try it, at least right now.

As Miller went around to the other side of the house, searching for another entry point, Michael headed back to the street and crossed it. He walked at a steady pace, like a utility worker who had a reason to be there, and slipped back between the houses.

When he got to the car, Cathy was sweating. "Thank goodness you're okay."

"He was trying to get in," he said. "But that place is locked tight, and apparently Miller didn't rate a key."

"What do you think it is?"

"Maybe he stored drugs there."

"Is that how it works? Do they store them?"

Michael thought for a moment. "Not for long. Just until they get them distributed. They have to be delivered somewhere."

"But why a residential area? I would think that would be too visible."

"There was a dock out back on the canal. And a landing."

"So you think they brought the drugs by boat?"

"That's a common way to traffic drugs. But customs

officials often stop boats, especially if they're coming from Colombia or the countries known for drug trafficking."

"But if they were coming from the Bahamas?" Cathy asked.

"They'd be less likely to be checked."

"But wouldn't that still be risky? I mean, customs agents board a lot of these boats, looking for drugs. If they got caught, they'd lose the whole load."

"That's part of the business. They lose a lot of loads. But most of them probably get through."

"No way. Bob wouldn't want to take a chance like that, would he? If the transporters got caught, Bob would be exposed."

"Nope," Michael said. "Bob wouldn't be exposed, because the transporters wouldn't know him. They would only know where they're delivering. They would park the boat and have somebody pick them up, and they'd be on their way. Somebody from this end would take care of receiving and storing the drugs until they could get them to the distributors. If the transporters got caught out in the Gulf, they just wouldn't show up at the delivery point. They probably wouldn't have anything on board to point to it. Officials would never have reason to suspect that place."

"We've got to get in there."

"Yep. I'll call Sid again." He pulled back onto the street and handed her his phone. "Look up Griffin Security in my contacts."

She found the number, clicked on it. "Ringing."

He took the phone back. "He must have landed if the phone's not going to voice mail anymore. Maybe I can catch him." He waited as it rang, then rang again.

"Sid Griffin."

Michael wanted to shout. "Sid, this is Michael Hogan."

"Michael! I was just about to call you. Just landed. I'm still on the tarmac."

"Can we meet you at your office? It's pretty important that we get access to this place as soon as possible."

Sid hesitated. "What's up with this place? Why does everybody want in so bad?"

Michael glanced at Cathy. "Everybody who?"

"I've gotten calls from some woman who claims she was Bob's business partner. I forget her name."

"Was it Amber Williams?"

"Yeah, Amber. That sounds right. Also a couple of calls from some guys who didn't identify themselves. I let them know that unless they had a legal claim to the building, I wasn't giving them anything. The house was empty when I wired it. It must have some important stuff in it if this many people want to get in."

"Did you replace the windows? Board them up?"

"No, not me. I just put in the doors and the computer system. He told me not to worry about the windows, that he would take care of those. I was worried, because that's a perfect place to break in. But he said he was going to take care of that."

"Looks like he did. Listen, there are some things in there that are important to the functioning of this family. We need to get in there as soon as possible."

"Okay, man. I was going to go home first, but we can meet at my office. I'll get his wife fixed up, as long as she has the paperwork we talked about. I trust you, man, but I have to follow my own rules."

"Right, no problem. We have what you need."

When Michael hung up, he looked at Cathy. "Better get Juliet on the phone. Tell her she has an appointment."

Cathy stared at him. "Is he really going to give her the code?"

"Looks like it. You got her paperwork ready?"

"I talked to her earlier. She has the marriage license and death certificate, and a copy of Bob's Revocable Trust, which is his will, naming her as his beneficiary."

"All right. Soon as we get the codes, we'll go in. I can't wait to see what's behind those doors."

CHAPTER 45

Sid Griffin wore jeans, a pullover golf shirt, and tennis shoes. He met them at the door of his security company, shook hands with Michael and gave him a quick bro hug, then walked them down the hall to his office.

It wasn't what Juliet would've expected. She'd been picturing the kind of office you'd find in the police department or the FBI, not this no-frills room with papers piled high on the desk and no pictures. Five computer monitors were lined up on the wall. Sid dragged in some folding chairs from another room, lined them up in front of his desk, then plopped down in his own chair and crossed his feet on the desk.

"So you guys need access to the Court Street property."

"Right," Juliet said, sitting too straight.

Cathy handed him the death certificate. "Her husband died several days ago."

"Yeah, I saw it on the news. I'm really sorry."

Juliet just nodded.

"So the woman who came the day after his murder was pretty convincing. At first I thought she was his wife, but she couldn't produce any documentation. She finally confessed that she was his business partner. Tried to bribe me, but I don't take bribes. Can I see your marriage license?"

Juliet slid it across the desktop, then stacked her other papers in front of him. "Here's a copy of Bob's Revocable Trust, listing me as the trustee and beneficiary of his estate. The Court Street property isn't mentioned specifically, but there is a clause that I inherit all of his property, whether it's listed or not. And here's my driver's license."

Sid scanned the documents. "Let me just get you to fill out a few forms and then I'll print out a list of the codes for you. I'll have to get your fingerprints and scan your retina, then program those into the computer. Then you'll be able to open the doors." He turned back to Michael. "We set it up like we do for classified areas on military bases. Pretty high-tech. There's a series of security cameras around the premises, and the doors won't open even with the codes unless Juliet puts her fingerprint on the pad and lets the system scan her eye. The interior and exterior can both be monitored."

"By who?" Juliet asked.

"Not by any of our monitoring companies. The feed went to Bob's computer hard drive."

"Was he the only one who got it?" Michael asked.

"Yep. That's how he wanted it."

"Which computer?" Juliet asked. "The laptop at home, or the one at his clinic?"

"I programmed it myself on his laptop. I think Bob was probably monitoring it pretty regularly. We also had a series of alarm systems set to go off if anyone made it past a certain point. Again, all those alarms went to Bob instead of the police."

Juliet couldn't help asking what had been plaguing her. "Did he tell you why he wanted all this security? And why he wanted the monitoring and the alarms going directly to him, rather than to you or a monitoring company, or to the police?"

Sid shrugged. "It's none of my business. The house was empty when I did the installation. But it seems like he mentioned something about storing high-priced medical equipment there. Sounded weird, since it was a house in a residential neighborhood, but I didn't question it."

He typed a few things on the computer, then had Juliet press her thumbprint on a pad. He followed that with the retina scan. He made sure the computer would take it, pressed the start button, and the printer began humming. "So you guys better be careful if there's something valuable in there that other people want. If I were going in there, I'd probably make sure I was armed or had a police escort."

"We'll be careful," Juliet said.

Sid pulled the paper out of the printer and handed it to Juliet. "There you go. Tell me, are you going to be renewing the security contract? It's paid for until the end of the year. We would have renewed it automatically, but if you're not going to be needing it anymore . . ."

Juliet looked at Michael. "I don't know. I need a few days to think about it."

"All right. Normally when someone dies, we start over from scratch with a new contract. If these people are so gung ho about trying to get in, it's better not to let it lapse."

Juliet felt a sense of relief as they walked out and got back into her van. "Well, that was easy," she said. "What now?"

"Let's go back to the house," Michael said. "Let's check it out and see what we have in there."

"But shouldn't we call the FBI agents first? We could have them meet us there."

"If we do that," Cathy said, "we might never be able to get in. I want to see what's there. After we've had a look, we can call them."

Juliet thought that over. She feared going in there, but if the FBI kept her out, she wouldn't be able to sleep, wondering what her husband had hidden there. "All right," she said finally, "but as soon as we've seen it, we call them."

"Deal," Michael said. "Whatever's there, we don't touch anything. And after it's over, I'll go look at my copy of Bob's hard drive. Now that I know the video went to his computer, maybe I can see some of the stored footage there. See who went into that place."

"Where will we meet?" Cathy asked.

"Let's leave your car and Juliet's car here and you two ride with me. We'll park away from the property and walk to the house."

Juliet got into the backseat of Michael's Caprice. She dreaded what she would find in that house, but whatever it was could change everything. Maybe it would help the FBI crack the case and arrest everyone involved.

She prayed it would soon be over.

CHAPTER 46

Juliet felt a slow nausea rising in her chest as Michael parked the Caprice. Cathy followed the two of them as they walked like neighbors toward the house with the privacy walls. Sweat beads sprang to Juliet's temples as they cut across the lawn and around the wall to the canal, where they could slip into the backyard.

"Are you okay?" Cathy asked her when they were safely on the property.

Juliet shook her head. "No, I'm scared. I don't think I want to see what Bob has in there."

"It's probably his drug supply."

"Yeah, but until now that was just a theory. Seeing it in person . . ."

"You can do this. Come on."

Michael gave them latex gloves and blue paper booties to cover their shoes, and they pulled them on.

Juliet had the paper with the codes wadded in her hand,

and she flattened it out and read, "Back Patio—Door 3—Print, Retina, Code #967854, 364192."

Michael pointed to the pad. "There's only a keypad here. Type in the first part, see if that works."

Juliet's hands trembled as she typed in 967854. "Do I press ENTER or the pound sign?"

Michael studied the keypad. "Hit ENTER."

She pressed it and heard a bolt click. She turned the doorknob and the door opened. Her heartbeat pounded in her ears as she looked inside.

There was a little entry area, about four feet by five feet, and a steel door with the scanners she'd expected, and another keypad. "Okay, so this is where the real security begins."

"Wow," Cathy said, stepping in. "This is some setup."

Juliet went in, and Michael followed her and closed the door behind them. A motion-detecting light came on. "Okay, now I scan my thumb, right?"

"Yes, but do it at the same time as your eye," Michael said. He tapped a small metal shelf below the retina scanner. "Put your chin here."

She put her chin on the shelf, making sure her eye was in front of the scanner.

"Wrong eye," Michael said. "Sid scanned your right one."

She moved over to expose her right eye, then put her thumb on the pad. "How do I make it scan?"

Michael studied the keypad again. "Okay, I think you have to type a code in first. Then it scans." He took the paper out of her free hand and read the code. He typed it in, and in a few seconds, a red line appeared in the scanner, then moved across, reading her eye. Juliet fought the urge to blink.

Again, a bolt clicked. "Got it," Michael said.

Juliet stepped back, and Michael pulled the heavy door open. They stepped into the pitch-black house. Michael felt along the wall next to the door and found a light switch. He turned it on.

This room was empty except for some tools lying on the floor. Several kinds of saws, screwdrivers, crowbars, hammers.

"Okay, not what I expected," Juliet whispered.

They waited as Michael made a quick search of the house, checking every room and every closet for occupants. "It's clear," he said when he came back downstairs.

Juliet breathed a sigh of relief and looked around. All the windows were covered with steel plates. The rooms felt stale, hot. She could hear the hum of air conditioning, but the thermostat was set high, maybe eighty degrees.

Michael went to the kitchen, visible from the room they were in. More tools sat on the counters, and a gray dust had been tracked in from the garage. "Come on in here, but avoid these tracks on the floor. Stay against the walls."

They did as they were told, and Juliet looked around the room. This place clearly wasn't used for cooking, but there was nothing obvious here worth noting.

Michael opened the door to the garage. He flicked on the light. "Bingo," he said.

Juliet hurried to the door and stepped out. It was a four-car garage, facing the back of the property. All she saw were some dismantled cigarette boats. "What do you mean, *bingo*? I don't see anything except for some torn-up boats."

"That's our gold," he said. "I'm getting a clearer picture of how they were using this place."

Cathy came into the garage and looked around. "You care to share it with us?"

He was looking into a boat, his eyes wide, checking out the damaged structure. "The favorite way to transport drugs from Colombia or other South American countries known for growing these crops is by boat. But it's dicey bringing a load into US waters, because customs agents are pretty tough. Anything coming from Colombia would automatically be searched. So they plot their course from the Bahamas or Mexico or some midpoint that isn't as suspicious."

"But there's still a high risk they could be caught," Cathy said.

"Right. So they have to get creative about how to transport. Larger cargo ships are more likely to be searched. They can carry more drugs, but the risk of losing a load is greater. With loads like cocaine and heroin, they can have smaller loads and make more money. So sometimes they build them into these cigarette boats."

"Build them in?" Juliet asked. "How do you mean?"

Michael pointed to one of the boats. Its hull had been sawn open. "The boat is made of fiberglass. There's a closed bow. It holds up to five people, but for a drug load, there would probably only be two guys. The smaller the crew, the better. These boats are thirty to fifty feet long. Mostly fiberglass. They could hide drugs inside the bow, the walls, the floor, and customs agents would have to tear the boat apart to find them."

"So you mean they literally manufacture these boats with drugs in them?"

"No, not at the manufacturing point. They would have a boat architect at their end, taking the boat apart, loading the drugs in, then putting it back together."

"So customs agents never look that far?" Juliet asked. "If *you* know about it, how come *they* don't?"

"They do. But in order to take the boat apart, Customs

would probably have to take it out of the water and dry dock it. And if the boat had Colombians on board, they might be suspicious enough to do that. Colombia is responsible for 42 percent of the cocaine in the US. But if the transporters aren't Colombian, and it looks like these are just boaters out having a good time, they might decide not to waste their time—or to risk damaging an expensive boat whose owners may not be guilty of anything."

Cathy walked to the garage doors. There were no windows. "So you think the transporters deliver the load here, on the water?"

"Right," Michael said. "They could pull up to this private dock in broad daylight. There's a boat landing here, so pretty soon after they dock, they can put the boat on a trailer and pull it straight into this garage. The garage opens to the back, and they filled the pool in so it would be easier to pull the boat across the lawn and straight into the garage. Then they take it apart and get to the drugs."

Juliet frowned, trying to envision the whole process. "But it seems like the neighbors would get suspicious if boats come, then disappear, never to be seen again."

"The neighbors wouldn't be that suspicious of boats docking at these houses. Besides, the boats might be seen again," Michael said. "Having them vanish or not return to where they came from could be a red flag for Customs. There have been cases where the traffickers have a dummy boat identical to the one they tore up, waiting to replace the one with the drugs. The new boat would go back into the water. Anyone who noticed would think it was the same boat, customs officials who might be tracking them would be satisfied, and the transporters would be on their way, safe and sound."

"So there would be someone here to get the boat out of the water and load it into the house? Was that Bob?"

"No, probably the same people who tear the boat up to find the drugs. They'd want to keep the crews small and segmented from the people above them. The same crew might transport the drugs to the distributors. Bob might never get his hands dirty. He might never even be here when this stuff is happening. He would only control the locks on the doors from his computer and monitor things from a distance."

Juliet found this all hard to believe. "How do we know this for sure?"

"Can you think of a reason that there would be remnants of . . ." He counted the boats in the garage. "At least three boats in here? And I saw pieces scattered all through the house. I didn't know what they were until I came into the garage, but now it makes sense. They probably cut them down into smaller pieces and dispose of them later."

"It just . . . it all seems so far-fetched. Crazy. That people would go to these lengths."

"If they get caught, they could serve upwards of twenty-five years. They would also lose a load of drugs worth millions. Yeah, they go to those lengths. You bet they do."

Michael went around the garage, taking pictures at various angles with his iPhone.

"Can we go through the rest of the house?"

"Yeah. The upstairs was pretty bare, but you might be interested in the two downstairs bedrooms. Just stay against the wall and watch where you step. The feds might be able to get footprints. Don't mess them up."

Juliet followed Cathy up the hall, stepping carefully—one foot lined up in front of the other—to the master bedroom.

There was no bed here, no furniture at all. But as Michael had said, there were smaller pieces of fiberglass and foam, boat seats, steering wheels, and other parts she didn't recognize. A stack of empty boxes stood against the walls.

"They probably take the parts out in these boxes," Cathy said. "A trunk load that they could dump into a Dumpster somewhere."

She opened the walk-in closet. "This closet has been converted to a vault," she said, looking back at Juliet. "It's a walk-in safe. Is there a code for this?"

Juliet pulled the wadded sheet out of her pocket and smoothed it out. "Yes, it's right here. It says there are two safes in the house." She saw that this one required a thumb-eye scan too. "Here, I'll type it in."

Cathy stepped aside, and Juliet typed the code in, then set her thumb on the scanner and placed her eye in position. The red line floated by, then she heard the click. Cathy pulled the door open.

Inside were boxes measuring three feet on every side, stacked to the ceiling. "What are those?" Juliet asked. "The drugs?"

The lid of one of the boxes close to the safe door was open. Cathy turned on the closet light and bent down. "No, it's cash. Lots of cash. Hundred-dollar bills, twenties, fifties . . ."

"There could be millions of dollars here," Juliet said.

Cathy shook her head. "I doubt it. But think about it. Why would they keep the drugs stored? They'd get it to the distributors as fast as they could. That's probably where this cash came from. From the distributors who bought the drugs."

"Then they'd get the drugs into the hands of the dealers."

"Right. And the dealers would never know about this place or any of the people involved above them."

In the other downstairs bedroom, they found the second safe. They opened it and found more cash.

Cathy snapped some pictures. "So this is why Miller was trying so hard to get into this place."

"And why it's locked down like Fort Knox."

They heard Michael coming in behind them. Juliet turned to him and said, "See what we found?"

"Yep," he said, unsurprised.

"So why would Bob keep this much money here?" Juliet asked. "It seems really unsafe, even with all these precautions. I'm sure there would be a lot of people willing to kill him to get to this."

"It's probably just a temporary storage place until he can launder it. After that, I assume he moves it to off-shore bank accounts."

"So do you think that's why he was killed?" Cathy asked. "For this cash?"

"I don't know. Maybe he wasn't paying the people he owed. He would have had to send the money for the shipments to his contact in Colombia. If he didn't pay, there could be trouble."

"But why wouldn't he pay? He had it. And wouldn't he pay in advance?"

"Could be another reason," Cathy said. "Maybe one of his contacts here turned on him."

Still a mystery, Juliet thought. But they knew more than they'd known before.

When they'd searched the rest of the house and taken all the pictures they wanted, Michael told Juliet to call the FBI.

"Do I tell them we've already been through the house?"

"Sure. Tell them the truth. Just leave the safes open."

Juliet called Darren and updated him. He told them to

get out of the house and wait for his and Agent Blue's arrival. They locked the house up and waited in the courtyard area in front.

When Darren and Blue arrived, Michael went to the gate and figured out how to open it from the inside. They pulled their car in.

"Sure wish you'd called us before you went in," Darren said, clearly irritated, as they got out. "There's evidence in this place that you may have contaminated."

"We were careful," Michael said. "Gloves and shoe covers."

"I have CSIs on their way," Darren said. "I didn't want to wait. I want to see what we're dealing with. Juliet, can you open this lock?"

Juliet typed in the code for the front door. As at the back entrance, another steel door waited just inside the foyer. She got them in, then waited in the front courtyard as they went through the house.

"How much money do you think is in there?" she asked.

Michael was pacing back and forth along the wall. "I've seen these boxes before, when I was on the force. They can sometimes pack half a million dollars in a box that big, depending on the denomination. I counted twenty-two boxes. That could be up to eleven million."

"Juliet?"

Juliet turned to the front door and saw Darren motioning her in. "Did Griffin give you a code for the back closet?"

Juliet consulted her sheet. "Yes. It's where his security equipment is stored."

"Come do your thing and let me in."

She went back in and followed him down the hall to the third bedroom on the ground floor.

She pressed her finger to the pad, let it scan her eye again, and punched in the code. The door opened and she saw the computer equipment that monitored the cameras around the place. "I thought Bob monitored it from his computer," she said.

"He did. But he would be able to change the direction of the cameras and so on from in here. If the remote link ever failed to work, he would have come here to reset it." Darren stood in the tiny room, studying the monitors that showed the areas around and inside the house.

"Have you found the video footage on his hard drive?" Juliet asked.

"Yep," Darren said. "But we didn't know where the place was." He checked out something on the computer, then glanced at her. "You can go on back out now. You guys never should have come in here before calling us. I could slam you for interfering with an investigation."

"We told you we didn't touch anything."

"It doesn't matter. Evidence could be contaminated just by your walking through."

His tone heated her blood, and she bit her lip as he typed something on the keyboard. "You know, Darren, this is my life. Bob was my husband. The father of my children."

He looked up at her. "I know that, Juliet."

"And all this affects me. It's not just a case. It's not a mystery to be solved. It's my life."

"But your life could be in jeopardy if you keep interfering. You have children to think about, Juliet. You need to back away and let us do this."

"You've had his computer," she said. "You have all the information the DEA had on him. Yet you didn't find this place. *We* did."

"You don't know what we've found or what we've done."

"So you knew about it? And you hadn't been here yet?"

He turned back to the computer. "No, we didn't know. We haven't been here. You want me to give you a trophy because you got to it first?"

"Of course not. But I'm trying to point out that we aren't interfering. We're helping. You have access to all this now, and you didn't before."

Darren shook his head. "Juliet, it's time for you to go." He took her arm and walked her to the front door. Tears stung her eyes.

Darren stopped before putting her out. "Look, Juliet, it doesn't matter how long I've known you or how long I knew Bob. I have to be objective. If you were any stranger who went into a crime scene and contaminated the evidence before we got there, I would treat you just the same."

"We didn't contaminate evidence! You can log our gloves and shoe covers to see if they have trace evidence. But we took those precautions."

"From this point on, I want you out of this. I'd like to put you and your kids in a safe house."

Juliet liked that idea. "Okay, but why now? We've been in danger all this time."

"If these traffickers learn that you've gained access to this place, they'll be even more desperate to force you to help them."

The thought made her sick. "All right. I'll do whatever you say. But how will you get back in here without my fingerprint and retina scan?"

"We'll do some reprogramming now, adding our prints and retinas to the mix. We can override what's there, now that we're inside. We're professionals. Unlike you guys."

She didn't know why that put her on the defensive. "Michael's not an amateur."

"No, he's not. But I still want all of you to leave this to us. Do you understand?"

Tears glistening, she nodded her head. "All right. And if someone contacts me or I trip over more evidence, do you want me to call you or sit on it? Because I don't want to get chewed out."

Darren closed his eyes and shook his head. "Obviously, you call me. But don't go looking for things. I don't want to have to investigate your death, Juliet."

She turned away, but Darren caught her arm and turned her back. "Juliet, look at me."

She met his eyes.

"I care about you, okay? You're my friend. I want you safe."

Her anger melted. "I'm sorry. I know you're just doing your job. So about the safe house. How does that work? I still have to get my kids from school and pack up their stuff."

"I'll send for someone to escort you when you leave here. They can let you go home so you can pack a quick bag. Hopefully you won't have to stay there long."

She couldn't help feeling relief. "Okay. Yeah, I guess that's best."

She stepped out the front door.

Michael and Cathy were standing at the edge of the yard, beside the wall. "You okay?" Cathy asked.

Juliet shook her head. "Not my best day," she said. "It's like an Alfred Hitchcock movie. That Bob could sit in church every Sunday and say his prayers with our kids at night and go to men's conferences and . . . act like he was some big Christian."

They both looked at their feet.

"How do I explain this to my children?"

"You don't have to explain anything," Cathy said.

"Yes, I do. Zach already knows. If it's going to be on the news, he'll find out about it."

"Maybe we can keep it off the news."

"There's no way a prominent doctor in town is caught in a drug ring, murdered for it while hiding a huge stash of money in a local upscale neighborhood, and it stays out of the news."

"Let's not worry about the media right now, honey. One thing at a time."

She drew in a long, ragged breath. "Well, the one thing that's going to happen next is that they're taking me and the kids to a safe house."

Michael's eyebrows lifted. "Really? That's good."

She nodded. "Things are starting to feel even more dangerous. I'll feel better when we're where they can't find us."

CHAPTER 47

Robbie was still sick. Amber had tried to take him to daycare that morning in spite of his fever, but they had refused to take him. She had to do something. Lenny hadn't been able to get into the house where the cash was, the delivery had been aborted, and the prospects of her walking away from this mess with any cash at all were getting slimmer all the time.

The babysitter Amber preferred was at school, so she called her neighbor across the street who homeschooled her children. "I need a babysitter," she said. "Could your oldest kid babysit for me? What's her name? Ariel? Allison?"

"Her name is Lizzy."

"Oh. Sorry. I need her to babysit right now. I have an emergency."

"But she's only twelve. Are you sure?"

"Yeah, I'm sure. She knows how to change diapers, right? You have a dozen kids."

"I have five."

"So she knows what to do. I'll pay her."

The woman hesitated. Amber wanted to scream.

"Why isn't he at daycare?"

"He was sick this morning, but he's better now." He wasn't, but Amber couldn't take the chance that the woman would refuse. "He's sleeping, anyway. He may sleep the whole time I'm gone."

"How long do you need her?"

"Just a couple of hours. Come on, I'm in a hurry!"

"All right. I'll send her over."

Amber waited, fidgeting, about to go crazy, until she heard the knock on her door. She opened it. The girl was smaller than she remembered. She looked ten at the most.

"Hurry up, come in," Amber said. "I have to go."

The girl looked up at her. "Well, where is his food? Does he take a bottle? Where are his diapers?"

Amber quickly gave her a rundown.

"My mom says he's sick. What if he has a fever?"

"Then call your mom. I'm sure she'll step in."

The girl just looked at her.

"Okay, I'm outta here. Call me if you need me, but if I don't answer, I'll get back to you when I can."

She went to her car and pulled out of the driveway. As she drove, she called Lenny on the disposable phone he'd given her.

He answered quickly. "Amber, did you forge the documents?"

"Yes," she said. "I worked on it all night. I think I can prove I'm his wife now."

"Amber, don't screw this up."

"I won't!"

Last night, he'd made her reset her phone, take the battery out, and throw it out the car window a few miles from her house, just in case it was wiretapped. But the question of who had pretended to be her plagued her.

"Lenny, do you think it was the police who had my phone? Yesterday they came to tell me not to leave the baby in my car. Maybe they've been watching me."

"Doubtful. Stealing your phone would ruin their case if there was one. But somebody had it. It's too much of a coincidence that you happened to misplace it at the exact moment somebody hacked into it. No, I think somebody stole your phone out from under your nose. They probably bugged it and put it back. Your head wasn't in the game yesterday."

"I didn't expect to have a sick baby with me!"

"It doesn't matter. It cost us a mint. We lost the load because of that, Amber. You have to pay attention or we'll lose the rest."

Amber closed her eyes. "But what if we can't get into those accounts? I'm not going to walk away with nothing!"

"There's cash in the house. We can settle for that."

"But we haven't figured out how to get in there yet! And that load is worth another couple of million."

"Amber, it's not worth the risk. You screwed up yesterday, and now somebody's onto us. Trust me, the transporters are going to call it off anyway."

She grunted. "Then what's your plan?"

"I think we need to get to Juliet Cole. She got the codes today, and they reprogrammed things to her fingerprint and retina."

Her mouth fell open. "How do you know?"

"I told you I have a contact at Griffin Security. But she's

low level—she doesn't have computer access and she can't get to the codes. She only knows that Juliet came in and got what she wanted."

"So Juliet has the address? How did she even know about that place?"

"Who knows, Amber? You've botched a lot."

Amber almost couldn't breathe. So Juliet knew where Bob's delivery point was? She would tell the police, take them there, and all that cash in those safes . . . This couldn't be happening. She had to get that money!

"Lenny, call your contact at Griffin Security. Threaten her if she doesn't get you the codes. We have to get in there before Juliet drags the entire Panama City police force in there with her."

"It's worse than that. She'll drag the FBI and the DEA in. Maybe she already has. Maybe we should just focus on the bank accounts."

"But there's no guarantee we'll get into those either! I'm not going to be penniless, Lenny. I earned that money. I worked with Bob on all of this. He couldn't have done it without me. I deserve it and I'm not going to walk away without it."

"And I'm not going back to prison. I haven't stayed under the radar all this time by taking stupid chances."

"There's got to be a way! Lenny, do you understand how much money we're talking about? It could be fifty million dollars altogether. More, even."

He was silent for a long moment.

"Lenny, we could take Juliet. Force her."

Lenny seemed to consider that. "What do you know about her?" he asked.

She tried to dredge up everything Bob had told her about

Juliet. "She's rigid. Unbelievably rigid. And she's been working as a PI, so she's not stupid, and she has a little training."

"What about her kids? We could use them."

Amber's eyebrows shot up. "Yes, that could work. Bob said she'd throw herself in front of a train for her boys. If we could just make her think that they were in enough danger. Threaten them somehow."

"We've done that."

"Yeah, you're right." She tapped her solar nails on the steering wheel. "It needs to be something more. If we could . . . take her kids. Then we'd have leverage. She'd do anything we told her."

"Do you realize what you're saying? If we did that, how would we end it? There's no exit strategy. It's not like we could let the kids go once we got her to do what we wanted. They'd know too much about us."

She hated this. Why did things have to be so complicated? Everything had gone so smoothly for so long when Bob was alive.

If only he hadn't turned on them.

"We could lock them up somewhere until we could get out of the country," she said. "Your friend who flies planes. We could hire him to take us to Mexico."

"Juliet and the kids would talk when they're found. The authorities would be waiting for us when we landed."

"Then we'll have to kill them!" The minute the words were out of her mouth, Amber knew that was the only possible solution. "We use them to make her give us the codes and the cash, and then we kill all of them. That's our only option."

Lenny thought it over for a moment. "It's too messy. Too much could go wrong."

Amber's plumped lips grew tight over her teeth. "The only other option is to walk away with nothing, and I won't do that. I had it all when Bob was here. Now he's gone and I have nothing. I'm not going to be left with nothing, do you understand, Lenny? I'm not going to be destitute. I'm getting something out of this." She tried to think. "Juliet will pick the kids up from school today. You could find her there and follow her to where she's been staying. Are you with me on this, or not?"

For a moment she thought he would balk, but finally, he said, "Yeah, I guess it's our only choice."

"Do you have guys you can trust to take them?"

"Yeah. You know which schools?"

"Yes." She told him the names. "She'll pick up Abe first. Go to the second school, the middle school, wait for her there. She'll either be in Bob's silver BMW or in her van. Bob said she bought a Caravan, but I don't know what color it is. Just drive up the line and look for her. Red hair . . ."

"I know what she looks like. She came to my trial every single day."

"Good. Follow them home after she's gotten Zach. Bob said they were outdoor kids. If they go outside when they get home, grab them then. If the kids don't go out, your guys might have to go in. Once you get them, we tell her that we'll kill them if she brings in the police. We'll have her meet us."

Lenny was quiet, and she held her breath, waiting. "Come on, Lenny," she said at last. "It's the only way. Millions of dollars. We could live the rest of our lives on an island in the Caribbean, eating shrimp and drinking margaritas."

Finally, he spoke. "All right. If we do it right, it could work. But the plan has a lot of moving parts. Things could go wrong."

"Things are already going wrong."

He let out a hard sigh. "All right. Let me get the Harper boys to help. I have enough to pay them some up front. We'll promise them more money than they've ever seen on the back end."

"Perfect. Call me the minute you have them."

"All right. Don't lose this phone, Amber."

Amber didn't find that funny.

CHAPTER 48

That afternoon, Miller went to pick up Caleb Harper, who was built like a linebacker. Caleb wasn't the sharpest tool in the shed, but he always did what Miller told him. As long as he kept him in dope, he was up for anything, usually with no questions asked. But today he had questions.

"You said if we made that call to that doctor, it wouldn't be traced to us. But it was, and the police questioned us. We could've gone back to jail."

"I didn't think they'd find you. It was a prepaid disposable phone. If you hadn't put your real address on that credit card, they'd still be in the dark. You never do that, Caleb. That's just stupid."

Caleb brought his cigarette to his mouth and took a long drag. "And you got Jerome to kill that guy, and it turns out to be some big-shot dude and it's all over the news, and Jerome's going down for murder one."

"Jerome's being taken care of. We're going to get him out.

Look, Caleb, there are risks. I paid him a lot of cash for that job. There's a lot to be made in this one too. You do this for me, and you can buy all the dope you want."

Miller knew that, to Caleb, that incentive was stronger than the risk. There were benefits to working with addicts. They didn't even realize they were slaves.

Just as he'd expected, Caleb gave in. "What do you want?"

"I need you and your brothers to pick up some kids for me and hold them until I get what I want out of their mother."

"What do you mean, *pick up*? Are we talking kidnapping?"

Miller sighed. "There's big cash to be made, Caleb."

"How much?"

"Ten grand for each of you up front. Ten more when the kids are released."

"Nope. Not enough. Twenty up front—each—and twenty at the end."

Miller thought about the millions of dollars he could get from that house, if he could just control Juliet Cole. And after he had what he wanted, he wouldn't even have to pay the rest of what he owed the Harpers. He'd be long gone.

Still, he had to pretend to negotiate. "Ten up front, twenty at the end. Final offer. I can get somebody else if you're not game."

He thought for a moment that Caleb might balk, but finally, he said, "All right. We got a deal."

He drove Caleb to pick up David. He, too, was huge and fast and had proven himself useful. Caleb told him what their task would be. The money quieted any debate, and when they called Steven, he seemed eager to score that cash too.

"So where are we going?" Caleb asked as Miller drove.

"To the school where the mother will be picking up her kid. Then we'll follow them to where they're staying."

He drove slowly past the front of the middle school. There was a long line of parents already there to pick up their kids. In the circular driveway, buses were lined up, waiting for the final bell to ring. Miller drove past the line, looking for Juliet's van. He finally saw her. She wasn't alone; he assumed the younger kid was in the car already. He went around the block and got into the back of the line, keeping his eye on her van up around the curve.

Just being here was risky. But he couldn't leave this part to Caleb and his brothers. He had to make sure they found the place where she was staying and came up with a good plan to grab the boys. He was tired of rookie mistakes.

Miller wished he could keep the distance Bob had always kept. Bob had rarely gotten his hands dirty, and few of his cohorts could even identify him. But Miller had started as a dealer and then had risen to off-loading and transport on this side of the deliveries. Finally, he'd become a distributor. His hands had been dirty from the beginning.

Killing a cop hadn't helped.

School let out, and Miller kept his eyes on Juliet's car. Her kid came out with his backpack and got into the car. "That's the oldest kid," Miller said. "He'll be easy. And the other one's only nine, so he's even smaller."

Juliet pulled out of line and drove away. Miller pulled out too.

Grabbing two at the same time would be problematic, but he knew the guys could do it. He trailed her, silent. The two men were also silent as he drove.

Miller followed Juliet to a different side of town than he'd expected and watched her pull into an empty parking lot. A sedan pulled in behind her. Had someone been escorting her all along? He hadn't noticed, and that worried him. He drove past and pulled into a parking lot across the street. From there he watched as she and the two boys loaded into another car. Then, abandoning her van, they pulled back onto the street. Miller waited until the sedan had pulled out, then he followed when it seemed safe.

Were those the cops, taking her somewhere? Was this a setup?

He followed cautiously for a few blocks, and the car pulled into the driveway of a small house set alone on a huge wooded lot. Perfect. This place was isolated. No one around to see them.

"All right," Miller said as they passed the house. "You come back here in the van, park in the trees. Hide until the kids come out in the backyard."

"What about the guard?"

He knew the brothers wouldn't agree to murder. "I only see one guy. Chloroform him first, then tie him up. Use your military training. Then watch for the kids to come out."

"And if they don't come out?" David asked.

"Then you'll have to go in. Just take all three of them if that happens. The mom too. We have plenty of chloroform." He pointed to the bottles in the back of the van and the pile of torn-up towels. "Pour some into a towel, get it good and wet, and press it against their faces. It'll knock them out. Grab them and throw them in the van. Then get out of there."

"Who are these boys?"

"Bob Cole's kids."

Caleb frowned. "Not him again."

Miller's jaw popped. "If you're cowards, tell me now. But you'll stay *poor* cowards."

He saw Caleb looking back at David. "We'll do it. But if we get arrested, I'm not taking the fall. I'll tell them everything."

"Then I'll have to kill your mother."

Caleb gaped at him. "You'll what?"

Miller grinned. "Don't worry about it. You won't get caught."

"Why aren't *you* doing this?"

"Because I'm not as big and fast as you. You guys are professionals."

Caleb grinned as if he'd just been awarded a medal of valor. "What do we do with them after we get them?"

"Take them to the trailer."

"That run-down rattrap? I hate that place. Besides, my uncle lives there."

"He's just a crazy old man. Don't worry about it. He doesn't know which end is up. That's where you're taking them. It's out of the way, where nobody'll look. Hold them until we get what we want."

"How will we keep them from ID-ing us afterward?"

Miller didn't tell them there wouldn't be an afterward. "I have ski masks in the back. They won't see your faces."

Caleb looked back, taking quick inventory of their supplies. "Where will you be?"

"When we pick up Steven, you guys take this van and I'll drive his car. Once you're at the trailer, we'll swap back. I'll need the van."

Caleb frowned as if considering that scenario.

"I don't know how long the chloroform lasts. But if you need to, do it over and over to keep them unconscious."

Caleb was quiet for a long moment. "I'm not going to prison again, man."

Miller shook his head. "Neither am I." But he also wasn't going to be poor. This was his ticket, but it wasn't theirs. He couldn't tell them he had millions riding on it, or they'd want more money—and they wouldn't let him out of their sight till they got it. He tapped the Bluetooth earpiece in Caleb's ear. "Wear your earpieces, and put your phones on vibrate. I want to communicate the whole time."

David pulled his Bluetooth out of his pocket, shoved it into his ear, and set his phone.

They went to pick up Steven. He was full of protests when he got into the van, but then Miller handed them each the ten thousand he'd promised. That shut them all up.

Steven would drive the van, and Miller would drive Steven's car. He didn't want to be anywhere near that van if the Harper goons botched this.

Uneasy about how all this would go down, Miller decided to hide the car off the road near the safe house. He hung binoculars around his neck and jogged toward the house. When he reached the woods adjacent to the house, he saw that his van was already there, tucked into the trees on the opposite side. He climbed a tree and sat on a branch, watching through his binoculars. He couldn't see David or Caleb. They were doing a good job of hiding. The guard pacing out front seemed oblivious to their presence.

He watched through the binoculars as David ran around the back of the house. He stopped on the side Miller was on, grabbed a stick, hit the side of the house, then stepped behind a tall bush. What was he doing?

As the guard drew his weapon and came to investigate, Caleb ran up behind him. He threw his arm around the man's neck and pressed the wet rag against his face. The guard struggled for a moment, then went limp. David came out and lifted the guard's feet. They took him to the side yard, bound him with rope, and stuffed the rag into his mouth. They started to leave him there, but David turned back, as if uncertain. Finally, he knelt beside the man, lifted his head, and gave a twist, snapping his neck.

Miller grinned. The Harper brothers had a lot of flaws, but their military training came in handy.

"Guard's down," David said into the Bluetooth.

"Good job," Miller said.

Minutes ticked by, and Miller kept checking his watch. If the kids stayed inside, this could get ugly.

Suddenly the back door opened. He strained to see into the backyard.

"Only one came out," David whispered. "The little one. What now?"

Miller watched as the younger boy came into his view, heading for a tire swing. "I guess if you just take one, we'll have the same result."

"Wait," David said. "We have two now." Miller saw the older kid walking out, wearing earbuds and thumbing his phone, never even looking up. He went to a bench in the center of the yard and slumped down.

"Now," Miller whispered. The kids were both facing the direction of the van, and Caleb and David were behind them.

David pulled the bottle out of the pack on his back, wet another couple of rags, and handed one to Caleb. They both crossed the yard, quietly stealing toward the kids. Abe looked up just as they reached him, but David mashed the rag into his face, grabbed him, and headed for the woods.

The older kid never looked up. Caleb came up behind him, slapped the rag against his face, and grabbed him around the front, pinning his arms against him.

The boy fought against Caleb's grip, but his fight was futile. Eventually he stopped struggling and went limp. Caleb threw him over his shoulder and ran.

Miller watched as they tossed the boys into the van and closed the door. The van pulled out of the trees and raced away. Only then did Miller jump down from his perch and run back to where he'd hidden Steven's car. He'd told them he'd meet them at the trailer. Now it was time to call Juliet.

She would do whatever he asked.

CHAPTER 49

Zach opened his eyes, and the world seemed to tilt. He tried to reach for the edge of the bed . . . but his hands were tangled and there was no bed. Slowly his situation came into focus. His arms and feet were bound, and he was lying on a dirty carpeted floor. He tried to focus. He was on the floorboard of a moving van. His brother lay nearby. His hands and feet were also bound, and he was curled up, unconscious.

Zach lifted his head. A man with a black ski mask over his face sat on a toolbox, staring down at him. There were two more men up front, also wearing masks, but the driver's was turned up. Zach tried to sit up. "Where are you taking me? Where are we?"

"Calm down," the man on the toolbox said. "You're gonna be okay."

Zach looked at his brother. "Abe! Abe, wake up." But Abe kept sleeping. Had they hurt him? Was he dead? He checked to see if his shoulders were moving. They were, so he must be breathing. "What did you do to him?" Zach asked. "How did we get here?"

"Just shut up and you'll be okay."

"Where's my mom?" He tried to think back to his latest memory. He was outside playing on his phone when suddenly . . .

Now he remembered. The hand slapping over his mouth. He couldn't breathe. Had they smothered him until he passed out? There had been a smell . . .

If there was a drug, Abe might be too little to handle it. "Abe!" Zach shouted again. "Abe, wake up!"

Still nothing. Zach moved until he could sit up, hands and feet bound. "If you kill him, I'll kill you both! Let us go or I'll make you sorry!"

The men laughed.

"The FBI knows all about you," Zach said. "My mom's been talking to them. They're gonna come after you."

"Hear that, Caleb?" the driver said, amused. "They know all about us."

Caleb didn't look quite as amused. "Well, you see, you're our ticket. They're not gonna do anything to us as long as we have you."

Horrified, Zach sat still for a moment, staring straight ahead. "What are you gonna do with us?"

"We're gonna keep you with us as long as you're useful. Then we'll go from there."

"What does that mean? Where's my mother?"

"Your mom is fine. She'll do exactly what we want her to do."

So that was it, Zach thought. They'd told her she had to do whatever they wanted if she wanted her kids back.

Zach lay back down and tried to think. His mother had been right about the danger she saw coming. He trembled as he tried to work at the bindings around his wrists to get them loose, but they were tight. He looked up at Caleb, memorizing his eyes in the holes of his ski mask, the pockmarked area around his mouth. The mask hid Caleb's hair, but Zach saw dark chest hair curled at the neck of his T-shirt. The dudes up front didn't look back, so he couldn't see their faces. He squinted to see the driver's eyes in the rearview mirror.

"Did you know my dad?" he asked. "Did you kill him?"

"I didn't have nothin' to do with that," Caleb said.

The driver looked at him in the rearview mirror. "Shut him up, will you? Give him another hit of chloroform."

Chloroform. Zach didn't know what it was. It didn't sound good. He stiffened as he watched Caleb pour something into a rag, then come toward him.

"No!" Zach fought. "No, please!"

"Quiet." Caleb mashed the rag over his mouth and nose. Zach held his breath. After a few seconds, he pretended to go limp. Caleb backed off. Then Zach let out a slow, shallow, unmoving breath.

"That ought to do it," Caleb said, and Zach heard him moving toward the front seat. "David, that won't kill them, will it?" Caleb asked. "I didn't sign up to kill no kids."

"You're acting like you're expecting to get caught. We won't get caught. We're being careful."

"I don't know if they're payin' us enough for this. I'm not going back to prison. It would kill Mama."

"None of us are going back to prison," David said. "Mark my words. And we're getting thirty thousand each, man!"

Zach kept his eyes closed. So they were brothers—Caleb

and David, and the other guy in the passenger seat. They'd been to prison. Somebody else was calling the shots. They'd been paid to kidnap him and Abe.

He didn't know if he'd be able to keep himself or his brother alive.

CHAPTER 50

The safe house wasn't what Juliet had expected. It looked like someone's home. There were even clothes in the laundry hamper and towels in the dryer. The two tiny bedrooms had dark sixties paneling. One had a bed with a thin knit bedspread pulled haphazardly over a pillow. The other was full of junk.

She would have expected the FBI to own a nice condo somewhere.

The house smelled moldy and stale, so when the boys had asked if they could go outside, she agreed, as long as they didn't wander off the property.

Darren and Agent Blue had left one man to guard the house. He hadn't said more than a few words to her and the boys, but she was thankful for the security.

She wet a dish towel and wiped down the sticky Formica countertops, just for something to do. When her phone rang, she dove for it. The caller ID showed a number she didn't recognize, but it could be one of the FBI agents trying to reach her. She clicked it on. "Hello?"

It was a man's voice. "Hello, my little Juliet."

Chills ran down her spine. "Who is this?"

He didn't answer that, just got right to the point. "Do you know where your children are?"

The question jolted her. She ran to the back door and threw it open. "Zach! Abe!"

They didn't answer. She ran into the yard and turned in circles. They were nowhere. Screaming for them, she ran around the house to the front door.

The man guarding the house was gone.

Panic rushed her like a tsunami. "Who is this?" she shouted into the phone.

There was only laughter. "The kids are with us."

No! Juliet ran around to the back again and stood in the middle of the yard, turning slowly as she screamed their names. The tire swing was still moving, as if it had been recently abandoned. Terror burst through her. They had taken them!

"What have you done with them?" she screamed.

"We've just tried to give you some incentive," he said. "If you contact the police or the FBI, we'll kill them. Simple as that. Don't even contact your sisters or Michael Hogan."

"What do you want?"

"I want you to follow my instructions step by step, and we'll both get what we want."

Sweat broke out under her arms, across her lip, her temples. "You give me my children and I'll do whatever you want," she said. "But I won't do anything until you bring them to me."

Laughter again. "Juliet, you don't call the shots here. You do what we say."

Her gaze darted back and forth across the yard. Had someone come out of the woods and grabbed them? They must be terrified! Had she failed to hear their screams?

"If you hurt my children . . . if you touch one hair of their heads . . . I'll hunt you down . . ."

The man was amused. "Juliet, your kids' safety is entirely in your hands. Now listen carefully. I want you to drive to the nearest store that sells prepaid phones. Buy one, activate it, and then text me your new number at this phone number. Don't put anything else in the text. Then I'll call you on your new phone and tell you what your next step is. Let me say it again. If you contact anyone, we'll know. And your kids will be dead."

She had no choice. "All right, but I want to talk to my children. Put them on the phone."

"Sorry, they're sleeping."

"*Sleeping?*" What had they done? Had they drugged her boys? Were they already dead?

Before she could speak again, the phone clicked off. Juliet stood there a moment, her hands and legs trembling. She thought of calling Max or Darren, but would the man on the phone know? She quenched the urge to call her siblings. She couldn't risk her children's lives. She had to do what the man said.

She ran back into the house, grabbed her car keys and purse, raced outside. Only then did she remember that she had left her van somewhere else. The FBI had left one sedan at her house with the guard, but he was gone. Had they killed him? His car was still there. Where were the keys? She ran out to the car, but it was locked. She didn't see the keys through the window.

Her van. She had to get to it. It was only a mile or so away. She took off running, trying to remember every turn they had taken. Sweat dripped through her hair into her eyes as she ran. She passed buildings and parking lots, but didn't try to wave anyone down. She could see her van up ahead in the empty parking lot. She ran as fast as she could, gasping for breath, until she reached it.

She got into it and drove like she was on a high speed chase, looking for someplace she might be able to buy a disposable phone.

The drugstore! It seemed like she had seen those Go Phones there. She headed to the nearest Walgreens, running a red light and almost hitting a car in front of her. She jerked to a halt and ran in, stopped at the cash register. "Those prepaid phones. Do you have them?" she asked the lady at the checkout.

"There." The woman pointed to the display.

Juliet grabbed one and pulled out her debit card. "I'm in a hurry," she said to the people in line in front of her. "It's really important. Can I go before you?"

The two people in line let her go. The checkout woman looked disgusted as she rang her up and put the phone into a bag. Juliet almost jerked it out of her hands. She rushed out to the van, struggling to open the packaging. Eventually she worked her way into it and pulled the instructions out. How did she activate this thing? She had no idea.

Skimming the instructions, she found a phone number. She had to call and give them the number on the phone and her credit card number, and then they would activate it. Quickly, she called the number and waited on hold as seconds ticked by.

What could they be doing to her children? While she was holding, she tried to imagine Zach fighting back, getting himself into more trouble. Abe would cry quietly, trying not to move or make anybody mad. *That's right, baby. Stay quiet.*

As she held, Juliet located her gun, tucked away in a lock-box under her seat. She pulled the box out, found the key on her keychain, and clicked it open. She pulled out the Glock and checked the clip to make sure it was loaded. Snapping it back in, she had no question that she could kill her sons' kidnappers if she had to. If she got close enough, she could do it, just like they had murdered her husband. They wouldn't get away with touching her children. They'd underestimated her.

The holding music cut off, and someone answered. "Would you like to activate your phone?"

"Yes," she said.

"Could you give me the activation number?"

Juliet read it, waited, then gave her debit card number. "How soon will it be activated?"

"Should be in the next hour or so."

"Could you put a rush on it?" she asked. "I'm in a very big hurry. It's a matter of life and death."

"It's not really up to me," the woman said. "But it might not take as long as an hour. That's just what we tell people in case the computer is slow."

She was getting a headache. She rubbed her temples. "Okay, thank you." She hung up and waited, hoping the phone was powered up. She found the battery icon. It showed 25 percent. It must have been charged at the factory.

It didn't have any bars yet. She tried to call her other phone, but it was too soon.

Minutes had never stretched so long . . .

Finally, she saw the bars. The phone was working! She looked on her original phone and found the number of the kidnapper. On the Go Phone, she texted him her new number, then waited.

More excruciating minutes ticked by before the phone rang. When it did, she jumped. She clicked it on. "I did what you said. Let me talk to them."

"Not yet, Juliet. But you did good. I'm very impressed."

"What do you want from me?" she bit out.

"I want you to meet us at the Court Street house. I know you know where it is. Bring your codes. We'll need your finger-print and your eye to get in."

"Fine," she said. "I can be there in ten minutes."

"Don't park at the house. We don't want to call attention to ourselves."

She prayed the FBI were still at the house. But what if they weren't? She wasn't sure they would be monitoring it in real time. And what if they'd changed the codes? What if she couldn't get in anymore?

She would have to try.

But if the man on the phone got the money, would it only fund more drugs that would wind up on the streets of her town?

She squeezed her eyes shut. "God, you've got to help me. I can't take it if anything happens to my babies. You know I can't! I need your intervention."

She started her car and headed to King's Point, determined to do whatever it took to save her children.

CHAPTER 51

The van finally stopped, and Zach pretended to still be sleeping. Through slitted eyelids, he'd checked on his brother often during the ride, praying that he was okay, that he wouldn't have brain damage from the chloroform. Caleb, David, and the other dude kept chattering about what they were going to do when they got the money.

From where he lay, Zach could see the assault rifles on their laps. There was also a pistol strapped to the driver's shin, partially visible under his jeans.

The van stopped, and he heard them get out. They opened the back doors. He heard one of them pick up Abe, and seconds later someone hoisted Zach and turned him over his shoulder like a bag of dirt. Zach tried to stay limp as the blood rushed to his head. He couldn't let them know he was conscious.

He slitted his eyes again to see where he was. He could tell by the pattern on the shirt that it was Caleb who was carrying him, following David up a dirt driveway. An old trailer sat far back from the street. How would his mother ever find them here?

Hanging over David's shoulder, Abe was red-faced.

Zach felt suddenly helpless. *God, I need you to show Mom where we are. Please don't let them hurt Abe.*

Someone opened the door, and they were carried from daylight into a dark trailer. It smelled musty, sour, smoky.

"I told you on the phone not to bring them here," a man's voice said. He sounded old, his voice weak and raspy.

"We had to."

"I ain't got food or electricity."

"You don't have to do anything," David said. "We just have to keep them here until we get our orders."

"Are they dead?"

"No, just sleeping."

"Sleeping mighty hard."

"Don't worry about it. They'll wake up before you know it."

The men carried them into the bedroom and dumped them on a mattress that smelled like urine. Zach didn't move.

"You wait here at the door," David told Caleb. "The minute they wake up, you let me know."

David's steps shook the trailer. Zach slitted his eyes and saw that Caleb's back was to him. Quickly, he glanced around. There was a window. If he could get it open, they might be able to get out. Abe was breathing, but he still seemed to be sleeping. Why hadn't he woken up yet? Had they hurt him?

Where were the police? Why hadn't anyone come to help?

I will never leave you nor forsake you. It was a verse that Zach had memorized in Bible Drill, and he'd been told it was true. God never left his children. So how had he and Abe been kidnapped and brought here? *You promised,* Zach prayed silently. *There's nobody else to turn to. You gotta be there for us.*

Caleb was holding his assault rifle, a strap around his back. What if Zach attacked him? Jumped on his back? Knocked him over? Would the element of surprise help, or would Caleb squash him like a roach? No, he would just have to wait. If he did anything, he might get Abe killed.

He closed his eyes and lay still, waiting for God to tell him what to do.

CHAPTER 52

J uliet dreaded going into the Court Street house again. She
passed it once, looking through the gates, hoping to see the
FBI's crime scene investigators there, but the courtyard looked
empty.

Now she wished she'd bought two Go Phones and used one
to call Michael. No, she wouldn't need to do that. She could
call on this phone. They hadn't had time to tap it, had they?

But what if Miller or Amber or whoever else had taken the
boys had bugged Michael's phone? Or Cathy's? They knew
things they weren't supposed to know. If she took the chance
and they found out, her kids could pay the price.

She parked in a common area near the water, about ten
houses down from the Court Street house. She pulled the page
with the codes out of her pocket—and noticed with surprise
that her hands weren't shaking. A strange resolve had come over
her, filling her with determination.

She didn't get out of her car yet. She looked around to see

where the kidnappers might be parked. There were no cars parked along the street.

She blinked back the tears in her eyes. What if the kidnappers murdered her after she got them into the house? Especially after they realized that the FBI had already been there? Was the money even still there? They might have taken it as evidence.

If they killed her, then Zach and Abe would grow up without either parent. She squeezed her eyes shut. She would gladly give her life if it meant they would be free. Jay or Cathy or Holly could raise them. They would be in good hands. They wouldn't be homeless; they would still have family.

But why would the kidnappers ever let them go? If they killed her, they'd kill them too.

She pulled in a deep breath as if drawing in courage. *Think like a detective*, she told herself. *What has Michael taught you?*

She thought of strapping her gun to her shin, but she knew they would pat her down. She couldn't take the chance of making them mad. In the end, she left it hidden in her van with her purse. Stuffing a phone into each of her front jeans pockets, she got out of the car and locked it. Clutching only her keys and the page of codes, she strode up the sidewalk, her posture purposeful and confident. She walked beside the walls to the canal and came up in the backyard as she'd done earlier. Then she went around to the front door and waited.

A few minutes passed, and suddenly Leonard Miller came around the house with a big man—a bodyguard?—with something in his pocket that looked like a gun.

"Hello, Juliet." Miller's was the voice she'd heard on the phone.

She stared up at him. "Let's get this over with so I can get my kids back."

He smiled. "We have a sniper with an assault rifle pointed at your head at this very moment, as well as a .357 up close and personal, so don't do anything stupid."

She glanced around and didn't see any place for a sniper to hide, unless maybe they were on a roof somewhere.

Miller knelt and patted her legs down, then her torso, then her arms. Juliet endured it, praying someone would drive by and look through the gate, see this, and call the police. He took both of her phones and stuffed them in his coat pockets. Apparently satisfied that she wasn't armed or wired, he nodded toward the door.

"Open it," he said.

She punched in the code on the paper, held her hand up to the print pad, then pressed her forehead against the scanner and let it scan her eye. The door clicked open—which surprised her. Hadn't Darren told her he was changing the codes? Or had he just added himself and Agent Blue to the people who had access?

Miller pulled it open and shoved her inside. As the other man stepped in, he closed the first door behind them.

She smelled their sweat and felt the sour dampness of their skin in the small area, keenly aware that no one could see them now. Holding her breath, she typed in the next code and did the scans again. She pulled the door open and they stepped inside the living room.

"Bob was a brilliant man," Miller said. "The security here is amazing."

She didn't have anything to say about her husband. "If you're looking for the cash, it's in the back, in the safes. I have access to those codes too."

The other man gave Miller a puzzled look. "What cash?"

"The cash I promised you," Miller said. "Wait here, Steven. Watch out the window and let me know if anybody comes."

Juliet looked at Steven, wondering if he bought that.

Miller followed Juliet to the back bedroom. The safe doors were closed now. She released the lock and he pulled the steel door open.

But the safe was empty. Juliet felt a surge of fear, then quickly quelled it. Surely the FBI knew these people would come for it. They had to be watching. She prayed they would show up while she was here, that they would bolt in and arrest Miller and force him to give her kids back to her.

"Where is it?" Miller bit out.

Her heart raced. "The other one," she said. "I must have gotten them mixed up. The cash must be in the other one."

He didn't look like he believed her, but she led him up the hall to the next bedroom and opened the closet. When he saw the safe, he shoved her toward it.

She tried the codes again, wondering what would happen if this safe was empty too. If Clement and Blue had cleaned out the first one, wouldn't they have done the same with this one?

But when the door clicked open, the money was still there.

Miller raised his fists. "Sweet!"

He opened a box and bent to count the stacks of cash. Juliet stood back, letting him work. She didn't care a whit about the money.

"Now that you've got it, it's time to give me my kids," she said. "Can you tell whoever's holding them to let them go?"

"We have to load these into the van. Do you know how to open the gate?"

She had seen Michael do it earlier. "I think so."

"Then I'll send my partner for the van and we'll load it."

"And then you'll give me my kids?"

He didn't answer. His eyes were like saucers. "When we get out there to Steven, don't talk about what's in the boxes."

"No honor among thieves?" she asked.

He breathed a laugh. "We're not thieves. I earned this money fair and square. It's mine."

"Does Amber get any of it?"

He shot her a narrow look.

"Does *she* have my children?"

"Just shut up and help me close these boxes."

She did as he said, folding the boxes shut, probably so Steven wouldn't see inside them.

Miller led her back through the house and told Steven to get the van and bring it in. Juliet went out and opened the gate. Steven brought the van inside the enclosure, and he and Steven brought out the boxes of money.

As they did, she scanned the inside of the van, looking for any sign of her sons. Had they used this van to take them?

She saw nothing, but the wheels were mud-covered. Where could they have taken them?

When Steven asked what was in the boxes, Miller diverted his attention and had him stand with Juliet, his gun aimed at her through his pocket.

"Are you one of the ones who took my children?" she asked him quietly as Miller loaded the boxes into the van.

No answer.

"I just want to know that they're okay. Did you hurt them in any way?"

He glanced toward the van, as if to make sure Miller didn't hear him. "No," he said. "They're not hurt."

She swallowed. "Are you a father?"

The man didn't answer.

"Because those two boys just lost their dad a few days ago, and they're grieving. They're having a really hard time." Tears sprang to her eyes, ruining her confident image. "I'm just so scared for them. Did they struggle?"

"They didn't even know what hit them."

She didn't like the sound of that.

Her voice trembled. "Will you tell them . . . My son Zach is twelve years old. He can be a smart aleck sometimes, but he's a good kid. Please don't hold his attitude against him. And Abe . . . he's only nine. He's really fragile right now."

"Your kids are fine," he bit out. "Just shut up."

When the van was packed, Miller told Steven to bring his car in. Then he locked up the van and the house, opened the gate as Juliet had done, and waited for Steven.

"How did it work?" Juliet asked in a dull voice. "Did Bob come here himself, or did he unlock things remotely to let you in?"

Miller just gave her a long look.

"Of course he did it remotely," she said. "He would never want to be here, in case things went bad. He would have let you take all the risks, right?"

Miller's lips tightened.

"Was he keeping the cash from you? Is that why he was killed?"

Miller said nothing, just opened the gate as the car pulled in. Steven got out.

"All right," Miller said, "let's go. I'll drive the van, and you take the car. She goes in the trunk."

Juliet sucked in a breath. "What? I can't get in the trunk!"

Steven backed the car up next to the van. It was a blue

Chevy Cruze, and the trunk was small. He grabbed her wrist and pulled her toward the car. She thought of screaming, but then they might kill her. She tried to see if anyone across the canal could see her, but the van was between the Cruze and the canal, cutting off the view.

Seeing no choice, she got into the trunk. It was tight, hard, and uncomfortable, but she could do this if they were taking her to her kids. "You *are* taking me to them, right? I won't . . . I won't tell anyone anything if you just let them go. We don't care about any of this. Let us get on with our lives. You got what you wanted."

Steven closed the trunk, locking her in the darkness. She heard the building's doors closing, then car doors. The engine started. She tried to record in her mind every time they went over gravel, every bump, every hill, but after a while she lost track.

What kind of PI was she? Michael would have been able to record every turn in his mind. It grew hot in the trunk as the sun beat down on the car, and sweat dripped from her hair into her eyes. Her neck hurt. She shifted her body so she could keep her head straight. But there wasn't room.

The boys were okay. She would know in her bones if they were dead. They were alive. She felt it.

Oh, God, please let them be alive.

She prayed that someone would realize that she and her boys were gone. Maybe if the FBI tried to reach their guard, the one who was supposed to be protecting her. Was he dead somewhere, or had they abducted him too? Or had he just walked away?

And surely Cathy or Holly, who thought she was at the safe house, would try to reach her soon. Would her failure to answer her phone be enough to alert them?

It could be hours before they realized something was wrong.

CHAPTER 53

Cathy tried Juliet's number again, but she still didn't answer. Juliet wouldn't just ignore her phone, today of all days. Not when her life was in danger and so much was going on.

Cathy tried calling Agent Blue, but there was no answer. Clement didn't answer either.

What if something had gone wrong? What if Amber had talked with the transporter by now and learned that someone had impersonated her? What if they figured out it was Juliet?

Unable to stand it any longer, she searched her mind for a way to locate Juliet. Her computer, she thought. Maybe if she could get on Juliet's laptop, she could use her iPhone's Find My Phone feature.

Jay wasn't home, so Cathy walked to the back of the house and used the key he kept hidden for family to unlock the back door. It didn't look like the kids had been home—no backpacks carelessly dropped, no shoes by the door. Juliet and the agents must have taken the kids straight from school to the safe house.

She heard the garage door opening—Juliet? She ran to the garage's side door and threw it open. It was Jay's car. She waited as he drove in, but as soon as he was stopped she pulled his car door open. "Jay, have you heard from Juliet?"

He shook his head. "No. When I talked to you earlier you said she was going to a safe house."

Jackson bounced out of the backseat. "Hey, Aunt Cathy!"

Cathy bent over to kiss him, then straightened. "Jay, I'm worried about them. She's not answering her phone. She wouldn't just not answer her phone. I can't reach the FBI agents either. I want to get her computer and see if I can track her phone."

"It's probably upstairs."

Cathy went back in and trotted up the stairs. She could hear Jay downstairs turning on the TV for Jackson. "You watch TV for a while, kiddo, and I'm going to be upstairs helping Aunt Cathy."

When Jackson was settled, Jay joined Cathy in Juliet's room, where she'd sat on the bed with the laptop. She navigated to iTunes and checked to see if Juliet had the Find My Phone app. "She has it. How does it work?"

Jay took over. "I had to do this a couple of months ago when I misplaced my phone. First I have to sign into her iCloud account."

"Are you sure she has one?" Cathy asked. "She's not the most technical person in the world."

"Yeah, she has one. I helped her set it up. Unless she's changed her password . . ." He went to iCloud, and her computer logged in automatically. "Perfect."

A map came up. "Okay, there she is. Looks like . . ." He zoomed in, staring at the screen. "There. She's on Bellamy Street. Looks like it's over in that area behind Costco."

Cathy felt the veins bulging in her temples. "What's she doing there?"

"Maybe it's where the safe house is. Come on," he said. "Let's go find them."

"What about Jackson? I don't feel comfortable taking him, in case this gets crazy."

Jay looked toward the stairs, then back at Cathy. "See? I told you this would get dangerous, but no, everybody insisted that all you do is make phone calls and do computer searches."

"This is different. We didn't take this assignment. It chose us. So what's your point?"

"My point is that my sister should be answering her phone. You stay here with Jackson. I'll go find her alone."

"No, Jay. You stay with Jackson and I'll go. I'll get Michael to help me."

He sighed. "You have to have an Internet connection to follow her."

"I can tether it to my phone. We can get a signal through that. I know what I'm doing, Jay, and I'm armed. I don't have time to talk about this anymore."

She left the laptop open and took it to her car, and Jay didn't try to follow her. Settling into the driver's seat, she used her phone as a hot spot, synced it with the laptop, and checked the screen. The phone wasn't moving. It was still at the location it had shown upstairs.

She drove to the location, using the map on the screen and praying that she didn't lose the signal. When she got there, she saw only a convenience store. She refreshed the computer page to make sure she had up-to-date information. The phone was still there.

She went in the convenience store and looked around. Juliet wasn't there, and her car wasn't outside. She went to the clerk at the cash register. "Have you seen a woman with two boys in here in the last hour or so? The woman has short red hair, and she's about five-eight."

The woman was opening a roll of quarters and seemed intent on peeling the paper off carefully. "I don't remember seeing her."

Cathy found a picture of Juliet on her phone and showed it to her. "Here. This woman."

She shook her head. "Nope, sorry. She's pretty. I think I'd remember that red hair."

"Can you check the gas receipts? Juliet Cole. Did she buy gas?"

The woman got on her computer, clicked through some things. "No, she hasn't used a credit card here today."

Cathy wanted to scream. She went outside and looked in all directions. Maybe the computer had it wrong. Maybe she was nearby. Across the street or something.

She quickly dialed Juliet's number again. "Answer, Juliet," she whispered. "Pick up the stinking phone!"

Suddenly she realized what she was hearing: the chorus of "Cathy's Clown," the ringtone Juliet used to identify Cathy's calls. She followed the sound toward the pay phone on the wall. There was a trash can next to it. She dug into the garbage and found the phone . . . still lit up and ringing.

Why would Juliet have thrown her phone away?

She wouldn't. Someone else had put it here so that it couldn't be used to lead them to Juliet.

Feeling sick, Cathy got back into her car and called the FBI agents. Finally, Agent Blue answered.

"Where is my sister?" Cathy said, her voice shaky.

Blue hesitated. "She's at the safe house, Cathy. You know that."

Increasingly frantic, Cathy told her about finding Juliet's phone in the garbage. "Has she tried to call you?"

"No."

"Well, aren't you monitoring her? Isn't there a guard or anyone—?"

"Yes, but we haven't been able to reach him for the last half hour. The cell phone reception isn't that good where they are. I'll call again now. Just calm down."

Tears filled Cathy's eyes, and she pictured the top of her head exploding right off. "Find her!" she screamed. "For all we know, Miller took her, took the kids—"

"Hold on, Cathy. Don't panic. I'm sure she's fine."

"Don't panic? You're telling me not to panic?" she shouted. "Where is that house?"

Blue wouldn't tell her, but she promised to do everything in her power to find her. Cathy hung up. Gripping the steering wheel, she dropped her head. "God, if you still listen to me, please take care of them!"

Her prayer was desperate, and her thoughts grappled with horrors rather than faith. She hoped God listened anyway.

CHAPTER 54

Cathy had just met Michael and Holly at his office when Agent Blue called her back. She put her on speakerphone.

"What have you found out?" Cathy demanded. "Where is she?"

"We sent someone to the safe house to check on them. They found the guard dead and . . . your sister and the kids are gone."

Cathy kicked Michael's desk. "I told you!"

"We just reviewed the security video at the Court Street building for the last hour. Juliet was there."

"What? Why would she go there?"

"She was with Miller and one of the Harper brothers. They used her to get inside."

"Where is she?" Cathy yelled into the phone. "Tell me where she is!"

"They took her with them."

Cathy wanted to scream. "You're telling me they kidnapped

my sister and took her to that building, and you guys weren't watching? That the safe house wasn't *safe*?"

Holly had started to cry, and Michael was on his feet bent over his desk, listening. "You find her and you get her back!" Cathy screamed.

"What about the kids?" Holly asked weakly.

"Were the kids with her in the video?" Cathy said into the phone.

"No, they weren't."

"Then where are they?"

There was a long pause. "It's possible they used the kids to manipulate her."

Cathy couldn't believe their complacency. "What is it you people are doing? This whole thing is going to pot and you're just sitting there—"

"We're not just sitting here, Cathy. We're doing everything in our power."

"Well, obviously you don't *have* any power if they could do this. So help me, if anything happens to her or the kids, I'll sue the federal government and make sure everyone knows—"

Michael stopped her. "What's the plan now?" he asked into the phone.

"We're working on broadcasting an Amber Alert."

Cathy saw Michael's face reddening. "Have you found out anything from tapping Amber's phone?"

There was a sickening moment of silence. "It appears that Amber is using an alternate form of communication. They had her buy a disposable cell phone. We haven't been able to get the number."

"So she's communicating with the traffickers and probably

the kidnappers, and you guys are out of the loop? How will you resolve this?"

"I told you, we're working on it."

"That means they don't have a plan!" Cathy shouted, knowing they heard her. "It means they don't have any way of tracking her down!"

"Oh, dear God," Holly said as she came closer and reached for Cathy. They clung together as Michael ended the call.

"What now?" Cathy asked.

"First we pray," Michael said. "Then we figure out a plan of our own."

CHAPTER 55

The car slowed, and Juliet braced herself in the trunk. It stopped, and she heard the car door slam, then a key in the trunk lock.

The trunk opened, light spilling in. She sat up, squinting.

Along with Steven, Amber Williams stood there with her arms crossed. "Did you have a nice trip?"

"Where are my children?" Juliet demanded, climbing out of the trunk. When her feet were on the ground, she lunged at Amber and screamed, "Where are they?"

Amber stepped out of her reach, and Steven stuck his arm between them, holding Juliet back. "They're safe for now," Amber said. "They will be as long as you do what we tell you."

"Are you going to take care of them the same way you take care of your own?"

Amber slapped her. Juliet gasped, and rage erupted in her head like boiling lava. As Amber turned away, Juliet pushed past Steven, swung and knocked Amber to the ground, then threw herself on top of her, satisfied that she'd drawn blood on her enhanced cheek.

"Tell me where my children are!"

She heard Steven cocking his revolver. "Get off her. Now!"

When Juliet made no move to get off, Steven grabbed her by the arm. Juliet got to her feet, her chin set tight and her shoulders rising and falling with each breath. She pointed to Amber. "I don't know what Bob told you about me, but I can guarantee you that you've all underestimated me!"

"He said you'd die for your kids. We might just arrange that."

"Wrong!" Juliet countered. "He should have told you I'd *kill* for them. What do you want from me?"

"You're going to help us get access to his bank accounts," Amber said, touching her bloody cheek.

Juliet hoped the wound would leave a scar. "I don't know anything about them. Just our joint account. I'll give you access to that, but—"

"We want the big ones. The ones that matter."

"I don't know how to get into those! I didn't even know they existed."

"You can help us figure out his passwords. You can answer his security questions."

"All right," Juliet said. "Let's do it now."

Steven tied her hands behind her back, and they pushed her toward the house. The place looked like a deer camp, set deep in the woods. She tried to figure out where she was. An address . . . a street . . . But she saw nothing. Only a dirt road leading to the house from who-knew-where. There seemed to be only one set of tire tracks.

They took her into a dusty, moldy room and set her down. She hadn't seen Miller. She wondered where he'd taken the cash. "Leonard Miller's going to take the cash for himself, you know," she told Amber. "He's using me to keep you busy while he does."

"Shut up!" Amber sat down at a computer and navigated to an international bank's website.

Juliet sat stewing, going back over the day's events in her mind. When she'd let Darren and his partner into the King's Point house, they hadn't called for backup. Shouldn't they have roped it off? Shouldn't the place have been crawling with feds by the time they'd left there?

And where was the cash that had been in the first safe?

All they had done was taken her to a supposed safe house—which turned out not to be safe at all. It had been someone's home . . . dirty, cluttered . . . not the kind of place the federal government would put an endangered witness in.

Were they bad cops?

She knew that Darren was in fact the regional bureau chief. He'd been recruited into the FBI in his twenties, had spent time in Washington, then other bureaus around the country, and finally had come back to Panama City.

Could he have been corrupted at some point along the way? If greed could change Bob, it could change Darren. What if the feds were in this with Amber and Miller? As it stood, it looked like Darren and Blue had taken most of the cash but left just enough for the crime scene investigators to log as evidence. No one would know they'd taken half of it.

But no, if they'd been working with Miller, he wouldn't have had to take Juliet back there. He would have had access.

She couldn't work it out in her mind. All she knew for sure was that her children were in trouble.

To the thieves, what would be the point in keeping them alive? If Miller planned to escape with the money, he'd be better off with Juliet and her children dead.

The reality of that blazed in her like a nuclear dawn.

CHAPTER 56

Michael had lost track of Miller, so he'd parked in Miller's parking lot, hoping the man would return. When he was about to give up, the white cargo van pulled in. Michael slowly sat straighter. He couldn't see the driver from so far away, but there was no question it was Miller's van. Same tag.

He watched as Miller got out, locked it, checked all the doors, then ran into his apartment.

Michael grabbed some plastic ties out of his console and shoved them in his pockets in case he got close enough to cuff the man. He considered taking the risk to cross the lot and look in the van for Juliet or the kids, but before he could make a move, Miller rushed back out and got back in, then pulled out of his parking space. Michael's heart raced as he followed at a distance, knowing in his bones that Miller was about to do something that would crack this case. If Michael could stay on his tail without being spotted, Miller might lead him to Juliet.

With every mile, rage pounded harder through Michael's veins. Miller had murdered Joe in cold blood—and now he had Juliet and her kids. He would pay this time. He followed, trying to keep several cars behind him.

Then Miller turned off the main road to a small street—it would be difficult to follow now without being seen. Michael didn't take that turn; instead, he went another block down and turned onto a road parallel to where Miller was, hoping he would find him at an intersection. When he came to a red light, he looked down the block and saw Miller's van turning right. Michael turned. There was one car between them.

Then the car turned off, and the buildings on the street grew farther apart, until there was nothing but trees, and there were just Michael and Leonard Miller on the road. Michael backed off about half a mile, and then just in case Miller had seen him, he turned off and drove up the parallel street again.

Michael checked the GPS to see what street it was, but the screen didn't show a road here. The asphalt was new; this must be a new street. He turned again and returned to the road Miller was on—but Miller had disappeared. Michael drove slowly, looking from one side to the other to see if Miller had pulled off anywhere.

The road was flanked by woods. No parking lots or buildings. There was an occasional dirt road. Maybe he'd turned onto one of those. Michael braked at one of them, then checked his mirror.

Miller was barreling up behind him—too fast.

Michael groaned and punched his accelerator. Miller had seen him! Now what? He wasn't able to accelerate fast enough, and Miller caught up to him, rammed his bumper. In the mirror, Michael saw that Miller was smiling and laughing, playing with him. Something burst inside Michael's chest. Gritting his teeth, he stomped his brakes, skidding to a stop. He braced himself as Miller bashed him from behind.

Michael jumped out of the car and ran back to open Miller's door. Miller's airbag had deployed. Michael grabbed him by his collar and threw him to the ground, going for his throat.

"Where is Juliet?"

Miller's face was turning red, and the veins on his face and chin bulged.

"Where is she?" Michael shouted. "Spit it out!"

Miller spat in Michael's face.

Michael flipped Miller over and twisted his arms behind his back, grinding his face into the asphalt. He pulled the plastic ties out of his pocket and bound Miller's wrists. Then he bound his ankles. Quickly he patted him down, looking for his weapon.

"You don't know what you're doing," Miller hissed.

"Oh, I know," Michael said through his teeth.

"They'll kill the kids."

Michael went back to Miller's van, pulled a pocketknife out of his pocket, and stabbed the airbag so it would deflate. He searched until he found a .38 revolver and a knife with an eight-inch blade in the door pocket. He took them both, cocking the gun and pointing it at Miller's head.

"Get up."

Miller struggled to his knees. "You'll go to prison for even touching that gun," he said.

"You're right," Michael said. "And it'll be worth it. Get up!"

Miller struggled, so Michael roughly helped him to his feet.

Michael bent and lifted Miller over his shoulder. The man

yelled and tried to fight, but he was bound and Michael was stronger. Michael took him around the van and opened the passenger door, then dropped him to his feet and shoved him into the seat. "I'm driving," Michael said. "If we're seen, your scumbag friends will think it's you."

He got into the driver's seat, the gun in his left hand across his stomach. "You make one move," he said through his teeth, "I'll blow out your kidneys and your liver."

"You're making a big mistake," Miller said. Blood was oozing on his lip and cheekbone.

"I don't think so. I think you and your thugs are the ones making the mistakes now. Take me to her before I blow out each of your major organs. And don't test me, because I've been dreaming about doing it for years."

Miller's forehead glistened with sweat. "Go up another mile. Take a right onto a dirt road. You'll come to a red mailbox. Take a right there."

Jaw popping, Michael pulled back onto the street.

CHAPTER 57

Amber and Steven cut the ties binding Juliet's hands and put her in front of the computer, her feet bound. Then Amber sent Steven to the kitchen to make her something to eat. Amber had already figured out Bob's password on the first account, but the security question had stumped her.

"Best Vacation," Bob had listed as his hint.

Juliet knew that the sooner she gave them what they wanted, the sooner she'd have her kids back. She closed her eyes and tried to think. *Her* favorite vacation was the one they had taken to the Smoky Mountains of Tennessee with the boys. They'd camped out on a lake and fished and boated and hiked. The place was called Dawn's View Campground. Could the answer be Dawnsview?

She typed that in. That wasn't it.

"They only allow four tries an hour, and then they lock you out," Amber said.

The answer probably had something to do with his vacations

with Amber. Somewhere in the Bahamas, probably. "Why do you need me? Where did he go with you?" Juliet bit out.

Amber shrugged. "Nassau. Mexico City. Kuala Lumpur. Peru."

Juliet swallowed the sour taste in her mouth. "Which one of those trips was his favorite?"

Amber's lips grew thin. "He didn't use those. I already tried them."

Juliet hoped that meant that his adulterous paradise wasn't what it was cracked up to be.

Juliet told herself not to care. Her children were depending on her to manage the next few minutes wisely and carefully. She racked her brain for other vacations. There had been the one they had taken to Hawaii on their tenth anniversary. They had rented a house on Kauai. Bob had spent their first day in Kilauea sleeping, but after that he'd done whatever she wanted. They had gone to Moku'ae'ae Island and watched the exotic birds, sat for hours watching the geysers at Spouting Horn, sunbathed at Waiakalua, snorkeled at Lawa'i Beach, hiked to Ho'opi'i Falls. One day they'd taken a helicopter tour over the Na Pali Coast. Juliet would never forget looking over at Bob as they hovered over the Wai'ale'ale Crater with its three-thousand-foot waterfalls, seeing his eyes tearing at the sheer magnificence of the sight. He had smiled at her and kissed her. "These are the good days," he whispered.

He hadn't had Amber back then, had he? Maybe that was before his descent. Maybe some of what they had then was real.

If his favorite was Hawaii, what would the favorite vacation clue be? She typed in "Kauai."

An error message came up again.

"That's two tries," Amber said, her voice growing sharper. "Think!"

Juliet tried. Maybe it was more specific. She tried to type in Wai'ale'ale, but the log-in screen wouldn't allow apostrophes. She backed up and tried it without them. She typed in "Waialeale."

Suddenly the beach ball began to spin, and Amber sprang to her feet. "It's working! What did you type in?"

"Wai'ale'ale, without the apostrophes. It's a crater in Hawaii, where we went together on a helicopter ride."

Amber's smile faded. She kept her eyes focused on the screen. The account came up, and Juliet clicked on it to open it.

All of Bob's recent deposits were revealed in living color: $75,000 in May, $190,000 in June, $235,000 in July, $400,000 in August.

The balance was just over fifty million. How in the world?

Amber pushed Juliet out of her chair and took her seat. "Move. I can make the transfer to our accounts."

Juliet went back to her seat against the wall, relieved that she'd given Amber what she wanted. But she'd said *accounts*. Plural. There were other hurdles yet to cross.

"Steven," Amber called as she worked. "Tie her up again."

Steven got a roll of duct tape and led Juliet to a chair. He bound her hands in front of her, then wrapped her ankles together. She didn't fight, hoping this was just temporary until they'd transferred the money and needed her for the next account.

As Amber worked on making the transfer, Juliet said, "My children. Call your partners now. Tell them I did what you told me to do. Tell them to bring my children."

"Shut up," Steven said. "We'll do it when we're ready."

Juliet stared at Amber. "If you loved him, why would you hurt his kids? You know he loved them."

"Call it payback," Amber said through her teeth as she typed.

"Payback for what?"

"Never mind."

Juliet dwelt on that for a moment. What did she mean? Had Bob betrayed Amber in some way? He must have, if she'd been part of the group who'd killed him. What could have caused her to do that?

Steven walked across the room and stood behind Amber, looking over her shoulder. "That's a lot of money."

Amber looked up at him. "I told you I'm hungry."

"You called me in here!"

"Well, go back. I haven't eaten all day."

Steven looked reluctant, but he went back to the kitchen. He glanced back over his shoulder as he left the room.

So Amber clearly didn't want Steven to know how much money was involved. And that meant that Steven wasn't intended to get this money, or not much of it, anyway. Miller had also kept him in the dark at the house, not telling him what was in the boxes he was helping load.

That must mean they paid Steven a set amount and had no intention of sharing Bob's cash with him.

Amber whispered, "Yes!" and leaned back in her chair as her transfer of funds processed. "For a while there, I thought it was all gone. He almost lost it all for us."

Juliet stayed quiet as Amber completed the transaction and navigated to another bank website. She used the same password and security question, and got in without Juliet. Juliet sat quietly until she couldn't bear it any longer. "You said he almost lost it for all of you. How did he almost lose it?"

Amber didn't answer for a long moment. Finally, she swiveled in her chair and looked at her. "He found out about the DEA probe and he wanted out. He threatened to burn the house down—close the accounts, give all that cash anonymously to some charity or something. He was going to cut his losses and dump everything."

Juliet frowned at her. "There still would have been a paper trail."

"Right. We tried to tell him, but he was panicked. He was making bad decisions."

"Then why is there a delivery on its way?"

Amber smiled. "So it *was* you. What did you do? Break into my car and steal my phone?"

Juliet didn't answer.

"Doesn't matter now," Amber said. "Bob would have aborted that delivery, but we wanted to take it. Thanks to you, we had to abort anyway. But we've got all this."

Juliet fought against the hope that Bob had had a change of heart, but she couldn't help herself. Maybe it was about repentance. Maybe he truly hadn't meant for it to go this far.

She thought back to his last days. He had been brooding, especially that Friday, but she'd thought it was about Holly moving again. Had there been a war going on in his mind? Had he been in over his head, fearing that there was no way out without going to prison?

Somehow, that helped her. It brought back a little bit of the real Bob, the Bob she'd thought she knew. Maybe his conscience had plagued him. Maybe he'd realized what he was doing to his kids and his wife. Maybe he realized how wrong this whole situation was.

Tears sprang to her eyes. That didn't justify any of it. It didn't make it easier to accept. But it was something she could tell Zach and Abe. That their father had cared about them. That he had tried to turn back.

Since finding out what he'd done, she had wondered if any of his Christianity was true. Had it all been a cover? A way to network and look honest?

Or had he truly loved Jesus, but found ways to compart-mentalize the sin in his life as so many others did? Could he have been a Christian and still been involved in drug traffick-ing? Could he have truly loved God and still done something that would devastate so many lives?

The corners of her mouth trembled. "Did he talk . . . about his faith?"

Amber looked back at her, eyes narrowed. "Give me a break. What do you care? He cheated on you, lied to you."

"I care about his soul," Juliet whispered.

Amber laughed. "That's priceless. So you'd rather he didn't rot in hell?"

Juliet thought that over for a moment. Did she want him punished eternally for his crimes? No, the truth was she didn't. She still loved the part of him she knew.

"I don't want anybody to rot in hell. Even you. I just want to know what he chose. If he was backing out, maybe he'd come to the end of himself and realized he needed a Savior."

Amber gave a disgusted laugh. "He said you were a reli-gious Pollyanna. It made him crazy." She executed the transfer, left that bank's website, and found the next one. "I swear," she said as she typed, "ever since Joe Hogan's death, Bob was the most miserable successful person I've ever seen."

Juliet couldn't swallow. "Then . . . was he involved in Joe's murder?"

"No. He didn't know about it until it was done. It all almost ended then, and he'd barely gotten started."

Relief flooded Juliet's heart.

"That whole belief system did a number on Bob's mind. It almost ruined everything."

"It's not just a belief system. It's truth."

Amber shrugged and focused on the computer. "Truth is different depending on who you're talking to."

"No, it's not," Juliet said. "There's only one truth. You can disagree with the truth of gravity, but if you jump off a twenty-story building, you'll find out real quick just how absolute gravity is."

Amber gave Juliet a mocking look. "So are you seriously trying to convert me? Trying to convince me to leave the money alone so God won't zap me?"

"God doesn't zap people," Juliet said. "He's actually ready to forgive you. I don't particularly like that aspect of God's grace when it applies to someone like you, but I like that it applies to me."

Amber shook her head. "He told me you were like this."

"Like what?"

"That you would try to convert a mouse you found in your attic."

So he'd mocked her. Why was she even surprised?

"He said you had a rigid sense of right and wrong. It messed with his head. That was part of his downfall."

Maybe it was his salvation, Juliet thought. She realized she might never know in her lifetime if Bob was a true Christian or not—the evidence proved otherwise—or whether he'd repented and called out to Jesus to save him in those last days. But the possibility was something she could give her children.

But Amber had told her too much. Why was she talking so freely, knowing that what she'd told Juliet could condemn her? There could only be one reason.

Amber didn't intend to give Juliet the chance to repeat what she'd said. They were planning to kill her and her children.

CHAPTER 58

Michael drove the van to the red mailbox, then pulled over and stuffed Miller's mouth with a rag he found in the van, and duct taped his mouth. Miller's eye was swelling and the skin of his face was scraped bloody. He seemed to have lost his fight, but Michael didn't take his stillness for granted.

Using his Bluetooth earpiece, he called Agent Blue, praying she would answer. Miraculously, she picked up the phone. "Special Agent Blue."

"This is Michael Hogan," he said. "I have Leonard Miller, and he's taking me to where Juliet is being held."

There was a pause. "What do you mean, you *have* him?"

"We had an altercation," he said in a level voice. "I wound up disarming him. Bottom line, I've got him bound. He's leading me to where they are."

"Michael, stand down. Tell us where she is and we'll assemble a SWAT team."

"The way you're handling it, Juliet will be dead by then and so will her kids. I'll do whatever I have to do to make sure that doesn't happen."

"Tell me where you are."

He gave her directions to where he'd left his car. "He said to turn at the red mailbox at the dirt road."

"Be careful. If they see you coming—"

"I'm in his van. If they see me coming, they'll think it's him. But I plan to stay hidden if I can."

"Wait out of sight until we get there."

"How long will it take you to assemble a SWAT team?"

"A little while," she said.

Of course. "Not good enough. If you don't get here fast enough, I'll have to do something. I'm not going to let them kill her." He cut off the phone, looked at Miller. The arrogance in his eyes was maddening.

Michael would have liked nothing better than to blow Miller's head off, but he had to stay focused. He turned at the red mailbox, then pulled down the dirt road slowly until he saw the house through the trees. Then he backed up into the woods until he wasn't visible anymore.

Miller's hands were still bound with plastic ties behind his back. Michael was sure he'd been working on them, trying to get his hands free, but Michael had bound him too tightly. He grabbed the roll of tape again and ripped off a long strip. Grabbing Miller's hair, he pulled his head back against the headrest, then wrapped the strip of tape around Miller's head and the headrest, rendering him immobile.

Miller tried to protest, but with the rag in his mouth the sound was muffled. Michael stripped off more duct tape and wrapped it around Miller's throat and around the bars of the headrest, around and around. Miller couldn't move or speak, and if he tried to get away, he'd strangle himself.

Michael got out of the car, quietly closing the door behind him. He made his way through the trees until he could see the house. He raised his binoculars and studied each window. He could see movement beyond the glass, but he couldn't make out any of it. He would have to get closer. He went from tree trunk to tree trunk, staying hidden until he was close to the house. Then he crossed the distance to the house and pressed himself flat against the wall in case anyone was looking out. He got under one of the windows and listened. He could hear voices, but they were muffled. No windows were open, and the air conditioner's hum made it difficult to hear the people inside. He pulled out his phone, turned on the video camera, and raised it until the lens was slightly above the window ledge. He filmed for a few seconds, then brought the camera back down and played the footage. He saw Amber sitting at a computer and Juliet behind her, bound in a chair. Amber had a gun lying on the table next to her.

He went to the next window and did the same thing. This time he saw a man in the kitchen. He'd seen him before—one of the Harper brothers. He was carrying a Glock .38.

Michael checked his watch. Ten minutes had passed since he'd called Blue. Would the FBI be here soon, or would it take them as long as it took the police department to assemble a SWAT team? Surely the feds had men at the ready.

He went around to the other windows but saw no one in the other rooms. The boys didn't appear to be here.

Ducked down and darting from tree to tree, Michael ran back into the woods, far enough away from the house that they couldn't hear him. He called Cathy—listening through his earpiece—and she answered on the first ring.

"Michael, where are you?"

"I found Juliet," he said in a low voice. "She's in a house off Highway 64. I've got Miller tied up in the car."

"Is she all right? Have you seen her?"

"Yes. She's in the house. She's with Amber and one of the Harper brothers. Steven, I think. They're doing something on the computer, probably bank transactions."

"Are the children with her?"

"I didn't see them. I'm guessing they're holding them in another location. I need you to get Max on the phone and tell him that the FBI says they're getting a SWAT team together—"

"Michael, I don't think we can count on the FBI. Something's not right."

"I agree, but Max thinks they're legit. Tell him the FBI may be too late. Tell him we need backup now."

"Can you get into the house?" Cathy asked.

"Not yet."

"Tell me where you are. Holly and I are on the way."

"No, stay where you are. I don't want you anywhere near this place."

"Michael, that's ridiculous. We can help you!"

"I want Max and his people to help me. Tell him to come down Highway 64," he said, and described the route he'd taken to the red mailbox and the driveway. "Halfway down the driveway, he'll see Miller's van. He's in it, but he's not going anywhere."

"Did you kill him?"

"No. Not yet."

"Michael, be careful."

"I will," he said.

"Don't hang up! Leave the phone on so I can hear what's happening. I'll call Max from Holly's phone."

"All right," he said. Leaving his earpiece in, he slid his phone into his jeans pocket.

He checked his watch again. How much longer? Suddenly something bumped the back of his head, and he froze. "Don't move or I'll kill you." A man's voice. "Drop the gun, right now." Michael hesitated. If he swung around, knocked the gun from the man's hand, kicked his groin . . . But he didn't know how many people were back there. If it was just Steven, he could take him. But what if his brothers were there too? What if there were others?

"Drop the gun now," the man said, his voice rising in pitch.

In the earpiece, Cathy said, "Michael, who is that?"

Michael couldn't answer. He tossed his gun to the side, out of the man's reach, and slowly turned around. "Steven Harper," he said.

Steven nodded. "Now hand me the phone."

Michael pulled it out of his pocket, glanced down at it. The screen was black. It wasn't obvious it was connected. He handed it to Steven. His Bluetooth had a thirty-foot range, so Cathy would still be able to hear. Steven didn't take the Bluetooth.

"Lean against that tree, hands over your head."

Michael did as he said, and Steven frisked him clumsily down his back, around to his chest, under his arms, down his legs.

Satisfied, Steven backed up. "We're going into the house now, nice and easy. And you're going to tell us who you called. Who's on their way?"

Michael kept his hands in the air—and his Bluetooth in his ear—as he stepped slowly toward the door, eager to get inside.

The door flew open, and Juliet gasped as Michael stepped in, hands over his head. Steven was behind him, prodding him inside with a gun.

"Michael!"

"Juliet! Are you okay?"

"Yes," she said. "My children . . . they kidnapped them!"

Amber shot out of her chair. "How did he get here? How did he know where we are?"

Steven shook his head and shoved Michael into a chair next to Juliet. "I don't know, but he was talking on the phone." He grabbed the Bluetooth out of Michael's ear and tossed it onto the desk.

Amber's expression turned rabid. "Who did you tell?" she demanded. "How did you find us?"

Michael's jaw muscle popped. "You have a mole in your operation," he said. "You can't trust anybody, can you, Amber?"

"Who knows?" she demanded.

"The FBI, the police department—they're on their way. If you want to leave, you better do it now."

Juliet breathed out relief. They were coming for her. They would rescue her and find her children, and Amber, Steven, Miller, and everyone else involved would be arrested and taken off the street. The nightmare would finally be over.

But . . . would the FBI help her? Or were they working with Amber and the others?

Enraged, Amber ran to the front door, still open, and looked out. From her chair, Juliet could see out too. She saw nothing but trees.

Amber turned back, sweat glistening on her face. "I have to hurry. Steven, just kill him!"

Steven hesitated.

"You don't want to do that, Steven," Juliet said. "She's

going to take the money and run. Miller already has millions in cash, and what'll you get? Life in prison?"

She had hit home. Steven winced and wiped his face with his wrist.

"Shut her up!" Amber said, going back to the computer and typing furiously.

"That was cash in those boxes he put in his van," Juliet said. "They're using you to do their dirty work, but you'll wind up like Henderson, taking the fall for murder."

Steven kept his gun trained on them, the one he'd taken from Michael tucked into his jeans. He craned his neck to see what was on the computer screen. Teeth gritted, Amber was working through another international bank's website, typing the password into the box.

Michael's eyes met Juliet's, and she understood his signal to get ready. She moved her feet under her, checked her hands. They were bound at the wrists in front of her, but she prepared to use them to clutch or scratch or swing. Anything she had to do.

As Steven cocked his revolver, Michael flung himself out of the chair, knocking Steven back. As the man fell, Michael stayed on top of him, kneeing his groin until he let go of the gun and curled up in pain.

Michael grabbed it, but Steven pulled the other one out of his waistband.

"Kill him!" Amber shouted.

Suddenly Juliet came off the floor, hands and feet bound, and hurled herself at Steven. He dropped his gun, and it slid across the floor. Amber dove for it. Juliet got her feet under her and hurled herself again, knocking Amber to the floor. The woman turned over and grabbed Juliet's face, trying to gouge her long fingernails into Juliet's eyes. Juliet turned her head and opened her hands as far as she could—just far enough to get her fingers around Amber's throat. The tape around her wrists cut into her skin, but she fought it, keeping Amber under control. As Amber's face turned purple, she groped for the gun. Juliet flung Amber to the side, away from the gun, and dove for it herself. She grabbed it in both bound hands and rolled to her back, aiming it at Amber. "Don't move!" she said. "I don't need another excuse to kill you."

A table overturned, a vase crashed. Michael was rolling with Steven, both struggling for Michael's gun. Juliet looked for a chance to shoot Steven, but he was too close to Michael.

They rolled and struggled for the gun until they were out-side on the porch, out of Juliet's sight.

"Put the gun down," Amber told Juliet from the floor, mascara tears staining her sweating face. "You can't kill the mother of a little baby. It would be on your conscience forever."

Juliet wiped the sweat from her forehead with her sleeve. "I don't have to kill you," she said. "If you tell me where my children are, we can all walk away from this. If not, I won't have any trouble pulling this trigger."

Amber lay on the floor, her lips curling in a sneer. "Bob said you couldn't hurt a fly. How would you explain murder to your church?"

Something snapped in Juliet, and lifting the gun, she fired into the wall, making Amber jump and scream. Juliet brought the gun back down to Amber's face. "Underestimating me will be the last mistake you ever make," she said through her teeth. "*Where are my children?*"

Just then she heard voices yelling out in the yard, and another gunshot fired. Amber looked toward the open door.

Juliet's heart sank. Had Michael been shot? Keeping her gun trained on Amber, she got to her feet and backed to the door to look out into the yard.

The FBI had arrived, their guns fixed on Michael and Steven.

She saw Blue and Darren in flak jackets, moving toward the house. Steven and Michael were still in a clinch on the ground, struggling for the gun.

Her chest tightened. Could she trust Darren and his partner, or would they turn on her and Michael?

"Freeze!" Darren yelled. "Drop the gun and get on the ground, arms behind your head! Now!"

Steven stopped fighting and fell back on the ground. Turning over, face down, he put his hands behind his head. "It was Amber and Leonard Miller. I'm just the hired help. I didn't even know what they were up to!"

Juliet took a deep breath, her eyes going back and forth from Amber inside on the floor to Steven and Michael on the ground. Michael took the gun he'd been struggling for and started to get to his feet.

Suddenly, Darren fired. Michael dropped with a thud.

"No!" Juliet screamed.

Darren ignored her and turned the gun on Steven. As if it were routine, he fired again, the bullet blasting through the back of Steven's head. Steven went limp, blood pooling around his face.

Juliet told herself to shoot him, then Blue, approaching right behind him. But she couldn't move. None of it made sense. Her brain couldn't grasp it. She stood holding the gun as her husband's high school friend, the local FBI bureau chief, stepped over Steven, came inside, assessed the situation, and aimed at Amber.

Before Juliet could make herself breathe, he shot Amber. Juliet screamed again as Amber's body jolted, then stilled. Juliet raised her gun to Darren, but immediately felt the barrel of a gun on the back of her head. "Drop the gun," Blue said.

She breathed in a sob and let the gun fall. "Whose side are you on? What are you doing?"

Darren had a vacant look in his eyes, void of compassion or interest. He picked up the gun Juliet had dropped and bent down to put it in Amber's limp hand.

Juliet didn't know what was happening. "Darren . . . she knew where my kids are. She could have taken us to them . . . Why did you shoot Michael? *Please!*"

Still stooped, he raised the gun in Amber's hand, aimed at Juliet, and put the dead woman's finger over the trigger.

CHAPTER 59

In the car by the red mailbox, Cathy and Holly heard gunfire, and Juliet's sobbing questions to Darren Clement through Michael's phone.

They heard her ask why Darren had shot Michael.

"Michael!" Cathy muttered as she leaped out of the car.

Holly followed her. "Cathy, wait!"

"No," she cried. "You stay here and call Max. Tell him everything we heard. Tell him to hurry!"

"But I'm coming with you!"

"You have a baby to think about!" Cathy shouted. "Please, stay here. I need you to call Max!"

Holly stood still and watched her go.

Cathy went through the woods instead of the dirt road, holding her gun in both hands, barrel pointing down, ready to fire if she needed to. She stepped over brush and broken limbs, crackling through dead leaves and dirt.

She saw Miller's car parked where Michael had left it. She

316

didn't stop to look inside. Instead she jumped over logs and leaped over holes, branches and thorns snagging her jeans as she ran. She paused, hidden in the brush at the edge of the clearing where she could see the house. Two men lay limp on the ground.

One of them was Michael. *Oh, dear God, please don't take him. I can't do this again. Please, God!*

She could see people in the house and heard Juliet's crying voice. Choosing an angle hidden from most of the windows, she raced to the building, stole up onto the porch, crept across it to the door.

She could see inside, Juliet standing in front of Blue, with Blue's gun to her head. Clement was on the floor, holding Amber's hand. There was a gun in it, and he was lifting it to Juliet. Cathy knew what he was doing—setting the stage for the story that Amber had killed Juliet.

Cathy planted her feet and centered her sights above Darren's vest. She fired and Darren fell back. She turned her gun to Blue just as the woman spun toward her. Cathy fired again. Blue dropped.

Juliet fell to her knees, weeping with relief. "Cathy . . ."

"Get up," Cathy told her, ripping the tape off of Juliet's wrists. "See if they're dead, and if they're not, tie them up. I have to see about Michael."

"Go!" Juliet said, bending to untape her ankles.

Cathy ran out to Michael. His wound was through his rib cage, bleeding out through his back. "No!" she cried. "Please, Michael! Stay with me." She touched the artery in his neck and felt a slight pulse. He wasn't dead. "God, please, you've got to save him!" she cried. She found the entry and exit wounds, applied pressure, tried to stop the bleeding.

CHAPTER 60

In the passenger seat of his van, Miller tried to turn his head, without success. He looked around the car for something, *anything* he could reach. His hands were behind his back, but he'd been working on them since Hogan dropped him into the seat.

He'd heard multiple gunshots, screaming. As the wind carried voices, he heard a woman shouting on the phone, saying that the FBI agents were dirty and that they were down. Then it hit Miller. It must have been one of the agents who had recruited Bob Cole into the drug business in the first place—the one Amber had described as a government official on the take. She had never met him, didn't know who he was, but Bob had told her that much one night when he'd been drinking. The mysterious man had called the shots with Bob, keeping a nice, safe distance, never getting close to the crimes until now, just arranging things with a contact in Colombia and leaving the dirty work to those beneath him who didn't even know his name.

Sweat made Miller's skin slick, making it easier to turn his wrists. He tried to move them under his body, but he couldn't slump enough. He kept stretching the ties and twisting his hands.

The console, he thought. He had a little Swiss Army knife in the console. If he could just get to it.

Miller twisted his body, letting the tape stretch across his neck like a noose, but he managed to turn toward the door, giving his hands room enough behind him to reach the center console. *Come on*, he thought. *Just open!*

Sweat dripped into his eyes, and the rag in his mouth gagged him. He could feel the veins bulging on his face as the tape choked him, but he kept reaching. Finally, he felt the latch, clicked it. The lid popped open.

There it was. From the corner of his eye, he could see the knife in a tray at the top. He twisted more and got his hands over the edge, gripped the knife.

Yes! He opened the knife and turned it upside down in his fingers, sawed at the plastic tie. He cut the edge, worked it more, and the plastic split.

He raised the knife and sliced the tape between his neck and the seat. He jerked the tape off his mouth and spat out the rag. Then he cut the tape around his head and around his ankles.

Free! Quickly, he dug back through the console and found another set of van keys. Slipping into the driver's seat, he started the van and backed down the long driveway. There was a car waiting at the entrance with a woman inside. He screeched the van out onto the road, threw it into drive, and punched the accelerator.

The woman jumped out of the car and fired, but she didn't hit the van. He would take the back roads out of this area, then call his pilot friend and offer him more money than he'd ever seen to load the boxes onto his plane and get him out of here.

The bank accounts were probably lost, but he could live comfortably for the rest of his life on this cash. He screamed out a victorious *Whoop!* as he made his escape.

CHAPTER 61

Holly didn't know what to do. Tears on her face, she jumped back into the car, started it, and screeched out in the direction the van had gone.

But by that time Miller had disappeared. He must have already turned off, and she wasn't sure where. She searched for muddy tire tracks. She tried one dirt road, but it was a dead end. She got back onto the main road and drove another few miles.

Where had he gone?

She heard sirens and decided to turn back. She had to know if Michael and her sisters were hurt. Back at the red mailbox, she saw the police cars and ambulances turning in.

She followed them, nausea roiling up in her chest. She felt the baby turn, kick.

Her hand went to her stomach, and she felt it again. Another kick.

She decided not to go in with the police. There might be more gunfire, more danger, more death. She had to stay here and keep her baby safe.

Sitting behind the wheel, she waited and prayed.

CHAPTER 62

Zach heard David's phone ringing. David picked it up. "Yeah? No! What do you mean? What about the money?"

He cursed, then cut the phone off and spat out more curses.

"What happened?" Caleb asked.

"It all fell apart."

Zach sucked in a breath, hope strengthening him.

"Who was that?" Caleb demanded.

"Miller. He got away, but the FBI came. There were a lot of gunshots."

Caleb's jaw dropped. "Is Steven okay?"

"He didn't know."

Zach peeked through the slit in his eyes.

David clutched his head, his eyes panicked as he tried to think. "It's over. We have to abort this whole thing. He said we have to kill the kids."

Zach's heart jolted.

"No!" Caleb said. "I didn't sign up to kill kids. I told you, I won't do that."

"It's the only way we have a prayer of getting the rest of the cash. Miller wants them dead. Just move out of my way. I'll do it."

Zach heard Abe stirring. He had to do something. He couldn't just lie here . . .

David pushed past Caleb in the doorway and stepped into the space between the beds, his back to Zach. He raised his gun toward Abe . . .

Zach sprang off the bed, jumped on his back, and bit the side of his neck. David tried to shake him off like a pesky fly, but Zach bit until he drew blood. Groping around the front of David's face, he gouged his eyes.

Gunfire shook the trailer.

David cursed and fell to his knees. Zach fell with him. Releasing his neck, he looked back toward the door. Caleb was holding a gun.

"I told you I ain't killin' no kids!" he shouted. "Kid, move back!"

Zach hit the floor, sweating and gasping for breath. He wiped the blood from his mouth and spat, then crawled over to Abe.

David's leg was bleeding, and his neck bled in a circle where Zach had bitten him. Crouching, he gaped up at Caleb. "What are you doing?"

Caleb fired again, jarring Zach. Zach covered his brother. When he looked again, David was slumped on the floor. He didn't move.

Shocked, Zach looked up at Caleb, his eyes pleading.

Caleb grabbed David's gun, then turned and left the room.

Zach heard the front door slam. Through the window, he saw Caleb running past the beat-up car that must belong to the old man, who was limping up the drive. Caleb dragged him into it and took off.

Heart racing, Zach turned back to his brother. Abe began to move, and slowly his eyelids opened. "Zach?"

"You're okay, Abe. We're gonna be fine." Zach left him and groped through the dead man's pockets. He found his phone and with trembling hands called 911.

"It's okay, Abe," he said as he waited for it to ring. "Just stay there. Keep your eyes closed. Don't move."

"I have a headache," Abe muttered.

"Don't worry. Help is coming."

CHAPTER 63

Juliet sat shivering as paramedics loaded Michael into the ambulance. FBI agents had swarmed the place. It was clear now that Darren and Blue's investigation into the case had been off the FBI radar. The two agents had been entangled in the drug-trafficking scheme. That meant that the agency had no information about where her kids might be.

She didn't know what to do to find them. Miller had escaped, and Steven and Amber were dead.

Forbes tapped her shoulder. She looked up at him.

The usually gruff detective smiled at her. "Got some good news for you, Mrs. Cole. Your son, Zach, called 911."

Juliet caught her breath. "Where are they?"

"He's on the phone. You can ask him yourself."

She grabbed the phone and brought it to her ear. "Honey?"

"Mom, are you okay?"

She broke into sobs. "Yes, sweetie, are you?"

"Yeah. They wanted to kill us. But I watched over Abe, and they didn't really hurt us."

She started to cry. "Where are you? I'll come get you."

"The police are here. They're gonna take us home."

Home, Juliet thought. Yes, home. They could go home now, wherever that would be, and they would be together.

But Michael's life hung by a thread. As the ambulance pulled away, Max and Cathy in the car behind it, she prayed that God would give them one more miracle.

CHAPTER 64

Cathy paced in the waiting room, her eyes constantly on the door through which the surgeon would come to tell them Michael was out of surgery. He'd been alive when they got him to the hospital, but he hadn't regained consciousness. She hadn't been able to talk to him before they'd whisked him off to the OR, and now she feared she'd never have the chance to tell him how much she loved him.

"Honey, come sit down." Juliet looked exhausted, and Zach and Abe sat on either side of her. She wouldn't let them out of her reach.

"I can't," Cathy said.

Holly came up behind her and rubbed her shoulders. "You're so tense."

"What if he dies?" Cathy whispered. "I can't go through this again."

Holly turned her around and hugged her. "He's not going to die."

But Cathy had seen blood spewing out of Michael's mouth as he'd tried to breathe. The bullet had blown through his lungs, and they had intubated him in the ambulance. She'd heard them call it in. *Collapsed lung, BP 60/40, pulse 50, chest trauma . . .*

He was slipping away, and there was nothing she could do but pray.

"Cathy, oh my heavens!" Cathy turned and saw Michael's mother coming in with his father at her heels. Becky Hogan cut across the room and pulled Cathy into her arms. "How is he?"

"He's in surgery," Cathy said.

"Max said he was shot in the chest! That he could die!"

Cathy nodded as tears pushed back into her eyes. Both of his parents pulled her into a crushing hug, and they wept with her. She wished Michael were here to see it. They'd treated him so badly ever since the trial, as if he were singly responsible for Joe's killer being set free. She had wanted so many times to remind them that even though one of their sons was gone, Michael was still here.

But now they had come. Maybe this was what it would take to remind them that they loved him.

They waited several agonizing hours with no word until finally, at 2:00 a.m., the surgeon came out. Cathy rushed toward him.

"He's stable and doing better than we expected," he said. "We didn't have to remove a lobe. We were able to repair the damage and give him blood transfusions. He lost a lot, but he's very lucky to be alive."

The family cheered as if their team had just won a pennant, weeping with joy and hugging each other.

His parents took Cathy aside before she went to see him

in recovery. "So much time wasted when we could have been with him," Becky said.

Cathy wiped her face. "Well, it looks like there will be time to make that up to him. I've wasted time too. I'm ready to move on with him and stop looking back. I loved Joe with all my heart, but I truly believe that he would be thrilled to know that Michael and I are together."

"We agree," Michael's dad said. "We've loved you all this time. You're already family."

———

Later, Cathy sat by Michael's side, watching him sleep with the endotracheal tube still in, the ventilator humming.

When he finally stirred and opened his eyes, he tried to talk around the ventilator, but couldn't. Instead, he took her hand.

She kissed his forehead. "We almost lost you."

He tried again to form words, but the ventilator got in his way. She brought him a pen and paper, and in a sloppy scrawl, he wrote, "Did we get him?"

She knew he meant Miller. She wished she could tell him that Miller was in prison, that he would never be released again, that even though he hadn't been convicted for killing Joe, there would be a sentence for all the other homicides.

Instead, she had to say, "No, baby. He got away."

Michael closed his eyes and shook his head.

"You did everything you could. The important thing is that Juliet and the kids are safe."

He nodded, tears welling in his eyes.

"And you're going to get through this. We're all going to

get through it. You could have died, but God answered our prayers."

He managed a smile and touched her hair. "I love you," he mouthed.

"I love you too. You're my soul mate. A gift from God. I believe that now. God knew I couldn't live without you."

His thumb stroked her face, wiping her tears. He pulled her close, and she pressed her forehead against his, basking in the warmth of his embrace.

CHAPTER 65

Two months later, Cathy chafed her arms, trying to keep from shivering. The courtroom was cold, but she could feel the heat of Michael's body next to her. He seemed calm, unruffled, as he had when he'd had his preliminary hearing just after being released from the hospital.

The judge looked at Michael. "Mr. Hogan, do you wish to continue with the guilty plea?"

"Yes, Your Honor."

"Then I'll proceed with sentencing."

Cathy couldn't stand it. "Your Honor, if I may . . . I know you're aware of why my client had possession of a gun. It's been all over the news. He's a hero, not a criminal."

"Miss Cramer, if he wanted to plead not guilty, he could have. He could have argued his case in court. It's not too late, Mr. Hogan. I'll ask you again. Do you wish to change your plea?"

"No, Your Honor."

Cathy tried not to cry. "I'd like to ask that you show mercy, keeping in mind that the greater good was served. He was wounded trying to save my sister."

"Duly noted. Now I've made my decision. For the crime of violating a court order and carrying a gun illegally, I sentence you to one year in the state penitentiary."

"No!" Cathy blurted.

The prosecutor turned to her in disapproval, as if she were nothing but an amateur. But Michael touched her hand. "It's okay," he whispered. "It'll go by fast."

She wasn't satisfied. "Your Honor," she said, trying to steady her voice. "We ask that you suspend his sentence."

"No, I'm sorry. I can't do that. We can't have convicted felons carrying weapons for *any* reason. If I let this go, I'll have dozens of other felons coming up with similar reasons."

"But you know the circumstances of his conviction!"

"The circumstances don't matter, Miss Cramer. Only the law matters. Again, if he'd wanted a jury to decide this, he could have pled not guilty and had a trial."

Cathy looked at Michael again. He shook his head. "I did it, Cathy. Let's just get this over with."

She had never been more frustrated with him. "Then we'd like to petition the court to give him house arrest for the duration of his sentence."

"No, I'm afraid not. As it is, he'll probably only serve half the sentence. I'm not going to change my mind." He hammered his gavel.

Cathy threw her arms around Michael's neck, and he held her. "It's okay," he said. "I'll call you every day. The time will fly."

"I love you," she whispered, touching his face.

"I love you too," he said. "Spend this time planning our wedding."

She stared at him as they snapped cuffs on his wrists. Had he just proposed to her? "Our wedding?"

"I'm going to marry you the minute I get out," he said. "If you'll have me."

Her mouth twisted, and she managed to nod. "I'll have you."

The bailiff pulled him away. Michael smiled back at her before they led him out of the room.

CHAPTER 66

Juliet sat with her hands in her lap, fidgeting with the strap of her handbag. The courthouse hall was empty except for three people talking quietly in a cluster near the bathroom.

Why was she trembling? She knew she was doing the right thing. Still, she felt unprepared. What if she wasn't up to this? What if she didn't have enough to give?

There had been so many decisions to make lately. First, she'd had to decide what to do with the money they'd found in extra accounts here in Panama City. The feds hadn't been interested in it since there was so much in the international accounts, but she knew the money hadn't come from Bob's practice. He'd probably kept some of it close so he could spend it as he wanted. She didn't want drug money. She would keep only the money in their joint account—the money Bob had earned legitimately through his medical practice. But any funds that had a questionable origin—whatever the feds hadn't taken as evidence—she had decided to give away.

She'd chosen to give it to a nationwide drug program that had a high success rate—one that honored Jesus, not just some ambiguous higher power. She loved the irony of using drug money to heal its victims.

But that hadn't resolved everything.

She heard voices around the corner at the security guard's station, then Cathy and Holly burst into the hallway. "There she is," Holly said.

As her sisters came toward her, Juliet looked away. She didn't really want them here. They would try one last time to talk her out of it, and she didn't want to hear it. They couldn't understand. They never would.

Cathy sat down next to her on the bench. "Juliet, you don't have to do this," she said in a low voice.

"I know that."

"It's too much of a commitment. No one would expect you to do a thing like this."

Juliet turned to her. "I'm not asking you to agree with my decision. But I am asking you to respect it."

Cathy wilted. "I do. I just don't want you to be more stressed out than you already are. It hasn't been long enough. You're still grieving."

"I'm not the only one." She looked toward the door that would open soon. "And too much time has passed already."

"But, Juliet—"

The door opened, and Juliet stiffened expectantly. A woman stepped out and held the door for someone else.

Another woman came through, holding a baby.

Juliet stood, and her sisters' protests hushed as her gaze locked onto the baby's little face.

Robbie looked so much like Abe and Zach. Like Bob. Like one of her own.

Tears sprang to Juliet's eyes, and she smiled as she stepped toward them. Robbie looked as if he'd been crying. His nose was red, his eyelashes wet.

"Hi, sweet Robbie," she said in a soft voice. "Can I hold you?"

The baby considered her, then leaned toward her, granting her the privilege. She took him, laughing through her tears, and kissed the top of his head. He smelled like baby powder.

"His things are in these bags," the temporary foster mother said.

The lady from the adoption agency passed the bags to Cathy and Holly. "We gathered up everything we thought he'd need. You're allowed to move his crib and other big items from his home, but you'll need to call me first."

Juliet nodded. "I think I already have everything I'll need from when his brothers were babies. But I may get some of his personal things so he'll feel more at home."

The baby touched her face, and she smiled and kissed his hand. "Are you going home with me?"

Cathy came closer. Juliet hoped she wasn't going to protest again.

"I'll take his suitcase," Cathy said softly.

Holly reached out for the diaper bag. "Does he take a bottle?"

"He takes formula," the foster mother said. "Also solid food. He's a good eater. But he's been crying a lot ever since . . ." Her voice trailed off.

Juliet hoped her boys would distract him. "Let's get you home," she said to Robbie. "You'll be getting hungry soon."

She started toward the door with Cathy and Holly flanking her. She glanced at her sisters. They both had tears on their faces.

They walked beside her as she bounced the baby to her car.

As she unlocked it and opened the back door, Holly stroked the baby's hair. "We'll help you," she said.

"I know you will. I'm counting on it."

Cathy opened the trunk and put the suitcase in. Then she took the keys out of Juliet's hand. "I'll drive so you can sit in the back with him."

Juliet smiled at her. "Thank you, Aunt Cathy." She slid into the backseat and put Robbie into his new car seat. As she buckled him in, she kissed his face. The baby smiled.

Joy entered her heart like a timid stranger. "These are the good days," she whispered.

A NOTE FROM THE AUTHOR

At this writing, I'm coming off an exciting weekend during which I have celebrated an abundance of riches—in the form of three grand babies born this year (2013). We already had one grandson who is two years old. We now have two boys and two girls, and all of our children are parents. That boggles my mind.

Three days ago, as my own baby went into the hospital to have a baby of her own, I read Psalm 139 and was reminded how perfectly designed every human on earth is. "For you created my inmost being; you knit me together in my mother's womb. I praise you because I am fearfully and wonderfully made; your works are wonderful, I know that full well. My frame was not hidden from you when I was made in the secret place, when I was woven together in the depths of the earth. Your eyes saw my unformed body; all the days ordained for me were written in your book before one of them came to be." (Psalm 139:13-16, NIV)

God doesn't make mistakes. He knew us before we were conceived, and he formed us and wired us exactly the way we are. He gave us each a purpose and a lifespan and timed it out precisely. That's why it plagues me that so many people are living on this earth, believing that they are accidents, that they are worthless, that they are useless. They believe they are trapped in the lives they lead, and that God is unaware of them. They believe that if God ever did notice them, he would be appalled.

But how can that be when God knew you before you were even conceived? When he wove you together himself in your mother's womb. When he wired you exactly the way you are. He knew you would try at things and fail. He knew you would struggle and be frustrated. He knew your life wouldn't be perfect, but that it would enable you to grow and mature. Like the process of birth that seems so dangerous and frightening, our challenges are uniquely crafted to help us fulfill our purposes. Each of us has to build up a different set of muscles for our unique tasks, so your struggle won't be my struggle, and mine won't be yours.

I constantly shake my head and grieve over those who can't or won't understand that. Some insist on staying in their daily state of supposed insignificance, only seeing themselves through the eyes of myopic humans around them, rather than through the eyes of their Creator, who sees them as he intended them to be.

I'll never forget hearing the song, "Touch of the Master's Hands," which tells of an old violin being auctioned off. No one wants it. It's worthless to the bidders—just a wasted instrument worth no more than two dollars, until an old man walks up from the back of the room, dusts the instrument off, and picks up the bow. He begins playing a beautiful concerto that brings tears to the eyes of everyone at the auction. As soon as he finishes, the auctioneer takes the violin and bow, and asks for bids again. This time the bidding starts in the thousands. The touch of the master's hand makes all the difference in the sound, use, and value of the instrument he created.

The fact is, you could be like that violin. You could be covered with dust and out of tune, forgotten and abandoned. But in the Master's hands, everything could change. You could be a redeemed child of the King, a joint heir with Christ, an overcomer, more than a conqueror. You can be among those who believe that God made provision for our failures and mistakes (and even our deliberate bad choices) and that provision was in the form of a man—God's only son—who stood in our place and took our punishment, so that we could have our sins wiped clean. You could be like a man condemned to death, waiting on Death Row for his execution, only to have the warden walk in and declare that a substitute has taken that sentence, that you are free to go. You can be among those who believe that Jesus' death on the cross in our place was enough to save and redeem us. You can be among those destined to spend their eternity with Him in heaven.

I hope you'll realize that today and embrace your uniqueness and your precious value to your Creator and join the family of God. But it's not just knowing that gives you salvation. It's *believing*. Believing what, you ask? Believing this: "For I delivered to you as of first importance what I also received, that Christ died for our sins according to the Scriptures, and that He was buried, and that He was raised on the third day according to the Scriptures . . ." (1 Corinthians 15:3–4 NASB)

And with that belief in your heart, you can know this with

all certainty: "For God so loved the world that he gave his one and only son, that whoever believes in him should not perish, but have eternal life." (John 3:16 NIV)

He loved you enough to give his son for you. You are not insignificant. You are not useless. You are not appalling. You are beloved.

Believe today.

Terri Blackstock

DISCUSSION QUESTIONS

1. If marriage is an illustration of Christ's relationship with the church, how is faith impacted when there is betrayal in a marriage?
2. Discuss the different faith journeys of Juliet, Cathy, and Holly. How does their level of faith cause them to respond differently to tragedy?
3. Discuss Bob's faith (or lack thereof) and whether he was redeemed by revelations at the end of the story. Did these revelations help Juliet in her grief?
4. Talking to kids about death is not easy. How does your faith help you deal with the death of a loved one when kids are involved? What about when the death is a senseless or violent one?
5. Holly is pregnant and unmarried. When Cathy asks her to come to church with her and her family, Holly feels uncomfortable: "I'm pregnant and I'm not married and

I'm walking into a place where people don't take well to
that kind of thing," she says. How about your church?
How comfortable do you think Holly would be made to
feel in your congregation?

6. The villains in *Distortion* threaten to hurt Juliet's children. How would you react if someone threatened your
kids or your nieces and nephews with violence? What
would be your first, gut reaction?

7. Bob was neither a perfect father nor a totally honest
man when he was alive. Juliet can't help but confront
those facts, even while she comforts her kids through
the loss. This causes some friction with her son. They
say one should not speak ill of the dead, but are we too
quick to beatify them? Do the deceased become ideal-
ized in our memories? In our words? What are the pros
and cons of telling children the truth about the sins of
their parents?

8. Juliet had developed a theology of rewards: "For so
long, she'd counted herself among the blessed, among
those who had been granted peace for obedience, mercy
for service, prosperity for generosity. God had rewarded
her for serving him." Are we rewarded for serving God
and punished for disobedience? Does Christianity work
like this? How so or why not?

9. The sisters do not show much faith in the police
department. Is vigilante justice justified in the face of
ineptitude? What about revenge? What does the Bible
have to say about authority? Vengeance?

10. Were Michael's actions with Miller appropriate or
wrong? What would you have done in his situation?

ACKNOWLEDGMENTS

There are lots of people important to the publishing process, people who work diligently to make sure that the book you're holding in your hands is worthy of your time and attention. Literary agents are chief among these people, and they often work behind the scenes with little recognition. They're the ones who encourage the writer at the very earliest stages, the ones who catch the spark of a story idea and help fan it into a mighty fire, the ones who take those burning embers to publishers and ignite even bigger fires in the hearts and imaginations of editors. They're the ones who do the "dirty work" of haggling and hammering out contract details, the ones who look out for an author's best interests while continuing to nurture a relationship with publishers who get authors' work into stores.

My agent, Lee Hough, passed away a few weeks ago after a two year battle with brain cancer. Lee continued to represent me through his chemo and radiation treatments, through remissions and relapses, through hope and disappointment. The day he told me that he had just a few more weeks to live, and that he was retiring from being an agent so he could spend that time with his family, I hung up the phone, stunned with grief. A few minutes later my phone chimed, reminding me that I had an appointment for a conference call with my publisher. I blew my nose and pulled myself together because Lee had asked me not to tell anyone his news until he'd had time to notify them, and I figured out what I would say to explain his absence on the call. *Lee couldn't be here because he's having a bad day.* They would understand. I took a deep breath and made the call. I punched in my conference call code and entered the virtual "room" where we'd all convene. The robotic voice told me who was already there. *Lee Hough.* He had interrupted his devastating phone calls to his friends and clients to represent me in that call . . . business as usual. With the professionalism he'd always shown, he took care of my miniscule needs. This act symbolizes my entire relationship with Lee over the last several years. He always put others first, even when no one expected him to.

The last CaringBridge update that he wrote himself was days before his death, when he asked us to pray for him as he shared Christ with a friend of his. He felt convicted to let this man know why he had such peace about dying and why he was assured of his passage to heaven. Again, Lee demonstrated his love for others and his selfless efforts to make others' lives better. After his death, his friends received a letter asking us to send the money we would have spent on flower arrangements to a struggling friend with cerebral palsy. He didn't worry for himself—he worried about his wife, Paula, and her well-being after his passing and the well-being of his children and grandchildren. Above all, Lee trusted God with their lives, as he trusted Him with his own.

I'm so grateful that I had the opportunity to work with such a godly man who so demonstrated the love of Christ, even after his final breath.

His work will live on in the hearts of those he touched and in the work of his clients. I am proud to be one of them.

AN EXCERPT FROM

TERRI BLACKSTOCK's

RESTORATION SERIES, BOOK ONE

LAST LIGHT

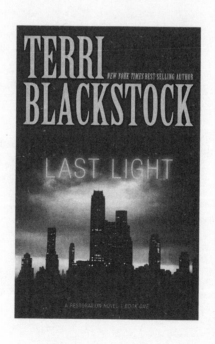

ONE

DENI BRANNING STEPPED DOWN ONTO THE TARMAC, PULLED out the handle of her carry-on, and glanced back up at her dad. He was just exiting the commuter plane as he chatted over his shoulder with the man who'd sat next to him on the flight. Doug Branning had never met a stranger, which accounted for his success as a stockbroker. He'd snagged some of his best clients on flights like this.

The oppressive Birmingham humidity settled over Deni like a heavy coat. *It's temporary*, she told herself. She wouldn't have to spend the summer here. Just this last week of May, and then it was back to D.C., her new job, and the fiancé she'd dreamed of for all of her twenty-two years. Yes, it was hot in the nation's capital, too, and probably just as humid. But its fast-paced importance made it easier to bear.

As her father reached the bottom step, his small bag clutched in his hand, the loud hum of the plane's engine went silent. A sudden, eerie quiet settled over the place, as if someone had muted all the machinery around them. The conveyor belt purging the cargo bin of its luggage stopped. The carts dragging the luggage carriers stalled.

She smelled something burning.

Her father seemed oblivious to the sudden change, so she fell into step beside him, rolling her bag behind her.

"Look out! It's coming in too fast!"

She turned back to see the airline employees gaping at the sky. An airliner was descending too steeply from the sky, silently torpedoing toward the runway. "Dad—!"

She screamed as the plane shattered into the runway, the impact vibrating through her bones. Time seemed to stop in a nightmarish freeze-frame, then roll into slow-motion horror as the plane tumbled wildly across the pavement and spun into a building.

Her dad tried to pull away. "In the building, Deni! Now! Let's go!"

Before she could get her feet to move, the plane exploded, flames bustling around it like a parachute that had finally caught wind. The blast of rippling heat knocked her off her feet, and before she could scramble up, her dad was over her, sheltering her with his body.

"Stay down, honey!"

She struggled to see through the shield of his arms. The fire conquered the broken fuselage, swallowing it whole. She imagined the people inside that plane, crawling over each other in a desperate effort to escape, slowly perishing in the murderous heat. Panic shot through her.

Her father got up and pulled her to her feet. "Come on, we're going inside!"

"But the people! Dad, the people—" She looked back, feeling the heat on her face.

"*Now*, Deni!"

"They're burning," she screamed. "Somebody has to get them out!"

"They're trying." His voice broke as he got back to his feet and grabbed up her suitcase. "There's nothing we can do."

She got up, staring toward the wreckage. The crowd of employees who ran to give aid stood helpless, unable to get close. Her father put his arm around her and moved her toward the building. They ran up the steps to their arrival gate.

They were greeted by darkness.

They hurried through the terminal to a window that provided some light. A crowd of people clustered around it, watching the plane burn.

Doug headed for two Delta clerks who stood talking urgently. "Where are the fire trucks? Has anybody called them?"

A distracted employee shook his head. "The phones aren't working. Everything's out."

He grabbed his cell phone out of his pocket, and Deni watched him try to dial 911. But the readout was blank. He shook his head. "It's dead. My battery must have lost its charge. Try yours, Deni."

She dug her phone out of her purse and hit the *on* button. Hers was dead, too. Had both their batteries died on the plane?

She looked back out the window. The plane continued to burn … engulfed in a conflagration that wouldn't be quenched. Helpless airport employees stood back, looking around for help. Someone had pulled out a fire extinguisher and was shooting white foam, but it was like squirting a water pistol at a towering inferno.

Deni thought of herself and her dad sitting on the plane just moments ago. It could have been *them* out there, trapped in a burning metal coffin.

Gritting her teeth, she pounded her fists on the window. "Where are the stupid fire trucks?"

"I don't know." Doug's whisper was helpless, horrified.

She watched the chaos on the tarmac as employees ran in different directions, looking confused and defeated, shouting and gesturing wildly for help. Some started pointing up to the sky …

"Another plane!" someone next to her shouted.

She followed the man's gaze to another airliner coming in. The others started to scream as that plane dropped too fast, too steep.

She couldn't watch as it hit the ground, but she heard the deafening sound of another crash, felt the impact shake the building. Screams crescendoed.

Shivering, Deni looked up. The plane was spinning and tumbling across the grass separating the runways.

"Daddy!" She glanced at him, saw the horror in his eyes. She followed his gaze to the sky. Was something shooting the planes down? Were there more to come? Deni slipped her hand into his and felt his trembling. For the first time in her life, she was aware of her father's fear. And though his strong, protective grip held her tight, she knew everything had changed.

TWO

DOUG BRANNING'S MIND RACED TO UNDERSTAND — PLANES falling out of the sky, crashing, burning, people dying ...

There was a power outage, but that wouldn't have caused planes to crash. Maybe there was some kind of battle going on in the air that they couldn't see. If someone was shooting the planes down, maybe they'd also knocked out the power on the ground. Was it some kind of terrorist attack?

In all his uncertainty, he knew one thing. He had to get his daughter to safety. The airport felt like a target for whatever evil hovered above them. He put his arm around Deni and pulled her from the window. He hoped she couldn't feel his trembling. "Come on, Deni, we're getting out of here."

For once in her life she was compliant as he pulled her up the long dark hall, past the empty gates. Several Delta ground clerks came running past them.

"Excuse me," he called out. "Can anyone tell me what's going on?"

"Power's out," one of them called back. "Nothing's working."

"Did the planes crash because the tower's electricity is down?"

"May have. We can't say for sure."

Doug frowned. That didn't make sense. Didn't pilots have emergency procedures for situations like this? Couldn't they land the planes without an air traffic controller talking them through it?

He walked Deni past another window and saw the ball of fire, still burning. The other plane hadn't caught fire, and men rushed toward it, fighting to get the door open. Still no fire trucks had come.

"Dad, what's going on? What would make two planes crash?"

He shook his head. "No power outage, that's for sure. One of the planes must have hit a power line."

"No, the power shut down *before* the crashes. That's why things went quiet. I heard our plane's engine power off at the same time everything else stopped. The luggage belt, the maintenance cars ..."

Dozens of people were at the second plane now, but they couldn't seem to get inside. He bit his bottom lip. The passengers had all probably died in the impact. How could anyone have survived? He didn't want Deni to see them pulling the bodies out.

"Let's go to the car." Still carrying Deni's suitcase, he headed to the exit. "Maybe we can get a signal on our phones after we leave the airport, and call your mother. She's probably heard about it on the news and can tell us what's happening."

Deni followed him at a trot, hiccuping sobs. He reached the front door, but it didn't open.

"Power's out, Dad," she reminded him.

He turned and found a manual door. As they pushed through it, he was struck with the silence in the street. No cars moved through, and the security guards were probably helping the rescue effort. Doug and Deni hurried across the street into the big parking garage. They'd parked on the fourth level, so they found the stairs and trudged up.

Doug was damp with sweat by the time they reached their level and made their way to his new Mercedes. He used the remote on his key chain to pop the lock on the trunk, but when he got to the car, the trunk was still closed. He pressed the button again, but it still didn't open. Frustrated, he jabbed the key into the lock, and opened it. He threw their two bags in, slammed the trunk, then tried to open his driver's door. It hadn't come unlocked with the trunk, so he manually unlocked it and got in, punching the power locks button to open Deni's door.

But Deni just stood there, knocking on the passenger window.

He frowned at the door lock. The power locks weren't working—how could *that* be? The power outage couldn't extend to his car, could it? He leaned across the leather seat, and opened the passenger door.

As Deni got in, he put the key into the ignition and turned it ... but nothing happened.

Deni just looked at him. "The car's dead, too? Dad, this is like the *Twilight Zone*. What could cause this?"

"Got me."

Doug looked around. Usually cars circled everywhere, competing for parking spots. But not today. He got out and walked to the edge of the garage, looked over to the roads that took them out of the place. There were a few cars lined up at the pay booth, but they weren't moving. No cars ran on the streets leading to the interstate, though several seemed stalled in the middle of the road. People stood outside their vehicles, opening the hoods ...

Doug went back to his car and tried turning the key again, to no avail. He tested the radio. Still nothing. "I don't believe this."

Deni found a Kleenex and blew her nose. "This is just great! Are we going to have to stay in this creepy place with planes crashing all around us? I want to go home."

He turned to the backseat and saw a Walkman one of the kids had left there. He grabbed it, shoved the headphones on, and tried to get a station.

All he got was silence.

"Nothing?" Deni asked.

"Nothing."

"Maybe it's all the metal in the garage, blocking the radio waves."

He got back out of the car, took it to the edge of the garage, and tried again. Still nothing.

Slowly, he removed the headphones as the stark realization took hold of him. Everything was dead. Electricity, phones, cars, radio waves ... even planes in midflight.

As he got back into his useless car, Doug Branning felt the world spinning out of control.

And he was powerless to stop it.

THE RESTORATION SERIES

In the face of a crisis that sweeps an entire high-tech planet back to the age before electricity, the Brannings face a choice. Will they hoard their possessions to survive—or trust God to provide as they offer their resources to others? Terri Blackstock weaves a masterful what-if series in which global catastrophe reveals the darkness in human hearts—and lights the way to restoration for a self-centered world.

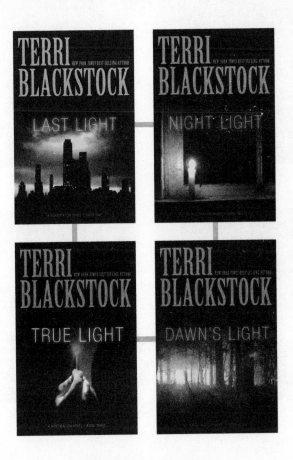

CAPE REFUGE SERIES

This bestselling series follows the lives of the people of the small seaside community of Cape Refuge, as two sisters struggle to continue the ministry their parents began helping the troubled souls who come to Hanover House for solace.

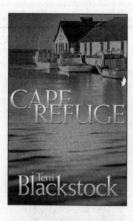

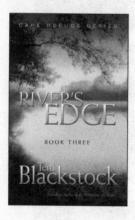

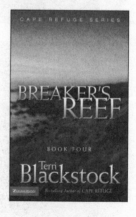

Available in stores and online!

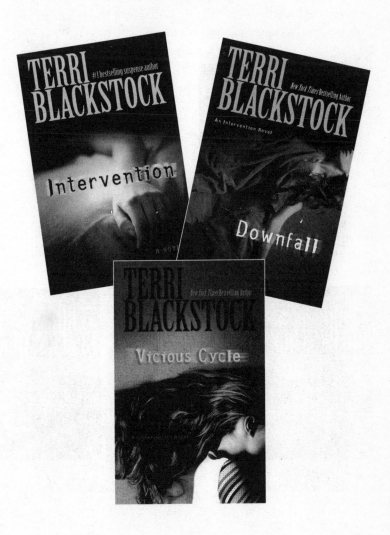

Other great books from Terri Blackstock

NEWPOINTE 911 SERIES

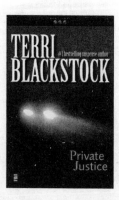

Private Justice

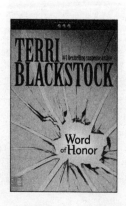

Word of Honor

Shadow of Doubt

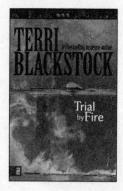

Trial by Fire

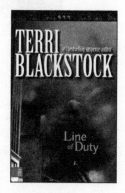

Line of Duty

Available in stores and online!

ABOUT THE AUTHOR

Terri Blackstock is an award-winning, *New York Times* best-selling author who has written for several major publishers including HarperCollins, Dell, Harlequin, and Silhouette. Her books have sold over six million copies worldwide.

With her success in secular publishing at its peak, Blackstock had what she calls "a spiritual awakening." A Christian since the age of fourteen, she realized she had not been using her gift as God intended. It was at that point that she recommitted her life to Christ, gave up her secular career, and made the decision to write only books that would point her readers to him.

"I wanted to be able to tell the truth in my stories," she said, "and not just be politically correct. It doesn't matter how many readers I have if I can't tell them what I know about the roots of their problems and the solutions that have literally saved my own life."

Her books are about flawed Christians in crisis and God's

provisions for their mistakes and wrong choices. She claims to be extremely qualified to write such books, since she's had years of personal experience.

A native of nowhere, since she was raised in the Air Force, Blackstock makes Mississippi her home. She and her husband are parents to three adult children—a blended family that she considers one more of God's provisions.

Blackstock is the author of numerous suspense novels, including *Intervention*, *Vicious Cycle*, and *Downfall* (the Intervention Series), as well as the Moonlighters Series, the Cape Refuge Series, the SunCoast Chronicles, the Newpointe 911 Series, the Restoration Series, and many others.

www.terriblackstock.com